INTRODUCTION TO
DIGITAL MEDIA
DESIGN

BLOOMSBURY VISUAL ARTS
Bloomsbury Publishing Plc
50 Bedford Square, London, WC1B 3DP, UK
1385 Broadway, New York, NY 10018, USA
29 Earlsfort Terrace, Dublin 2, Ireland

BLOOMSBURY, BLOOMSBURY VISUAL ARTS and the Diana logo
are trademarks of Bloomsbury Publishing Plc

First published in Great Britain 2022

A catalogue record for this book is available from the British Library.

A catalog record for this book is available from the Library of Congress.

ISBN: PB: 978-1-350104-93-8
         ePDF: 978-1-350104-95-2
         eBook: 978-1-350104-94-5

Typeset by Typo•glyphix, Burton-on-Trent
Printed and bound in India

To find out more about our authors and books
visit www.bloomsbury.com and sign up for our newsletters.

INTRODUCTION TO
DIGITAL MEDIA
DESIGN

TRANSFERABLE HACKS,
SKILLS AND TRICKS

DAVID LEICESTER HARDY

B L O O M S B U R Y   V I S U A L   A R T S
LONDON • NEW YORK • OXFORD • NEW DELHI • SYDNEY

COMPANION WEBSITE

The companion website features exercises, sample files and templates, videos, and complementary material to extend what you learn in the book. Check it out at:
introdigitaldesign.com

For my wife Molly, and my daughters Juniper and Beatrix, who allowed
me many an evening to devote to this text. With many thanks to Aaris Sherin,
Robin Landa, and Dan Wong of *Design Incubation*, for helping me to fully realize
this concept and move forward with it. And with gratitude to my editor,
Leafy Cummins, whose patience saw me through to the end.

Contents

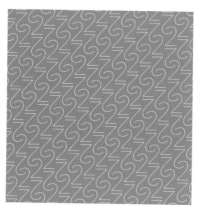

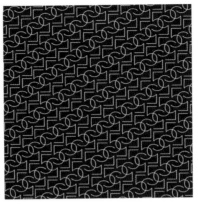

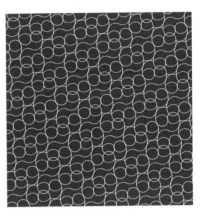

Introduction: Convergence with Tech, Divergence of Media

Imagine what a graphic designer from the 1960s would feel like if they stepped into a contemporary studio. Most of us can't because we've grown up with technology. In the space of twenty years, we've gone from tactile compositions to a completely digital ecosystem. The digital shift of the early 1990s empowered designers to produce richly layered compositions in a fraction of the time. Layouts that took days to build by hand could be knocked out in an afternoon with a Macintosh computer. This, no doubt, empowered designers to create the lush,

densely packed compositions that defined that era. Computers became sleeker, hard drives smaller and more affordable, and monitors grew larger and much crisper. Yet, the thing that had largely stayed the same since the 1950s was the scope of work and medium of output: printed matter. Graphic designers applied their craft using type, color, form, and a set of principles that had remained unchanged for nearly a half century. The fruits of their labor were reproduced in books, magazines, brochures and other collateral, and packaging.

Figure 0.1
Before digital methods were introduced, designers used a tactile process to create camera-ready art.

Figure 0.2
The Macintosh allowed design layouts to be produced much faster.

By the start of the new millennium, many designers had figured out how to embrace a digital workflow while also migrating to digital media. Transcending digital illustration, image-making, and computer layout meant learning a bit of coding, manipulating moving images on a timeline, and connecting design to inter-actions. Digital design is more or less connected to the *output* rather than the *process* in the way the term is typically used.

Many art directors I worked with at my first few design jobs hadn't learned the software, and many scribbled sketches and instructions on a sketchpad for junior designers to execute. My first job in college was outputting film for offset printing from a machine that filled a small room. In the short interval since that job, the design workflow has changed tremendously. A modern-day art director might find themselves shifting between creative direction, client interaction, and hands-on design in a variety of media.

From pixels to precision

Early websites were crude because of the limited fidelity of technology in the 1990s. They were puzzle-piece layouts that were strung together with spaghetti code. In 1996, Flash was introduced as a way to show animation on the Web without using heavy programming. It was immediately embraced as a creative tool, and many designers began to heavily experiment with it. Joshua Davis was one of those at the forefront of this new medium, hosting open-source Flash files on his website *Praystation.com*. Flash-based experiences enabled artists and designers to work more freely, but they were near impossible to update if not set up properly. CD-ROM designed experiences were often the best quality of that decade, but the format slowly disappeared in the wake of a more reliable Web. Early touchscreen design often needed dedicated hardware to run and was mostly limited to interactive kiosks. The 2000s were a time of new standards in digital media. The iPhone spawned the smartphone revolution, and this bore *responsive design* for different size screens in 2010. Apps appeared almost out of thin air, and interaction design took a giant leap from its Flash beginnings. Motion graphics, which were once strictly the domain of broadcast media, became a niche for many graphic designers eager to explore digital output.

In the time since, digital design has caught up to traditional graphic design in terms of craft. Websites and apps now have the same level of polish that you would expect from a professionally designed and printed piece. Many designers vacillate between traditional processes like sketching and development processes like coding, with tools both dictating the work processes and offering new ways to facilitate idea creation and refinement.

Who is this book written for?

This title is for:

- students enrolled in, or just out of, university who want to jump into a design discipline quickly without necessarily mastering it right away
- professionals who are burning the midnight oil in attempting a lateral move in their career
- creatives who are curious about digital design but don't know where to start.

There are myriad books on each one of the topics addressed in this text. There are likely millions of articles, tutorials, and videos that cover them. Consider this the missing manual that fills in gaps. Those who are curious about learning a variety of workflows and outputs quickly—without wading through a sea of information—will find this a good resource.

In part, my aim is to provide my former self with a tool I desperately needed at one point in my career but didn't have. I was a print designer so eager to get into web and interactive design that I oversold my skills during a job interview and figured it out through many long nights of trial and error. The encyclopedia-sized books I bought then might as well have been boat anchors. I needed a way to get things working quickly and then build on that. In the interest of ease of use and utility, this book will avoid deep dives. More useful is the perspective I'll present and the approaches I've found invaluable in navigating the bleeding-edge. Although this text will lean heavily on technical skills, there are some very lo-fi activities and hacks that will help bring the esoteric bits into perspective.

What disciplines will this cover?

UI and UX: The differences between these are lost on many designers, although there's some overlap between them. You'd be surprised by how far some functional knowledge and a few proof-of-concept projects can go in breaking into these sought-after fields.

Motion graphics seem especially difficult to many young designers. The software used is complex and doesn't invite experimentation. However, learning the five basic transformations can unlock about 90 percent of what the average designer would want to accomplish.

Interaction design also forces us to reframe what we know about how to effectively utilize a composition, not to mention crafting a set of interactions that need to all seem natural. But learning about commonly used design patterns and how motion can elicit a tactile response gets us more than halfway there.

Design for the Web is especially tricky for those not familiar with code, but there are analog and digital techniques that can help you more clearly visualize what otherwise might seem completely abstract at first glance.

Extended Reality: If those betting on (and investing in) the future of emerging technologies are right, they're going to change the way we work. Knowing the differences between them, and the methods for creating for these experiences, is a huge first step in beginning exploration and staying relevant.

What roles does this translate to?

Visual designer: This term is now routinely listed on creative job boards, and while it might range in specific methods required, the output is the same: digital experiences. It's somewhat of a hybrid between graphic and UI design, with traditional skills being translated into content that's crafted for a device or screen.

Motion designer: A shortened version of *motion graphics designer*, this job deals with framing elements (form, shape, type color, etc.) that are moving in space and time, often synced to audio. Title sequence design for film immediately comes to mind, but designing and producing explainer videos, short visuals for social media, and animated logos for use on devices are all within the realm of this discipline.

User interface designer: UI designers are responsible for the look and feel of an app or website. From designing the actual interface from an aesthetic point of view (hierarchy colors, type, negative space) to considering usability as a form factor, this job melds creativity with understanding best layout practices across all screens and devices. UI designers work very closely with UX designers.

User experience designer: A UX designer is involved in making digital products useful, usable, and viable for its users. They specify an audience, develop profiles, and determine user flows through an app or website. They may be involved in initial research, creating personas, and developing information architecture through wireframing and prototyping.

Web designer: This job involves wearing many hats, from being able to design the look and feel of a website, to rendering the content and style in code via HTML and CSS. This requires a sense for digital aesthetics and the ability to write basic mark-up and style it effectively with code.

Creative technologist: The term creative technologist has been in play for the last few years, referring to jobs that integrate technology into the creative process. These roles are often very experimental and nimble, allowing those involved to tinker with technical prototypes while still in the design phase of a project.

Money isn't everything, but it's nice

These new jobs place a premium on technical proficiency and staying up to date. Therefore, the salary ranges are typically higher than a similar role where the output is print based. According to The Creative Group, the midpoint salary for a *visual designer* is up to 50 percent higher than their graphic designer counterpart.

The fact is, making a living doing traditional design work is becoming more difficult for those coming into the job market. Those roles have been democratized through the reach of the internet and are difficult to break into while earning a livable wage. As design's convergence with tech continues, increasingly diverse skills are going to be valued as much as basic skills learned as a graphic designer.

This book intends to ignite exploration of these pathways, with the realization that finding your niche is still important within the scope of experimentation and proficiency across a variety of digital platforms. So read on, explore everything you can, and build from a generalist approach. While design continues to move into a larger popular context, a unified message across an ever-increasing array of media continues to be a competitive advantage.

User Interface and
Digital Design

Although everything we produce using creative software can be thought of as "digital design," *user interface (UI) design* refers to content produced for viewing on a digital screen; for example, websites, apps, wayfinding kiosks, smart TVs and other appliances, smart-car and in-flight interfaces, tablets, phones, and so on. It has a clear focus on visual style and feel, something that comes naturally to designers. And because of that, it's a good place to start. UI design visually communicates functionality and content. While already a decades-old niche, the demand for skills in this discipline of digital design has surged in recent years. UI design touches on most of what we can interact with on various types of screens. Imagine using an app, website, or smart device, with no menu or intuitive layout. You'd have to think pretty hard, because most digital content has some implied sense of UI design. A smartphone uses icons for apps. A TV has some sort of on-boarding menu that a first-time user can navigate. A digital streaming service displays thumbnail photos for each selection.

User interface specifications

A core principle of UI design is anticipating what the user might need to do from a visual perspective. Providing a set of options with clarity and precision is paramount. Any functional element on a screen, whether a menu, button, or link, is within the domain of UI. A user might interact with a mouse, trackpad, finger, gesture, or even eye movement. But UI design transcends its obvious interactive elements. It also considers basic layout, relationships between elements, typography, and color schemes. Here is where what most of us conceive of as *graphic design* factors enter the equation. UI is deeply steeped in traditional design principles, making it an easy transition into the digital realm. In fact, a core competency for UI design jobs is the ability to translate the look and feel of an existing brand or entity to a digital product. The visual hallmarks of that brand should extend to the digital experience and feel like a unified part of it. In the early days of digital design, this was more or less slapped on in the form of an online banner ad and ported out as an extra deliverable. We've now come full circle, as social media has fully embraced the ability for entities to interact in more informal and authentic ways. The full-page ad with a logo and tagline, while still appropriate in certain contexts, has been

Figure 1.1
These are app on-boarding screens that match the accompanying brand: clear, delightful, and fresh.

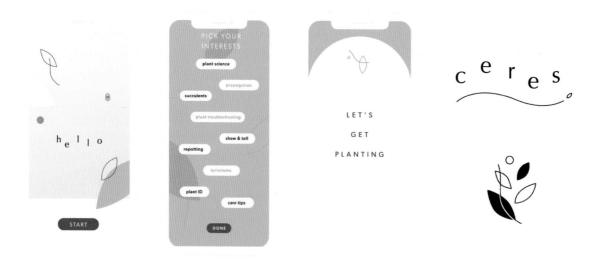

Figure 1.2
An app that facilitates collective discovery boasts a user interface that's both mysterious and striking.

replaced by the direct ability for users to digitally interact with a brand. In this way, users can play a part in the advertising themselves, but they can also freely complain if they want. The classic one-way presentation of branded content has shifted to a complex dance of platform-specific digital media. The user interface design not only weaves together all these experiences, but if done well it can *become* part of the brand. For instance, a whimsical UI using muted pastel colors, delicate typography, and quirky visual content might be appropriate for a lifestyle brand. A financially concerned entity, however, would require something more subdued and serious. All this to say: user interface design is the visual backbone of digital design.

UI AND UX

Many of the decisions made in the UI design process will be informed by user experience (UX) design. Questions small and large, from how many menu items are needed for a particular function, to what's the user demographic for a certain product, will be answered through that process. To be clear, UI and UX are distinct disciplines that demand separate skills. Increasingly, though, the same person might be performing both roles. Why? In a nutshell: money. A company might not have enough work to employ a UI designer full time, so it's usually bundled with UX design since they're so closely tied-together. That's not always the case though, and the separation is more pronounced in larger creative studios and agencies. While we'll take a deep dive into UX in the next chapter, keep in mind that many of the UI principles that follow depend on solid research, strategy, and attention to goals and outcomes.

Familiar controls and their uses

With printed and tangible items (like signage) in the physical world, the interactive possibilities, or controls, are usually nonexistent. If controls are in place, they're passive, a byproduct of the experience. For example, while driving a car, how do you view the next road sign? You simply continue driving. While reading through a magazine article, how do you advance through the content? Keep turning the pages. For digital products, advancing to the next screen requires a reliable interface. Controls for navigating the experience are crucial. These controls need to be intuitive, show visual contrast, and be memorable. Stickiness in these elements can lead to universal implementation.

Take a website, for example. What's the most basic control available? A link, right? In its most basic un-styled state, a link shows as blue text with an underline. You know that if you interact with a link, you'll likely end up on another page. Group a series of links together with some visual arrangement, and they become a menu. Add a background color and defined edges to a link, and it becomes a button. These visual variations provide some context. And while creativity does exist here, designing interfaces isn't high art. They need to be easy to learn in order to invite user interaction.

UI inventory

The best way to start building a user interface is to conduct an inventory of needs. This lets you assess what kind of elements you'll need to consider, both individually and as a whole. If the project is a redesign, this is obviously a quicker task. It involves sorting through existing components, confirming their functionality, and deciding if they're needed moving forward. For example, many websites have built-in search functionality. While this may be useful for large-scale sites with a lot of information to wade through, it's likely overkill for smaller projects. Back-end coding is required to implement this function, and the results might be disappointing to users. Is it a portfolio or lead-generation site? Ditch it. Are you building a project with a lot of text content that might get added-to over time? Probably worthwhile.

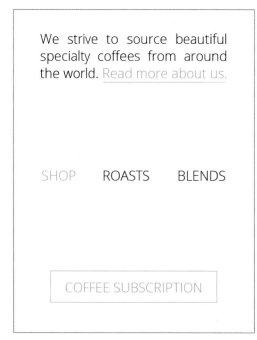

We strive to source beautiful specialty coffees from around the world. Read more about us.

SHOP   ROASTS   BLENDS

COFFEE SUBSCRIPTION

Figure 1.3
Some basic variations and groupings can convert text into a link, menu, or button.

HACK

Web designer Brad Frost has come up with an ingenious idea for speeding through a UI inventory: the grab-and-paste method. Start by taking screenshots and pasting them onto a blank document. Then, start sorting them into categories to easily compare. It's not high finish by any means, but it's the quickest way to get it done.

In creating a UI inventory for a new project, looking at competitors in the space will help with creating a list of possibilities. Seeing what works or doesn't work for others can be very valuable at this stage. The following categories are the common ones to consider:

- navigation (primary, secondary, breadcrumb)
- typography (headings, subheads, lists, body copy)
- images (logos, icons, photos, illustration)
- other media types (video, audio, carousels, slideshows)
- interactive elements (buttons, inputs, menus and controls).

Menus and patterns

Menus that transition to a new screen or experience need to offer the most reliable look and feel. They present information and options at different levels of complexity, depending on the number of functions they are meant to perform. A digital kiosk in a building, for example, might need to look fairly simple in order to be noticed from afar. The initial screen might start by offering an open-ended search or widely used functions like a map. These screens can be measured in inches instead of pixels. There's more room to spread out and use both word and image together in assisting navigation. You're bound by the user's physical reach, which can be substantial.

On a laptop, a website might display several overarching content areas as navigation items. These may look like a horizontal bar across the top. Once a user navigates to that content area, a sub-navigation menu is revealed on the next screen. These sub-nav items might appear smaller and further down the page,

after a large header or graphic. The user learns that general items, close to the top, are easily scanned. As they move deeper, scale and contrast become factors. This hierarchy is like the text layout on a business card: name, title, and contact

Figure 1.4
A digital kiosk requires menus that both invite users from a distance and allow them to explore deeply.

details revealed in order of importance as the reader's eye scans the card.

A navigation menu for an app might look like the familiar three-line icon with controls hidden until it's tapped. Here, screen size is precious, and spreading out usually isn't an option. Getting to a specific screen on an app might involve two or three taps. Now, consider what those three lines mean. At its most basic level, it represents lines of content in a list of menu items. Visual shorthand and iconography play an even more important role in UI menu patterns. Consider the shopping cart icon for the transaction function of an e-commerce website. By visually linking the transaction process to a familiar real-world object—the shopping cart—users are immediately able to recognize an action: "checking out."

Mentally scroll through the list of visual icons you use with digital devices. You'll be quite comfortable in recognizing functions for each one. A magnifying glass indicates the search function. An outright "X" indicates the ability to close a menu or content box. A downward-facing arrow lets you know that you can download something. This is the essence of user interface design, and UI design is the core of all digital design because it is what makes the medium dynamic, essentially different than design for the print and physical world.

Hierarchy and visual flow

A user interface can channel expression through design. At a visceral level, we process the design or layout of a digital experience from a holistic point of view before looking at fine details. This is known as Gestalt theory. This assessment is hyper-sensory and happens very quickly. We might think that a UI feels a certain way but aren't sure exactly why. Being able to deconstruct and tune into these details is key to harnessing this phenomenon. Controlling the hierarchy in a user interface

also relies on determining importance. Principal actions should have the most obvious visual contrast. Whether it's a sign-up widget on a website or a call to action at the end of an animated video, this should stand out. Secondary action should be subordinate to the principal action but still be accessible. For instance, using the same visual form but reducing contrast by stripping away a bright color. Any minor actions should be subdued but function when a user *looks* for them. Unadorned links in the footer of a website are an example of this: information that's necessary but not crucial.

Visual flow for digital design takes cues from traditional 2D-design methodologies, like scale. However, unlike print, size is a flexible concept for many digital experiences. A layout might adapt for different screens and scrolling can be a factor. Knowing this can help play up contrast for many situations. The constraints of the printed page might be absent, but you still need to account for things like cultural reading practices. In the Western world, we read top to bottom, and left to right. This affects our screen-viewing habits. On a content-heavy screen, users read the first few lines, and then vertically scan the left side. This is called an *F-pattern*. On screens with less content, our eyes travel diagonally after the first scan. We then track right again and repeat the process. This is a *Z-pattern*. Taking advantage of these natural eye behaviors can help with a layout's visual flow.

Proximity

This is one of the Gestalt principles of perception. Proximity states that elements closer together are perceived to be more related than those farther apart. For UI design, utilizing proximity helps us lay out content that's easily scanned. This can be applied to typography at a basic level.

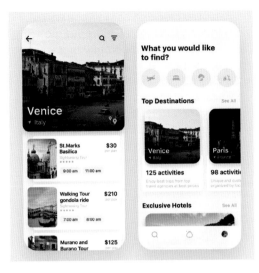

Headings, subheadings, and copy blocks should be grouped together. Placing them next to accompanying visuals helps users connect word to image. And for body copy, two-to-three sentence chunks are about the most you can ask of users to scan effectively. This is especially true of users who are interacting with content on mobile devices. For content containing a diverse range of elements (copy, images, buttons, and controls), proximity can also guide layout. Let's use a city guide app as an example. For a screen of tours and activities, start by pairing images with short bits of fine-grain details that are separate but related such as location, tour type, and price. Follow that with something to break it up, like a rating system. Available tour times become functional buttons, so color is used to give contrast. On more general category screens, photos that are paired with body copy offer a bit of room for a description. Here, the text is concise enough to be viewed as a unit. This kind of natural progression works well with our ability to visually combine and separate content.

Negative space

In the constant effort to squeeze in as much as possible on our digital devices, we've crammed our layouts to the brim with content. Adding contrast often means adding negative space to temper this noise, and sometimes that requires treating it as a design element itself. In the early days of digital design, everyone was concerned with getting all the important content before the user needed to scroll. This concept is referred to as *above the fold*. Rooted in traditional print publications, it historically referred to where the bottom half of the newspaper would fold. In digital design, it simply means what the user sees before they start scrolling. We know now that scrolling is no big deal, and tons of digital experiences feature a permanent scroll of unending content. I'm not advocating for something that severe, just that there's room for negative space. Moving content to another screen—further down after scrolling, or paring down core messaging—will give the user some breathing room to engage in a more meaningful way.

Grid systems

A grid is an underlying framework that helps to connect bits of content in a logical or intuitive way. Layout in traditional graphic design is heavily dependent on the use of grids. They're the hallmark of well-known movements such as the Swiss Style. In the pre-smartphone era of digital design, applying grids was pretty cut and dry. Why? Because of the lack of so many different devices, most digital content was viewed on desktop or laptop computer screens at a fixed size. The grid could easily be locked in. It's a bit more complicated now, since a product might extend across many screens and devices. Grids can (and should) be broken when it's necessary to create a more organic flow—meaning the

Figure 1.5
This travel app shows how the proximity of content can help guide the overall flow of a layout.

content doesn't have to abide by strict rules of alignment. But there is no arguing that grids are crucial to delivering the kind of thoughtful and consistent experiences we've come to expect. Their components include the following:

- *Columns* help define the width of design elements, which can span across them. An element like a photo might be three columns wide, for example.
- *Gutters* are spaces between the columns and help ensure that content isn't too crowded or touching when aligned. To increase horizontal spacing between elements, simply increase the width of the gutters.
- *Rows* dictate the height of elements, including images, text, and buttons. They tend to be less defined than columns, because in large part, they're dictated by the flow of content.

A grid utilizing both columns and rows is called a modular grid.

HACK

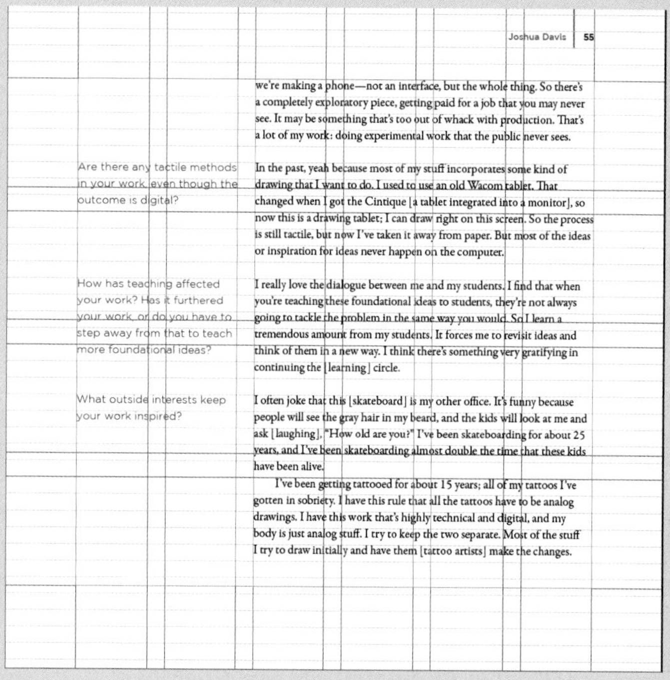

Figure 1.6
A column grid with gutters illustrates horizontal spacing, while a repeating baseline grid offers vertical alignment.

Rows are best organized by the baseline leading of the type. If you use a repeating grid of 6 pixels for your rows, it allows precise control over the vertical spacing. As long as the leading is set in multiples of three, your type should align nicely to the baseline grid. You can now align other graphic elements to it for more consistent vertical spacing. The alignment seems more intentional when set this way, rather than adding random vertical spacing above or below elements.

Joshua Davis | 55

we're making a phone—not an interface, but the whole thing. So there's a completely exploratory piece, getting paid for a job that you may never see. It may be something that's too out of whack with production. That's a lot of my work: doing experimental work that the public never sees.

Are there any tactile methods in your work, even though the outcome is digital?

In the past, yeah because most of my stuff incorporates some kind of drawing that I want to do. I used to use an old Wacom tablet. That changed when I got the Cintique [a tablet integrated into a monitor], so now this is a drawing tablet; I can draw right on this screen. So the process is still tactile, but now I've taken it away from paper. But most of the ideas or inspiration for ideas never happen on the computer.

How has teaching affected your work? Has it furthered your work, or do you have to step away from that to teach more foundational ideas?

I really love the dialogue between me and my students. I find that when you're teaching these foundational ideas to students, they're not always going to tackle the problem in the same way you would. So I learn a tremendous amount from my students. It forces me to revisit ideas and think of them in a new way. I think there's something very gratifying in continuing the [learning] circle.

What outside interests keep your work inspired?

I often joke that this [skateboard] is my other office. It's funny because people will see the gray hair in my beard, and the kids will look at me and ask [laughing], "How old are you?" I've been skateboarding for about 25 years, and I've been skateboarding almost double the time that these kids have been alive.

I've been getting tattooed for about 15 years; all of my tattoos I've gotten in sobriety. I have this rule that all the tattoos have to be analog drawings. I have this work that's highly technical and digital, and my body is just analog stuff. I try to keep the two separate. Most of the stuff I try to draw initially and have them [tattoo artists] make the changes.

Typography

It seems like a rite of passage for designers to use small, delicate type when learning how to control it. I thought I'd achieved type-nirvana in my university days by using 8-point body copy on a business card. While that may still have a place in design for print, the fact is, type is bigger when used for digital devices. Several things contribute to this:

- eye strain when looking at increasingly brighter screens
- the physical size of a pixel across different devices
- improved standards and advocacy regarding accessibility
- the fact that we're often multitasking while interacting with digital design.

Twelve pixels is the smallest size text you should be using for any digital element. Sixteen to eighteen pixels is my minimum recommendation for body copy. And any touchable or clickable object should be at least 50 pixels wide or tall. This includes links, buttons, and selectors. We read a little differently on digital devices. That is to say, we scan more. Short two-to-three sentence chunks are the norm for holding a user's attention. Typefaces designed for screens have existed for decades, but few options existed for much of that time.

Legibility issues plagued delicate serif fonts in the late 1990s and early 2000s. Hinting, which is a way of optimizing fonts for screens, solved that problem. Now, not only are serifs fair game, but some are designed specifically for screens. We've seen web type embrace flexible formats like variable and parametric. These challenge the idea that type is static content, allowing them to shift with respect to screen sizes and specifications. They also look ahead to the augmented and virtual spaces, where responsive manipulation is possible.

Styling type to create a focal point, add contrast, and improve hierarchy is at the core of graphic design, and it's even more important in the digital landscape where attention is at a premium. Increasing the impact of text where it's needed (headlines, important instructions, branding) can be achieved by using larger font sizes, thicker weights, and applying space liberally around it. You can also apply contrast to individual words by shifting to a lighter weight or alternating from uppercase to lowercase. It's classy when done well. Sometimes, you want to decrease the impact, or downplay the text. Boilerplate copy, sub-menu options, and captions all need to be toned down a bit. Smaller sizes, muted colors, and neutral font selections will make the job easier.

HACK

If you need a refresher from your Type 101 class, search for Type Connection, an online tool that sends fonts on "dates" to show you if they work well together (or not). It effectively explains how to use type families, visual consistency, letterform contrast, and contextual history in type pairing. I have yet to see this done in such a fun, engaging way.

Figure 1.7
Chunky stylized text becomes form at this size, and it creates strong contrast with a bit of disarming style.

Color

A designer relies on contrast to deliver the call to action for the layout. This might involve scale and negative space but can also lean on color. Distinct use of color for functionality is highly effective when the overall palette is minimal. This fact transcends digital design itself. Think of the various brands you grew up with as a child. Most of them used one or two brand colors, then sprinkled a highlight color here or there. Would Coca-Cola be so iconic if the brand's identity and label included four or five colors, rather than just the iconic red background and white type? You should also be aware of color associations that have been established over time: How many financial institutions use a deep blue primary color? What about an organization concerned with the environment? My money is on a shade of green. Knowing these established defaults is an advantage, because opportunities abound for creatively

flipping them. There are numerous tools available to generate color swatches and schemes quickly and effectively.

You should also pay attention to cultural cues if building a product for an international audience. Red can mean danger in the West, whereas traditional Chinese culture views red as a color for good luck. Purple is associated with royalty in European cultures. In Latin America, it can serve to represent mourning or death.

COLOR SWATCHES

Adobe Color (color.adobe.com) is synchronized with Creative Cloud and lets you save palettes and search publicly saved ones. This is both a blessing and a curse: there are a lot of great and terrible options to choose from. The ability to apply various color rules (complementary, monochromatic, analogous) against a chosen swatch is perhaps the most valuable part of this tool.

Colordot (color.hailpixel.com) is a pretty intuitive tool. It allows you to explore hue and saturation by moving the cursor (or finger, for the app) left and right, or up and down, respectively. It's a full-screen experience, and you can easily save a swatch and lock it in place before moving on to the next one.

Coolors (coolors.co) is a color-scheme generator that allows you to quickly shuffle through automatically generated palettes. Once you select the first swatch from the results, new colors will then be served based on your selections. It's by far the fastest option, and it seems to work well in getting to an appealing color scheme in a pinch.

Color models and profiles

In digital design, we use the RGB color model, which is additive (combining wavelengths of light), resulting in a wide spectrum. This contrasts with the typical CMYK color model for print, which absorbs (subtracts) wavelengths of light. Simply put, colors for digital screens "pop" in a way most printed collateral doesn't. If the project you're working on needs to work in concert with a print campaign, this is something that needs to be considered. If a co-branded print piece uses Pantone colors, that's another issue to tackle. Those are custom inks that can't quite be replicated by either CMYK or RGB, although the latter does a much better job. There are two major color profiles: sRGB and Adobe RGB. In 1996, HP and Microsoft collaborated to create sRGB, which came before Adobe RGB. It has become standard because it was developed for a wider audience. Adobe RGB was created specifically for designers, and it has a wider range of colors. There are pros and cons to using each.

ADOBE RGB

- has a very wide range (gamut) of available colors
- more saturated, vibrant color
- can be easily converted to sRGB
- major culprit of monitor colors not matching printed pieces
- won't be utilized on most screens

sRGB

- more consistent across various monitors and devices
- the standard format for web browsers
- color range is slightly duller with less contrast
- if you start with sRGB, you can't convert to Adobe RGB to get a wider range of colors later
- if you commit to it, there is no need to change anything later

So, ask yourself: What audience are you designing for? If it's the general public, sRGB is the easy choice. It's the standard, and you can rely on its consistency across the board. But what if you're pitching your skills for a job or to a creative community? Chances are, they might have higher-gamut monitors and appreciate the dynamic contrast of Adobe RGB. In the end, choose what works best contextually.

Grayscale and focus

A good UI design rule is to design your digital layout in grayscale to assess whether there's enough contrast and hierarchy. This simplifies the complexities of layout and allows you to focus on usability. If your methods of showing functionality are already in place without color, it's even more effective when added. Using distinct colors for important functions (like making a purchase) can funnel users toward a path. A call-to-action, such as a submit button, is a great place to add color after overall contrast has been fine-tuned. If that involves three or four steps, using that same color can increase confidence.

Figure 1.8
This color palette adds subtle variations through the use of light and saturation.

HACK

Add color by selecting a hue. Make copies of it and edit their saturation and lightness. You can create highlights and accents with this method, and the overall effect is harmonious and unified because it's rooted in light and shadow. If you want a darker complement, up the saturation and tone down the lightness; vice versa for a lighter color variation.

Black saturation

This is one thing that's easy to gloss over: select the default 0,0,0 (in RGB) black swatch when you want a black color. That's totally flat, devoid of any light waves. When you insert a pure black swatch into a color scheme, it instantly overpowers the theme. In real life, there's rarely anything that totally absorbs light: stealth technology, black holes, and little else. Even the things that appear to be black are likely reflecting some surface light, making them a (really) dark gray. One design trend in apps and software is to have a dark-themed layout. This is ostensibly to cut back on the ultra-bright light from our devices that prevent us from sleeping well, but I digress. All of those themes are actually varying levels of gray when you inspect them. Some are very close to pure black, but none go the full measure.

HACK

Try examining just how saturated black colors are for yourself: take a screenshot and open it in Photoshop. You won't likely see 0,0,0 when sampling it with the eye dropper tool. Another RGB combination to try that still looks black but is softer and much more balanced is 16,15,14.

Texture

The use of texture can help make a cold digital interface into an inviting, organic layout. The balance is finding a background that both juxtaposes and enhances the foreground. Tactile-looking textures can strike a deeper bond between the interface and user. A background that allows for interaction with the foreground can also create dimension. When choosing a texture, thinking about how it ties in with the concept is important. Photography, abstract design, and hand-drawn textures all have unique visual connotations. For example, a whimsical illustration might be a poor choice for a layout presenting architecture. Likewise, striking photography would not be a good choice for an interface made for children.

visual element to quickly communicate the subject, simplified messaging, and hopefully, a call-to-action. Everything supporting that becomes the signal. Tertiary elements, boilerplate copy, repetitive or excessive content, mere decoration—all of these things become noise. Using contrast, alignment, and negative space intentionally can help your layout become more scannable. Remember the F and Z patterns previously mentioned. The call-to-action should have the highest contrast in the layout. It's the reason everything else on that screen exists.

HACK

To add a bit of visual depth to your project, search online for "subtle patterns." This website hosts thousands of textures and patterns available under Creative Commons licenses—meaning they are free to use with proper credit.

Figure 1.9
The two media buttons have the highest contrast in this app user interface, followed by the back and download icons.

Signal to noise ratio

The term "signal to noise ratio" relates to science more than design, but it's a convenient way of measuring how effectively your visual messaging is cutting through clutter. In thinking about what the most important function of a digital layout or screen is, all other elements should support whatever goal that is. The hierarchy and flow that aids it is the signal. Anything else that doesn't directly support that function (or competes for attention) is noise. Asking what's absolutely necessary for the layout is a good starting point. Is this an interface for a website? You'll likely need some sort of logo or branding, a navigation system, a

Iconography

Digital products have come to rely on pared-down icons for almost every conceivable product, service, niche, or community. Though the first digital icons date back to 1981 (for the Xerox Alto), they've hit a tipping point in recent years. Many people would agree that there's an oversaturation of icons in the design landscape. The websites, apps, and operating systems we use are chock-full of them. A common mistake is using too many in one context. Icons can improve understanding and enhance scannability, up to a point. Blending them with text can work to understand a concept quickly if they're used in concert with that text. There are thousands of icon kits available for free download, and these would indeed save a lot of time if you're in need of many. However,

designing a custom set can be a nice opportunity if you're only in the market for a few. You'll be able to ensure a consistent look and feel with the rest of your content if it's done well. Several important factors should be considered when designing icons, such as stroke width, consistency, negative space, and overall aesthetic. They need to work well together, and either complement or juxtapose your content. Be careful to take common visual conventions into consideration. If you use a familiar icon that has a new or alternate meaning, it's frustrating and confusing for users. In terms of usability, the general public has already come to a consensus on what many icons mean. Being too creative could negate any visual value, instead creating a larger cognitive load for the user.

Accessibility standards

Many governments require their agencies to offer digital products that are accessible to people with disabilities. In the United States, this falls under Section 508 compliance. Essentially, all digital media produced or distributed by the federal government needs to be held to certain accessibility standards. User interface design has many implications in maintaining this standard, including color and contrast, typography, and layout. Using accessible color palettes is a good first step. This ensures that color is distinguishable for most of your intended audience. Light, bright, medium, and dark combinations can be found at the website: accessibility.digital.gov. Color shouldn't be used as a strict method of assigning meaning, though, as it still may be missed by those with color insensitivity. A contrast ratio of 7:1 is ideal for maintaining current accessibility standards. To understand what that means, if text and a background are the same color, the ratio is 1:1. On the flip side, pure black text against a white background comes in at 21:1.

LOGO

ICON SET

Figure 1.10
These are branded icons that feel customized yet easily understood.

HACK

Several digital tools can help with calculating contrast between colors. Search for "contrast grid" online to find one.

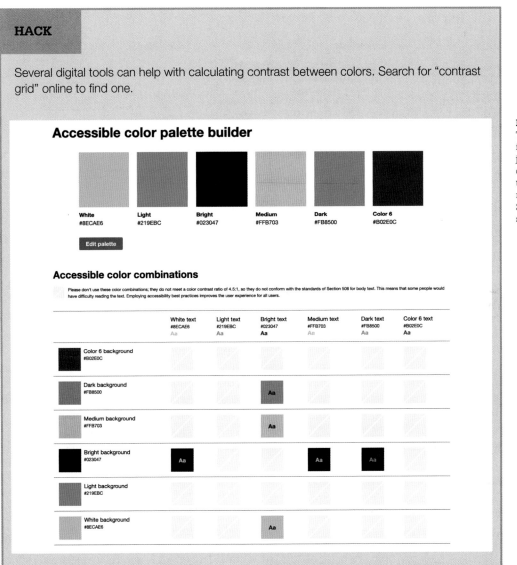

Figure 1.11
The gray squares in this grid show just how many color combinations are deemed non-accessible by Section 508 standards.

Type is a big consideration for accessibility design, and 18 pixels should be considered a starting point for body copy. Line lengths are important in maintaining a comfortable pace of reading. Very long line lengths cause fatigue in finding the next line; very short ones break words and phrases awkwardly. The range of ideal characters per line (CPL), including spaces and punctuation, is somewhere between 45 and 75. Choosing highly legible type is also a consideration: fonts with a larger x-height (the height of the lowercase "x" in relation to the ascenders) perform better for digital media because they're more visually impactful.

Typically, sans-serif fonts are used for interfaces, and serifs are used for longer content. This isn't pure doctrine though; common sense and context apply.

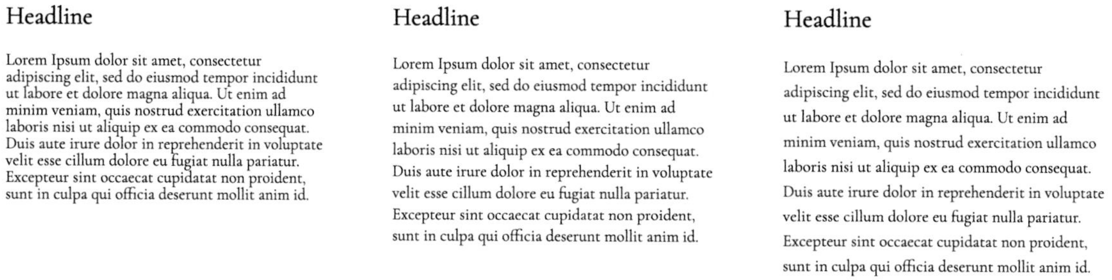

Headline

Lorem Ipsum dolor sit amet, consectetur adipiscing elit, sed do eiusmod tempor incididunt ut labore et dolore magna aliqua. Ut enim ad minim veniam, quis nostrud exercitation ullamco laboris nisi ut aliquip ex ea commodo consequat. Duis aute irure dolor in reprehenderit in voluptate velit esse cillum dolore eu fugiat nulla pariatur. Excepteur sint occaecat cupidatat non proident, sunt in culpa qui officia deserunt mollit anim id.

Headline

Lorem Ipsum dolor sit amet, consectetur adipiscing elit, sed do eiusmod tempor incididunt ut labore et dolore magna aliqua. Ut enim ad minim veniam, quis nostrud exercitation ullamco laboris nisi ut aliquip ex ea commodo consequat. Duis aute irure dolor in reprehenderit in voluptate velit esse cillum dolore eu fugiat nulla pariatur. Excepteur sint occaecat cupidatat non proident, sunt in culpa qui officia deserunt mollit anim id.

Headline

Lorem Ipsum dolor sit amet, consectetur adipiscing elit, sed do eiusmod tempor incididunt ut labore et dolore magna aliqua. Ut enim ad minim veniam, quis nostrud exercitation ullamco laboris nisi ut aliquip ex ea commodo consequat. Duis aute irure dolor in reprehenderit in voluptate velit esse cillum dolore eu fugiat nulla pariatur. Excepteur sint occaecat cupidatat non proident, sunt in culpa qui officia deserunt mollit anim id.

Figure 1.12
The image shows body copy with three varying line heights. The example at the center works best for most uses.

Leading—or line height—is also important for legibility. Too tight and the text becomes very dense, too loose and it feels exaggerated. Aim for 1.3 to 1.5 for body copy and adjust as needed for headlines and captions. Clear and focused layouts are important when considering hierarchy. Placing content in logical reading and visual order can help users complete important tasks. Indicating the intended focus order when designing wireframe layouts can help you determine what you need to revise or highlight. Grouping related items in chunks can assist people with vision or focus issues.

Light and shadow

Design for screens has taken a meandering path over the last few decades. In the beginning, everything looked quite bad because of crude tools and displays. The late-1990s deconstructionist aesthetic that followed relied on pumped-up colors and textures, heavy strokes, layered graphics, and a punk-rock spirit. The mid 2000s was all about skeuomorphism, trying to design things that mimicked real-life objects (faux-leather stitching on the edges of a screen, for instance). The short-lived flat design trend followed that, where gradients and shadows were faux pas. It seems that digital design feels a bit more comfortable in its own skin right now. It's matured

enough to embrace itself and show off the medium. I'd say we're in a *sensory* design phase, where geometric shapes and saturated colors are still alive and well. They've been tempered with the use of light and shadow, though, creating meaning through (implied) depth and surfaces. Google's Material Design Language has certainly capitalized on this shift. The scale of their entire style library is a bit daunting to a first-time user. And truth be told, if you follow their specifications to a T, your work will just end up looking Google-esque. However, their attention to interface surfaces is worth exploring. UI elements in the foreground are treated with imaginary light sources. An ambient light creates a soft contour shadow around flat surfaces, called "cards." A second light is expressed through additional light above, casting a drop shadow at the base of the card. The effect is subtle, layered, and adds a lush dimension to the layout. If there's any singular takeaway from Material Design Language, it's that light can bring much needed depth to a 2D layout.

Figure 1.13
This button has two drop shadows that mimic ambient and directional light, giving it subtle dimension.

BUTTON

Overlaying text

Other than dark-colored text on a neutral background, or light text reversed out of a color, there's often a need to run text directly over an image. It's rare that you can do this without any manipulation. Doing so requires some art direction before the act of creating the image, like intentionally including negative space in a photo composition, or illustrating an asymmetrical layout with some breathing room on either side. Most of the time, an image will need some kind of treatment for text directly over it to be legible. The three basic ways to do this are screening, blurring, and fading the image.

Screening is fairly straightforward: think of a composition in three dimensions. The image is the background, the type the foreground, and the middle ground is where you need to add some contrast. A typical example is a dark-colored shape that's semi-transparent (so you can still see the background image through it). It might be a rectangle fitted closely around the text, or it might fill the width and height of the entire image, thus muting the overall contrast.

Blurring an image behind the text is also another way to render it legible. It's like a frosted-glass effect, and it really makes the text pop. This is best done with images that have an atmospheric quality, since a lot of details are lost. Using a Gaussian blur at a low level (3–4 pixels) is usually enough to soften the image and provide needed contrast.

Fading the image is just that: applying a color gradient that creates some negative space for the type to exist in. The best method is usually to fade to a color towards the top or bottom of the image. This is a nice alternative if you don't want to blur or screen the entire image.

Modularity and affordance

Applied to digital design, modularity is a method of creating smaller components that work within an overall system. Visual widgets that are customizable, scalable, and work consistently within a larger system become even more important as devices become more interconnected with our daily lives. We expect the same consistent visual aesthetics across a range of media (i.e., easily knowing what's interactive and what's not), and designing with a set of modules can add speed to that consistency. Think about an e-commerce experience, where you're looking at a layout featuring items for sale. You'll likely see an image of the product, a description, price, and a call-to-action in the form of a button. If you drew an imaginary box around all these elements, you'd have a widget. That widget can easily be repeated using a modular grid, which displays other items for sale. Editing the content for each item is the same, so you save time. Once the visual grouping has been decided, it can be used many times over.

Figure 1.14
The product image, title, description, price, and "add to cart" button can be visually grouped as a modular unit.

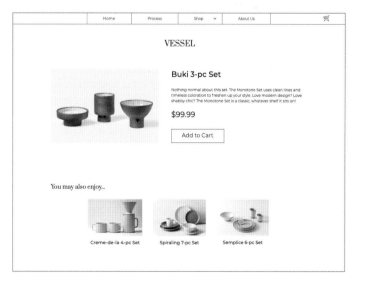

Affordance refers to the characteristics of an element in reference to its function. Things in the real world—door handles, chairs, tool grips—afford functions like pushing, sitting, and grabbing. We can leverage the knowledge that users have with past digital experiences. For instance, buttons are often enclosed with a border and fill, resembling a tactile, pressable button. A toggle switch on an interface often looks like a physical switch through the use of light and shadow. It looks like it *can* be pressed and is a great example of a learnable interface. Pattern affordance happens when a UI element's behavior becomes expected. Clicking or tapping a website logo takes us back to the homepage. Doing the same with an arrow icon initiates a download. These kinds of affordances don't win design awards, but they make interfaces fast and usable. Imagine using an app with a set of unfamiliar icons. Since they haven't been learned yet, you might be reticent to randomly tap them. Abstraction from the known also takes demographics into account. A button labeled "menu" might ease older users fears. Digital natives will assume that anything at the top left or right of an interface is a menu.

Trends

It's easy to say "build something that's timeless" when addressing current UI trends, but it's much more difficult in practice. Tastes shift almost monthly in our media-obsessed culture. Flat design is hot one minute and passé the next.

Gradients are out, then back in again. Tight grids are favored, then asymmetrical layout is king. What I *can* tell you is that interfaces that reveal information in chunks won't be leaving us anytime soon. Our ever-decreasing time and ever-increasing competition for it are forces in play. Here are some examples: interfaces that help break up content into chunks, thematic bands of sections on a website, or an onboarding process for an app. Interfaces that are purely task-focused can look visually stale, so using the UI to set up and enhance storytelling techniques feels like a trend that's spot-on. Treating content as distinct chapters involves juxtaposing words and images, using negative space, contrast, and distinct color. Inviting users to engage with content that's authentic includes them as part of your brand. If it's also consumable in bite-sized chunks, you've played to their emotions as well as their attention span. Trends that contribute to a goal rather than a fleeting visual moment will always feel classic.

Storytelling really helps to create positive emotions and relationships between your brand and users. Storytelling might also make your brand a lot more memorable and enable users to feel like they are part of our products or services, so they would like to associate with them. Having said that, storytelling is also an efficient and effective marketing tool that might increase the sales of your products or services.

User interface workflow

Sketching UI

The interface design process usually starts with sketches. Many designers want to begin iterating digitally as quickly as possible, but sketching holds a lot of value. The lack of detail can actually promote more creativity. I mentioned Google's Material Design Language earlier, with the caveat about following it verbatim. The same is true with jumping into digital design right away. You can end up cribbing from your own aesthetic, maybe even copying and pasting from a previous file. Sketching lets you work out all of the wild (and maybe great) ideas before sweating details like alignment and hierarchy. It lets you embrace an experimental mindset, something that's much needed in digital design.

HACK

There are several free printable templates available with dotted grids, pixel measurements, and even outlines denoting different devices. This is a great way to speed up your initial sketches without worrying about making straight lines. I advise my students to use these when starting out because the features let you design at actual size. When was the last time you saw a ruler with pixel measurements? There are too many websites to list here, but just search for "printable UI templates." Showing clients or stakeholders work at the sketching stage can be a toss-up. Known partners who value the process and trust the designer to work through it could benefit from early access to the UI layout. Their input at this stage may offer insight from their perspective. An example would be a navigation menu, showing six options. A client might see a sketch and realize that this could be cut down to four options (even though they stressed six options during the research and discovery phase). This lets you save time at the digital stage as you cut back on the need for revisions.

However, some clients might see this as an opportunity to flex their own creativity, whether it's valuable or not. This can be disastrous if a stakeholder sees you as a layout technician rather than a true designer. Trust your intuition during the early stages; you'll learn when to show your cards early and when to wait. While I don't advocate sketching every iteration of a layout, it's good to block out the basic ones in the beginning. For instance, if an experience is going to contain thirty screens, how many of those will be unique? Getting a representative number of layouts to work from is what you should focus on.

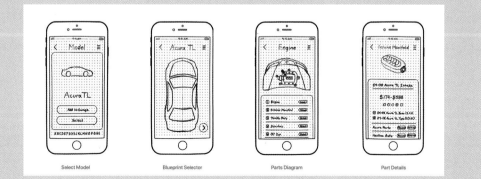

Select Model   Blueprint Selector   Parts Diagram   Part Details

Figure 1.15
Templates with outlines and dotted grids let you start sketching quickly.

Wireframes

It is important to be able to create a visual roadmap through a digital experience. Adding fidelity in stages ensures that form follows function. Wireframes are the next step. These are created digitally and map basic architecture. Physical sizes of buttons, navigation, and general elements are considered. The contoured black lines and lack of real content evoke the name.

Often, placeholder text is dropped in to give a better visual idea of space. Usually, this stage produces enough of an idea to begin testing basic functionality. It's important to bookend visual experiences here—to work out any questions in the process while it's easy to reconsider decisions. Buttons and menus are labeled with annotations (notes on functionality) and linked to subsequent screens by using lines and arrows.

Figure 1.16
Wireframes allow you to block out screens quickly and holistically across a digital experience.

HACK

Keep compositions in the same file or artboard while designing them early on. You can easily compare and contrast them when they're all on one screen together and separate them later as needed.

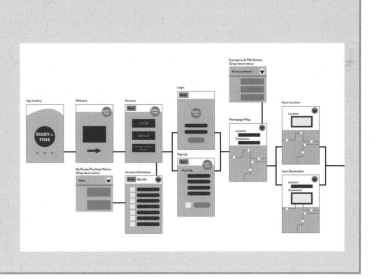

Measurements and resolution

It's familiar territory for designers to think about a composition size and resolution. For print output, we're usually working in inches or millimeters, depending on whether it's for the US market or the rest of the world. And for high-resolution printing, 300 dots per inch (dpi) has long been the standard. It's reliable and straightforward to think about this, because the unit (dots) and size (inch) are fixed. These are then paired with the layout size such as a US letter, A4, tabloid, etc. Simple, right?

For most digital design applications, you'll be working in pixels. For a long time,

pixel resolution for digital design followed the resolution for the Web, which is 72 pixels per inch (ppi). The lineage goes back to lead type for the printing press, where 72 points equaled an inch. The original Mac displays in the 1980s carried this over, displaying 72 pixels per one inch of screen. Finally, design for the Web has long used 72 pixels per inch as a holdover from these displays. But what is a pixel really? It turns out that it's not a fixed unit but is dependent on the size and density of the screen. Meaning, some devices still display 72 pixels in one inch of screen, while other high-end screens are now well over 300 pixels in one inch of screen. Apple introduced *retina displays* with the iPhone 4, and resolutions for all platforms have been climbing since. So, screen resolution has now eclipsed the typical high-resolution printing specification. What does this mean for you? First, digital design applications allow for 2x and 3x export beyond the actual artboard size, meaning you can automatically batch your final files to be output at twice or three times the scale. This is extremely helpful when designing for high-resolution displays. We could go on for an entire chapter, but here's what you need to know in short: work with

vector-based images (made with points and paths) when at all possible, which are infinitely scalable. Vector-based images scaled up will look just as crisp.

If you need to use raster images (like a photo), make sure the source is at least three times larger than you need. If you want to use a 300px square image at a standard 72ppi, it's ideal to start with a 900px image and scale it down when designing at your original size. Use file suffixes when exporting images. This is easily automated through saving or with scripts. A common naming convention is: navbar.png, navbar-2x.png, navbar-3x.png.

HACK

Most software allows for easy reuse of common items like buttons and menus. It can save a lot of time versus manually hunting them down and pasting them in each screen.

Figure 1.17
Adding annotations to your digital mock-ups can communicate functionality and intent.

Digital mock-ups

Designing the UI with color and fidelity is the next step after the wireframing has been completed. A mock-up adds a layer of visual design to the architecture in place and doing so gives you a detailed map of everything that needs to be designed and built in a more finished-looking product. At this stage, there might be placeholder content still left. The goal is to design for real content, so make sure you have an idea of its direction before spending valuable time styling it. The feedback from the previous step will provide some insight as to how to treat things such as typography, color, images, and light and shadow. At the end of the process, you should have full-color digital versions with some real content in place. Annotations are the last step in the digital mock-up phase. They add insight about functionality and intent, and show that you've carefully considered the UI.

Pattern libraries

This is like a UI inventory in reverse order, because you're designing something that didn't already exist. After individual elements are designed in a consistent aesthetic, you can use them like modules to quickly prototype and build. It's like Lego blocks for designers. Large systems can be broken down into smaller chunks this way. An example is the individual components of a form: text inputs, select menus, radio and check boxes, and submit buttons. This is also very valuable if you're working on a team; everyone has access to the same styles.

HACK

One of the easiest ways to access a UI inventory later is to build them all into one file. You can organize artboards by category and easily copy and paste them into a new project. You can test drive how this might work for your own project by searching for one of the free UI kits available all over the Web. Example:

Large screen landing page:
   Navigation
      links, toolbar

    Body
       Sans-serif heading
       Sans-serif sub-heading
       Serif body copy
         1/3 column CTA Widget w/border
           Screened background image
           CTA sans-serif copy
           CTA button

    Footer
       Copyright content
       Chat widget
       Contact link

Digital prototyping

After proper mock-ups are created, it's time to string them together in a way that's interactive. The digital prototype can be quite portable, allowing visual assets to be easily shared and tested in this phase. This process has grown more sophisticated in recent years, as various companies have designed competing software in this space. Early software allowed you to import static screens and draw rectangular hotspots throughout the UI. The hotspots act as a hyperlink that could send a viewer to any other specified screen. More software followed this trend, and functionality improved across the board. Another feature of digital prototyping apps is the ability to design content for vertical scrolling on a device. Testing out the content while being able to scroll through it feels very real.

There have been hybrid applications released in recent years that offer the highest fidelity possible. Some allow you to build fully interactive prototypes—visually or with code. These prototypes can run on their own, outside the software. They also allow you to import finished code into the application and use it to prototype future components. As the technology becomes increasingly precise, we can expect the design and development processes to further comingle.

HACK

It might make sense to build the digital mock-up directly with prototyping software, depending on the scope and stakes of the project. Here, explicit actions can be tested with realistic behaviors: the snappy accordion effect of a mobile app menu, for instance. Whatever software is used to produce the prototype, functions designed at this stage can be handed off to developers to produce the final product.

Development and handoff

Ultimately, a user interface is created in its native digital environment. That might be an app, a website, a digital kiosk, or a virtual interface. Many of these end uses have their own development methods, which can be time-consuming and costly. For instance, the iOS and Android operating systems are quite different, though their visual experiences are similar. Most developers specialize in just one or two coding languages, so choosing which experience to produce first is essential. Handing off files for final production is becoming increasingly easier because of the ability of software to translate design to code.

There are several pieces of software that specifically exist as a last stop between design and production. They allow you to build style guides and share specifications for developers. And by production, we're specifically talking about a designed experience that's coded for whatever digital ecosystem it's created for. For instance, building digital screens and a prototype using creative software is on the design side of things, while coding it for official release on an app store is on the production side. Production is industry vernacular for the final iteration of a digital product or something that's released to the public.

As this software evolves, we can expect the

pipeline to finished digital experiences to be smoother than ever. In some digital design disciplines, as we'll learn in later chapters, the lines between design and development are becoming increasingly blurred. The term *front-end designer* describes a job title for a user interface designer who can write markup for the Web. This isn't the case across the board, but as time goes by, we can expect development skills to increasingly make their way into the expectations of a user interface designer's role.

Takeaways

Whether a simple sketch or a fully functional interactive prototype, the content and scope of a project will determine the level of complexity. Many clients or stakeholders will want to see iterations at every level for large-scale engagements. Nonprofit clients or small businesses might concede to save some money and start development straight from the digital mock-up phase. Keep your business sense about you when it comes to defining the process. Don't overcomplicate a small project by over-phasing it, and practice due diligence for large-scale projects by thoroughly prototyping. Wherever the workflow leads you, knowing when and where to implement various tools and stages gives you the advantage to work with confidence.

UI DESIGN EXERCISE

Create a travel dashboard that includes a digital hub, which can host items such as popular destinations, weather, itineraries, travel times, receipts, local activities, popular photos, points and rewards, upcoming trips, delays, dining options, packing lists, etc.

DESCRIPTION

Design a travel planner dashboard for a digital experience. The client can be a travel provider (airline, rail line, bus company), booking agency, or an independent organization. Include layouts for a specific device or screen, whether it be a laptop, tablet, or smartphone.

RESEARCH AND METHODOLOGY

Consider functionality first. What's important to you when traveling? Use this question to decide what to include and how prominently to display that content. What kinds of tasks would you want to accomplish? This will inform any actions that would link to other areas with the travel planner. Download a few travel apps and visit a few websites for inspiration to try to find a niche or useful feature that might be yet unexplored.

INTENT

What do you think would motivate a client to create such an experience? There needs to be some sort of functionality to serve this need, and the goal is to incorporate it in a way that looks and feels consistent with the rest of the content. For instance, a credit card company might sponsor such a dashboard if it allowed users to see how their reward points might be used for travel.

CONTENT

This can be borrowed to get started, but resist the urge to use generic placeholder text. Some headlines, sub-headlines, general copy, and instructive text for action items and menus will get you started.

SKETCH

Draw some basic layouts based on what you've defined as important content and functionality. Spend some time making notes to label action items like buttons and anticipating the length of headlines and such.

WIREFRAME

Using your sketches as a guide, create wireframes that are sized for various end devices. Consider how much real estate you might have for content on different screens and prioritize content and actions for each. This will let you figure out the proper size of menus, buttons, and important call-to-action items. Add increased space for media (photos, illustration, video) as you move up in size. It's important to use the wireframes to glean insight before continuing. Input from someone who understands the process is ideal, but you can self-critique if needed. Walk through the experience by engaging with the visual content. Try to mentally complete actions that lead to new screens or processes.

IMAGERY

Find royalty-free stock photos or illustration to use for mock-ups: unsplash.com, gratisography.com, pexels.com, creative commons, public domain, etc. Alternatively, you can create this content yourself, but try not to spend so much time that it becomes a project itself.

MOCK-UPS

Create digital mock-ups based on feedback from the wireframes, adding real media, color, typefaces, and fine-grain visual details. Repeat the walkthrough you did at the wireframe stage to confirm hierarchy, visual flow, and consistency are in place. Make sure that commonly used items (logos and menu icons, for instance) are locked in place where they're expected. Finally, make sure that whatever business goal you've incorporated as part of the intent works with the visual aesthetic.

Figure 1.18
This app features a card-style layout using light and shadow. There's a visual hint of scrollable horizontal content.

**Figures 1.19
and 1.20**
This whimsical UI
is both fun and
serious, allowing
the ability to plan
trips and reflect
on past travels.

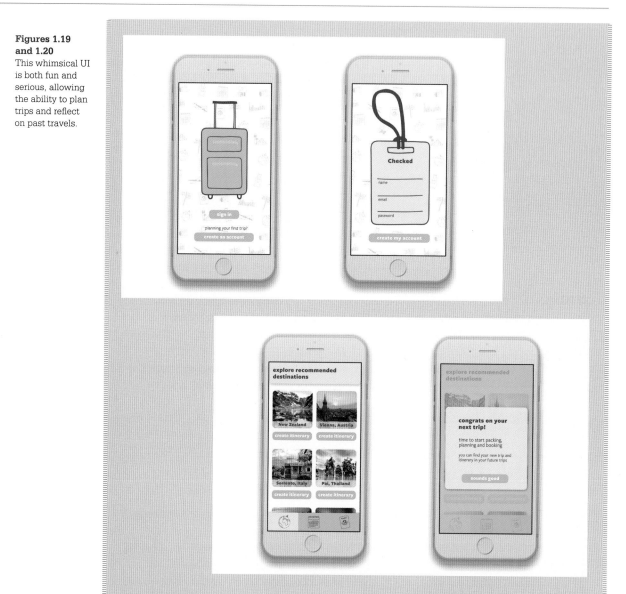

PROTOTYPE

Link the static screens together using prototyping software. Add functionality to menus, make buttons tappable or clickable, and allow content to scroll when necessary. Test this across the actual devices you'll be using for the end product.

ANALYSIS AND TESTING

Use prototyping tools to create an experience, starting with the smallest screen. Design two options, and have friends or family give it a try. Take notes. Let them use it straight away without too much explanation, because this could skew their feedback. Record their unsolicited comments and observe how they see and interact with important bits of content.

REFLECTION AND REVISION

Were there any instances where the call-to-action for any screen or layout might have been overlooked? If so, how can the contrast be increased, and the focal point emphasized? Are there too many actions on a particular screen? Decluttering the interface might provide clarity towards visual goals. Does the visual intent from the perspective of a potential client make sense? Compare it to the products you researched at the beginning. Does it look real? Are there any obvious differences in terms of it being perceived as professional work?

BONUS STEP

Export visual assets using development handoff software. Experiment with presets and the steps needed to package the project for final production.

GOALS AND OUTCOMES

A successful outcome of this exercise should be revealed by the reflection and revision stage. It should be obvious as to whether this visually communicates the importance of the functions you deemed significant through your research and conceptual steps. It should be portfolio quality, meaning it should have the same visual finesse of the products you researched it against. The user interface should highlight actionable content, embrace consistency, and have a pleasing visual flow. The tie-in that you imagined during the intent step should represent a realistic business outcome from a client's perspective. It should also fit the visual needs of that client, meaning the branding should be on par with a client that's tangentially related to this product. Have you imposed a visual style that seems at odds with the entire experience? Use your holistic design lens to make sure it meets your own gut check.

Figure 1.21
This is a dashboard that features search functionality, upcoming trips, and ticket information at a glance.

User Experience Design

Within the disciplines discussed in this book, user experience (UX) is a bit abstract compared to traditional graphic design. It's also one of the most important factors to consider for a digital project because it's directly connected to results. UX is a term that is often conflated with user interface design. This is partially because many entry-level jobs in the field bundle them together as a "one-stop shop." Whereas UI focuses on the visual, UX goes beneath that layer to examine *how* a digital experience works. It's psychologically driven and is deeply concerned with enhancing the user's journey through a digital product. Usability, accessibility, and the general cognitive experience are important to this discipline. Balancing business goals with user needs and technical constraints forms the three important aspects of UX design. The overall skill set is also broader than that of a UI designer. The core of user experience design is a question and answer: What is the user's goal or challenge? And how can you solve that in a way that best considers their needs?

One reason that UX continues to mystify designers is that many of the assets we produce are packaged up into familiar deliverables. Designing layouts for screens and exporting them seems relatable to a traditional graphic design workflow. Writing personas and creating experience maps and user flows doesn't. These UX assets are in one way counterpoint to UI design and at the same time greatly inform the visual design. Because of their dynamic nature, digital products are much more complicated than legacy media (an umbrella term that print-based design and broadcast TV fall into), and the time and effort that goes into development is significant. With the stakes this high, you simply can't design based on intuition. Although an often-overused buzz phrase, the "design thinking process" can help to explain how UX is involved throughout the cycle of a project. The core of design thinking rests on these steps, and UX has implications in all of them:

- defining the problem or goal
- empathizing with the user's needs
- ideating quickly and often
- prototyping and testing.

User experience specifications

Initial discovery

A project lands in your lap. What's the first step? Get more information about the potential client or stakeholder: What industry, discipline, segment, or niche do they operate in? Do you know anything about it? What's familiar, and what's totally new? How might it connect with your background or experience? Search for things that can shed quick insight, like a mission statement, organizational history, or any current or past visual media. Doing this before the next step can save you from embarrassment, and the initial effort will be appreciated.

Client interview

Sending a list of questions ahead of time can help the interview be more productive and comfortable. The questions should be broad, focusing on general points such as:

The outlying problem or opportunity
This doesn't need to be overly specific yet, but it should be answered without lingering questions: "create an augmented reality app that renders home products at actual size," for example.

Identify key performance indicators
These are goals that can be measured. For instance, increasing the ratio of items in an e-commerce cart to items purchased by 20 percent. Even goals that might seem initially holistic can be tracked. Creating public awareness of a new product, for instance, can be tracked very specifically on the Web.

Target demographic
Who are the typical customers or users from the client's perspective? They may have a base of existing loyal customers, which is concrete data. If it's a start-up or new company, they may have conducted some research themselves. It's also possible that they don't yet know or are off by quite a bit in their estimation.

Market research
Who are the competitors? What differentiates them from others in the same space? A client is likely to be very tuned-in to their market, but you can expect to push on this question a bit if they're just starting out. You'll want to identify a niche or competitive advantage with this question. For example: "Is there a short-term rental booking platform that serves remote workers?"

Brand philosophy
What values or ethics define the culture of the company or organization? How are their practices informed by these values? These humanistic traits should bleed through in the tone, voice, and visual communication. For instance, the online retailer Zappos states their purpose as "To live and deliver WOW." They're known for outstanding customer service; their public communication is very transparent, and their visual aesthetic is no-nonsense and casual.

Existing guidelines
Are there visual practices or standards already in place that need to be considered? This may seem like a question where answers will be revealed naturally, but this isn't always the case. Asking bluntly will prevent you from having to revise later. Sometimes a project or product needs to be on-brand and align very closely with existing styles. Other times it might need to look and feel like more of an offshoot of the main brand. That decision may be arrived at through conducting the rest of the UX process, but in the end there should be an obvious visual connection made.

Project brief

This is the first step in understanding the goals for starting a new project. Design exists to solve a problem or simplify an experience. So, what's the problem that's being tackled, and how can it be solved in a way that meets the client's goals? Sometimes these goals might be clearly defined, like buying a product or service via an app or website. However, they're often a bit more complicated, like finding an available rideshare bicycle based on user location, rider preferences, and station availability. A project brief differs slightly from a typical graphic design creative brief, where a client might simply state needs and expectations. Here, the brief is created collaboratively as a group. This involves client and creative stakeholders and is often created as part of an initial meeting. The aim is to create a list of shared goals, roles of those involved, and steps outlining the workflow.

To complete the project brief, you'll want to address the following:

Vision statement
This should clearly define the objectives of the project from the perspective of users. This is the bottom-line call and response:

- What's the problem or opportunity?
- Whom is the project serving?

- How will this project solve the problem or fill the opportunity?
- Why will it be better than any existing competitors?

From there, you should be able to craft a statement that defines the value proposition by answering these questions. Here's an example for a company in the digital payments sector:

> Stripe is a platform that helps customers accept web and mobile payments for their digital products. The product ultimately serves clients, but it also serves software developers who are building the products and influencing the client. It solves the problem of integrating payment software into existing products while allowing for total customization. It's better than its competitors because of the ability for complete control over functionality and presentation.

Specifications
What kind of functions must the product include? What medium(s) will it be designed for? Examples are "app-only" or "both app- and web-driven." Are there any technologies that must be used or existing technical requirements? The answers to these questions will start out broad and become more granular as the project evolves.

Design strategy
This is familiar territory for most visual designers because it's concerned with look and feel. What adjectives describe how the product should be perceived? What kind of visual goals would support those adjectives? What kind of tone should the overall experience convey? Are there effective examples that can be referenced? The answers to these questions will likely be in the form of word and image. If a traditional design brief already exists, visual direction can be gleaned from it.

Stakeholders
Who is involved from the client's perspective? What's their role and authority over the project? How involved are they in terms of collaboration and investment of time? The same should be answered for the design team. For example: "The marketing team will oversee the project, but the CEO will ultimately sign off."

Timeline
Defining the development stages and a realistic schedule is important, as is clearly stating that all parties involved affect deadlines. This ensures that no one person or group is holding up the process with a "hurry up and wait" mentality. I cannot stress just how often schedules get delayed because the time needed for a particular stage isn't well considered.

PROJECT BRIEF

What's the problem or opportunity?
The problem is not being able to find your terminal at an airport, actively engage with flight changes in a safe way, and finding a way to leave the airport if no one can pick you up.

Who is the project serving?
This serves users from 16-45. I personally used to fly alone as a teen, so this app would cater to those who know how to use technology but may not know how to travel. It also can help those who are familiar with travel and can make their experience more efficient.

How will this project solve that problem or fill that opportunity?
It will help guide you to the right terminal, find your luggage, and keep up-to-date on any flight changes. Additionally, you can use it to catch a subway or bus at your next destination. If this were real, it would offer all forms of transportation since it would have to cater to different areas; however, since this is a mock-up, I will just be focusing on air travel and the subway.

Why will it be better than any existing competitors?
It will be simple, but all-inclusive. The airport navigation feature that is based on my own personal travel experiences will effectively set it apart.

What kind of functions must the product include? What medium(s) will it be designed for? Are there any technologies that must be used or existing technical requirements?
It could easily be web-based but I am just going to focus on an app for now. It will be designed on an iPhone 6s but is opeable on any iPhone or Android.

I want the app to:
1. Include a profile component just so you can safely store important information (I.D., tickets, luggage pass info) on your phone without worry
2. Have a GPS function for moving around airports and finding terminals
3. Provide updates on any layovers or change in flights
4. Allow you to purchase bus/subway tickets and plan your route

What adjectives describe how the product should be perceived? What kind of visual goals would support those adjectives? What kind of tone should the overall experience convey?
1. Chic, simple, all-encompassing
2. I want simple but fun imagery, use of dark and neon colors
3. It should feel all-inclusive no matter what country you're in or where you're from

Figure 2.1
The project brief should include a synopsis of the client interview and vision statement.

Engaging stakeholders

Aside from the end user, there are several involved parties that need to be considered in early-stage research. Those who have the power to affect and influence the project, and those who are affected. Client stakeholders can include:

- executives and managers
- marketing directors
- in-house product and development teams
- legal departments.

On the design side, the stakeholders consist of whatever individual(s) or group is leading that end of the project and their collaborators. This can include:

- account executives
- creative directors
- art directors
- technical developers
- designers.

Individuals at the "top of the food chain" usually have the ability to affect change in one fell swoop, so it's important to fully engage them and inspire early buy-in. How to do that? Reiterate desired outcomes of a digital product and ensure design decisions connect back to them. Leaning on research is often effective, but when that alone doesn't convince them, user testing might. UX is often a totally abstract concept to high-value stakeholders, as their day-to-day duties are concerned with macro decisions. Don't get bogged down in micro details when communicating with high-value stakeholders. Time will be critical here; you'll need to hit your mark quickly and succinctly. Think bullet points. Stakeholders with less power can be motivated through collaboration tools like strategy meetings, individual interviews, and demonstration of research. Sometimes, simply cueing them in and answering questions along the way are enough. Others with a more direct connection to the end product will want their concerns validated. An interview might yield requirements or expectations that were left out of the project brief. Here are three key pointers that can help with consistent goal alignment:

- Ask them about their role in the project. They could simply be issuing a rubber stamp, or they might be someone who will use the product on a daily basis.
- Have them state the project goals. What problem is it solving? These will likely shift between stakeholders and form a range of answers.
- Ask them about the end user of the product. What's the demographic? What are some of their sticking points in using similar products or experiences?

Engaging stakeholders on your own team is usually more straightforward, because you likely already know them. That said, there's skill in understanding the myriad roles of a design business: those who bring in the money, those who direct the creative, and those who build and develop the experiences. Client-facing individuals need to be reassured that the creative is in service of the business goals. They are more likely to back design work if they're armed with the information to present toward those goals. The creative team needs to feel like their skills are being utilized beyond their roles as production artists. Allowing time to fully explore concepts is key, as is embracing ideas that are bold and innovative. Nothing truly inspiring comes from repeating past solutions or copying successful ones. Those involved on the technical side will want to be apprised of specifications and requirements and know that they aren't trying to hit a moving target. Development often takes significant

time, so "building it once" is a great goal to strive for here. Patching a finished product together with a technical Band-Aid would be a failure from their perspective. Forcing them to pull late nights because of a last-minute detour in specifications might inspire mutiny as well.

User research

UX design starts in earnest with conducting user research. Depending on the scale of the project, this might be done directly. For large projects, collaboration with a business or product analyst is usually necessary. The goal here is to glean information and requirements from potential users. What does this digital product need to do? And how might people use it? Extracting product needs at a basic level is critical in bookending the scope of the project. This becomes the basis for the information architecture, or the art of organizing and structuring needs and content. It's important to mention the popular phrase "you are not your users" here because it's easy for a designer to insert themself into the equation. So easy, that they might opt to make an educated guess. Conducting real user interviews is always better than this. Your client may balk at them for budgetary reasons or tell you that they already know their users well enough to answer themselves. This mistake can cause the project to miss the mark entirely, and unless the stakeholders have conducted independent unbiased research, their information may be based on assumptions or old data. Having access to actual users lets you see the project from their perspective.

Conducting user interviews

Typical methods for conducting user interviews include surveys and in-person interviews. The survey can be more convenient as it can be digital and portable. This method also tends to gather more information, but you can't adjust questions based on the user's answers. A survey for a digital banking app might start off by listing several digital products in that industry and asking the user to rank them by familiarity. You can home in on specifics by asking things like, "What frustrates you about the login experience?" or "What features do you use most?" In-person interviews are more difficult, although they can take place via videoconference if needed. Depending on the complexity, you can interview users one by one or in small groups. The latter seems to facilitate a more relaxed setting and perhaps more authentic answers. The interviewer introduces key points related to the user experience and lets users discuss them openly and

naturally. Here, the moderator might extend one of the earlier questions about the login experience by asking, "Would you prefer another kind of authentication method like a fingerprint scan?" Insight like that is more difficult to extract in a survey. Whatever you do, please don't use generic language like, "On a scale of 1–5, how likely are you to …" Successful user interviews will reveal their level of familiarity with the product, their motivations for using it (or not), and their sticking points and frustrations. The information gleaned here will help you develop personas.

Personas

A persona is a detailed model of a typical user for a product. It's designed to represent a segment of users and features as much realistic information as possible: a fictional name, demographic info, a profile, and often a photo. The user's goals related to the product can also be listed, as well as motivations and frustrations with products in

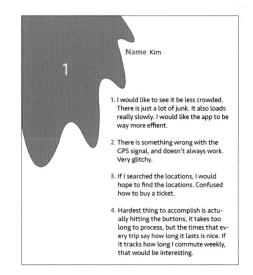

Figure 2.2
User interviews are sorted and compiled to develop personas. This example relates to questions about a competitor's app.

Figure 2.3
A persona is a realistic model of a user, built with information gleaned during interviews.

ABOUT
Ankit is a young IT professional working as a Software Developer in an MNC. He is an avid traveller who likes to explore new places, cities, food and cultures. He regularly plans his travel every 2-3 months. His prefered mode of booking tickets is through the IRCTC website or app.

TECH SAVVY

GOALS

- A trip every 2-3 months
- Get train fares & timings in least number of steps
- Easily book tickets
- Get personalised travel packages

NEEDS

- Better online booking experience
- Remember passenger profile for autofill
- Save travel history for repeated bookings
- Modify or cancel the booking easily
- OTP based login

PAIN POINTS/ FRUSTRATION

- Lengthy process to look for train details
- Resetting password
- Information clutter across channels
- Outdated design language
- Multi city travel planning
- Uncertain cancel & refund process
- Train status, PNR and route details are difficult to find

- Some vital features like save route details, search train by name are missing
- Slow loading website
- No review available for trains

Ankit Jain
30 years
Software Developers
New Delhi, India

that market. The idea is to define real user behavior, wants and needs, sticking points, and short quotes or phrases. All of this information is inspired directly from interviews and user research. Building a list of qualities around this persona helps the designer build features that best serve the needs of their users. For example: if a persona model dictates a user in their mid-twenties who lives in an urban environment, works in an office, and lists increased productivity as a goal, we can assume that they're technologically proficient. This information has a waterfall effect on the rest of the design process and helps inform everything from the size of buttons and touch targets to the kinds of imagery a digital experience might use. Depending on the overall scope, somewhere between three and eight personas are usually the range required to cover most intended audiences.

Understanding your market and typical user is paramount to being effective at UX design. Early in my career, I took on a design project where the client had identified their user demographic with a span of fifty years in age range. Not being experienced (or brave) enough to question this, I designed based on this information. Without question, the resulting work was some of the most mundane and uninspired output I've produced. An effective UX designer faced with the same challenge would press the client or stakeholder for more information in an effort to refine the user profile. As the adage goes, "When you try to be everything to everyone, you accomplish being nothing to anyone."

User empathy

UX has an important distinction within the digital design disciplines in that user empathy is at its core. This must be balanced against the need to look at the scope of a project from a bird's-eye view, so to speak. User empathy means being able to put yourself in the shoes of a user and navigate through the information architecture you've mapped out. This is easier said than done, because when we try to abstract this experience, we still end up negotiating the steps through our own subjective lens. While imaging yourself as a user faced with a choice to make, you might make an educated guess based on the choice that you would make. "Would the user press this icon to navigate to the next screen, or is that something that I'm assuming they would do?" Extending the personas and using the research collected during early stages is critical in framing the decision-making process from a user's perspective.

User flow

Mapping out the timeline of user goals within an experience is done with user flows. These are simple schematics that show individual actions and illustrate how many steps it takes to complete the task. They don't take any underlying technology or personal factors into consideration, just goals and steps. They often have accompanying user interface visuals in very basic form (sketches or blocks and shapes). They need to include the following:

- The name of the particular user goal or function. This should be labeled as a heading.
  Example: "Sign up for an account."
- They show a progression between screens or experiences in a linear fashion, from start to goal. This fundamentally separates them from related documents like site maps.

ACTION: Look up route

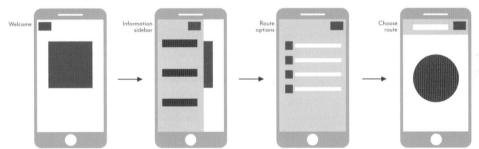

ACTION: Display fares for route

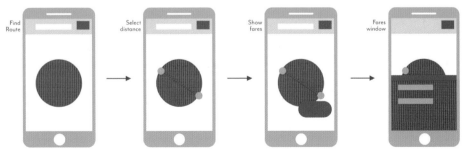

Figure 2.4
A user flow combines basic descriptions with simple graphics to illustrate the path through a single action.

- They include text that describes the actions of each step.
  Example: User starts at account sign-up page > fills out name and email > receives confirmation message and is directed to dashboard screen.
- Tasks should be singular and not show more than one path. If there is a point at which a user needs to make a choice that will diverge into multiple tasks, show each one as a separate user flow.

User journey

There's often much confusion about the differences between a "user flow" and a "user journey." The latter should be created afterwards, and it deals with both the emotional frustrations and motivations of the user. The user flow should be completed before all of this is contemplated. It's not concerned with the specifics of task or goal functionality but more with identifying and examining stages to get to a goal. Start by creating groups of related actions (in chronological order) that form a scenario leading up to the end goal (for example, user picks up phone > opens app > types in passcode, etc.). A user journey is mapped out by adding notes to each step in the scenario and visually grouping them. The notes should convey emotional motivations and frustrations with the experience. Have you ever used an app that required a numerical code yet displayed a full alphabetical keyboard on-screen? That's a frustration. You can make notes about the high and low points throughout the journey. For instance, a high point for using a ride-share app is the satisfaction of being matched with a driver. A low point would be updating a stored credit card that had expired. A user journey map shows all of this information in an organized way. The user and specific scenario is identified at the top, showing the journey moving horizontally across the page below. At the bottom of the page, insights are noted.

Figure 2.5
A user journey is much more holistic than a user flow, and includes external factors related to an experience.

HACK

You don't have to create a user journey template from scratch. Search for "when and how to create customer journey maps" to find a clearly labeled document developed by top-notch UX firm Nielsen Norman Group.

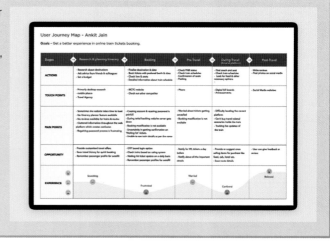

Content inventory and audit

This step helps plan your content needs with respect to the project objectives and design direction. The content that the client or stakeholders want or need might already exist in some form, though it might not be fully realized at this point. A content inventory involves cataloging and categorizing any existing content. After all, not all projects will start from zero. Some clients may hire you to jump in midway or to resurrect a failed project. When conducting an audit, sort any existing content into type (instructional, narrative, etc.), general description, topic, and date. Once you've had a chance to organize the content, you can begin evaluating it. What is its purpose and message? For whom was it created? Does it relate to a function or goal? A content audit can help with the decision of what to keep and what to scrap. The product needs and scope that were identified will likely open up opportunities for new content to mesh with anything that currently exists. At this early stage, establishing a common style for the content can be advantageous.

HACK

As much as designers hate spreadsheets, a content inventory and audit is a good case use for one. Try not to waste time on the layout of a content inventory. This is just a place to collect and organize information.

Categorization

Card sorting is a UX method used to examine how a user might scan, categorize, and sort content. Index cards with topics and themes relating to the content are given to users to sort out and organize. They should be shuffled to be randomized from the start. Whenever possible, representative users should be performing the sorting. This helps to understand the needs and intentions of the target audience. The groups that the particular content falls into become the basis for overarching themes in the digital project. Ideas for a navigation menu is an obvious outcome from this, but the exercise can also be helpful in confirming your content thus far. If users are fuzzy on the differences between topics (organizations vs. enterprises, for instance), you might revisit the personas to further hone your content. Cards might also be used to delineate category grouping for a retail experience, functionality for an app, or make a site map for web pages. For example, if you're creating a digital kiosk for a shopping center, sorting content into groups such as "Home Goods," "Clothes and Shoes," and "Electronics" would make sense. The reverse order also works, if functionality or categories have already been dictated. Meaning, the users would sort content into already existing categories instead of making the categories from the content and then sorting.

Market research

After the basic goals are framed out, the UX designer creates a competitive analysis to define the features. What do examples of existing products look like? What kinds of features do they have? We might be talking about an app, a website, a navigation device, or a smart appliance. How could those features be improved upon? What kinds of problems might users have with them? This is where UX really comes into its own because interviews and user observations are at the heart of these discoveries.

Figure 2.6
A site map illustrates logical relationships between screens in a progressive order.

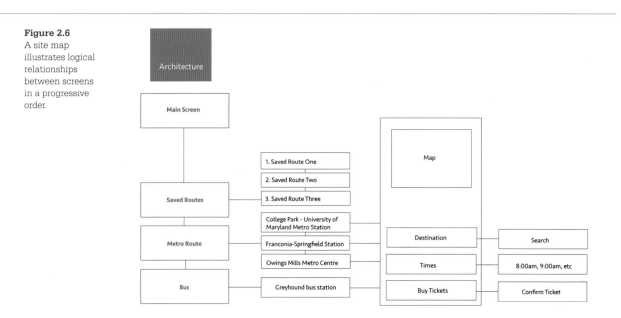

Information architecture

The steps leading up to this point all work toward creating the information architecture. It's an overarching map that classifies content in a way that's understandable and meaningful for the user, with respect to the functionality and project goals. The IA is largely composed of a site map or mind map. The former is an outline of screens or steps in hierarchical order. Think of a website with a home page, five major sub-pages or categories, and several pages beneath each category. A mind map is not as vertically structured, and it focuses on tasks, functionality, and the various relationships of digital assets to that end. Site maps obviously lend themselves very well to websites, but a mind map can provide some much-needed abstraction if you find that you're thinking too linearly (i.e., it allows you to envision the screens serving the functions rather than fitting the functions into screens). If you've conducted a card sorting session, the information gleaned could apply directly to the information architecture process.

User experience workflow

Sketching

Quick iteration is hands down the primary reason to sketch. As fast as you are in any digital design application, I can guarantee that you're faster with a pencil or marker. There are other benefits that might not be immediately perceived. One of these is collaboration. There's nothing more awkward than a team huddled around a designer's computer, with each person adding their feedback to include in the design. With sketching, not only team members can be included in the process, but clients and stakeholders as well. Again, the fidelity is absent at this stage, so you won't have to worry about a client art directing you.

Another benefit is the ability to write notes directly in the margins. This is hugely beneficial when considering the importance and scope of functionality. For instance, jotting down a note saying, "UI designer: this function is what we want the user to complete first and foremost on this screen."

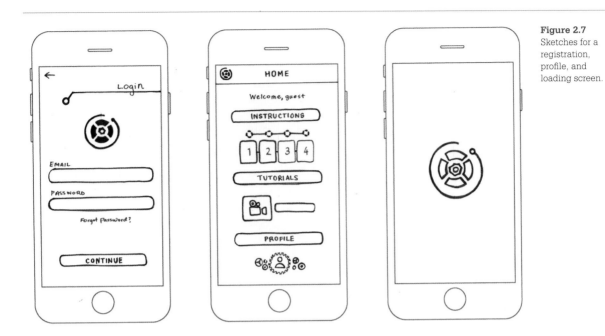

Figure 2.7
Sketches for a registration, profile, and loading screen.

That can then be carried forth to the visual design stage without having to constantly repeat it. Lastly, starting with paper allows you to bookend the functionality of the project. It quickly allows you to see what can and can't be done and highlights any dead ends in the functionality. For instance, after a purchase is completed through an app, what does the user see next? A confirmation might be obvious, but some additional information about the next steps could also be useful. After several screens are sketched, you can visually walk through the proof-of-concept.

Prototyping

If there's any part of UX that has an overlap with UI, it's the prototyping process. In fact, UI design is likely to be considered at this stage. Wireframing and prototyping are also both within the domain of a user experience designer. The difference? While a UI designer is tasked with crafting a consistent interface, a UX designer is concerned with the user's perspective. This is an important distinction, showing that

UX transcends the functional role it has been cast in. The prototyping process for UX design focuses on the user's journey and is decidedly low-fidelity when compared to a UI prototype. The user flow through screens or experiences and completion of a task or function is paramount to this step. If you haven't quite figured out how a task will play out, prototyping won't help yet.

Writing UX copy

A lack of attention to writing exists across the design disciplines. As a visual practice, look and feel takes center stage while the nitty-gritty details are left to copywriters. Writing with the intent of convincing a user to take some kind of action is a classic component of the advertising industry: crafting intoxicating headlines that identify a brand with your lifestyle. But writing for UX is distinct and relatively new: instead of writing to sell, it focuses on writing to aid. In fact, the two processes can be seen to bookend a digital experience. One is convincing users to try it, and another is helping them to complete it. As interfaces have evolved, you might have noticed the attention to UX writing becoming more apparent. Humanizing the experience is highly sought after in a landscape that's rife with automated messages. The effect of writing can have a big impact on the UI, especially if it's considered throughout the design process and not simply tacked on at the end.

Writing for specific functionality in UX is known as "microcopy" and can range from a sentence to a single word. Many times, the instructive microcopy for call-to-action functionality is left as a default: "more info" or "next." This is the bane of digital design products because it screams generic boilerplate copied from somewhere else. It's crucial to dial-in these details if you want to connect with digital natives; they'll smell the lack of authenticity from a mile away. So how do you start writing effective UX copy? First, establish a consistent mood or overarching attitude that will connect with your audience. The digital marketing platform Mailchimp serves as a great example: their copy is refreshingly crisp and casual when walking you through the steps involved in their services. They use bits of humor as well, something that's lacking in digital marketing and very effective if presented tastefully.

HACK

Mailchimp hosts a publicly available web document on "tone and voice" on their website. It's very thorough and super helpful in thinking about how to approach your own writing style. Just search for their name and that phrase. Copy needs to be effective beyond an emotional connection to your users. They need to feel like steps (even complicated ones) that are easily understood and manageable. The best-case scenario is to advance users through the use of UX copy in a way that makes them feel like they've guided themselves (meaning the copy feels familiar and honest to them). Harmony with the visual elements in the layout is important too. Sometimes a bit of copyfitting is necessary to avoid awkward line breaks or clutter. This simply means trimming the copy to fit the available space.

Wireframe

After paper prototyping and some UX writing, a project usually goes through a wireframing phase. This is a low-fidelity presentation of the experience that may include much of the functionality discussed and discovered during the paper prototyping phase. The goal of the wireframe is to present the content in a slightly more formal manner while outlining a basic structure for it. It should also give some attention to needs and wants for a user interface. The following are being presented at this stage: structure, layout, content, and functionality.

HACK

We've already talked about wireframes in the UI workflow, so there might be some confusion as to why it's mentioned here as well. The fact is, there's often a lot of overlap in the UI/UX process. The wireframing might be completed at either end or collaboratively. Since these two jobs might be combined in a single role, it's often a moot point.

Visually, the name gives a good description of what is produced. Generally, screens are designed using contour lines, basic geometric shapes (boxes and rectangles for photos or visual art, circles for icons) and shades of gray to add some depth. At this point, not all the content will be fully developed. Not only is the process of digitally creating the wireframe fairly quick, but the low fidelity forces stakeholders and clients to focus on functionality, user flow, interaction, and usability. Since all aesthetics are flattened, feedback is generally more objective and focused. You can't spend thirty minutes debating the color of a button if it has none.

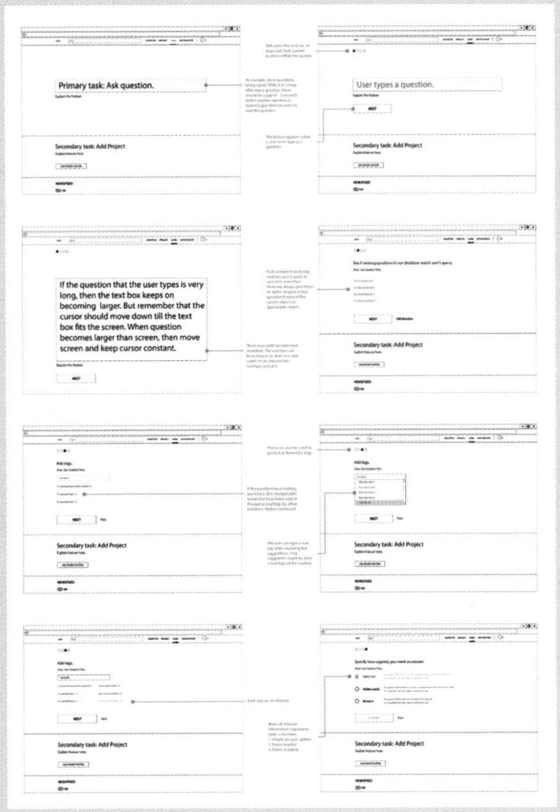

Figure 2.8
Wireframes that are specific to UX should be low fidelity and include annotations related to actions and flow.

The following is a checklist of considerations when wireframing:

- What are the functional goals when interacting with this experience? To purchase a product or service? To donate time or money? To enter an email address?
- How does the content support the goals? The headlines, sub-headlines, text, instruction, and call-to-action copy should make sense.
- What kind of imagery will be used (photos, illustrations, graphics)?
- How will any branding affect the layout? Will it heavily dictate the content, or will it be minimized?
- What is the first level of hierarchy? What is the first thing the user should see or interact with? What should be seen last?
- What is the call-to-action? How will you direct users toward that goal?

Consistency

Once the basic wireframe structure is decided, content blocks can be added. If there's a navigation system being used, where will it live? You'll need to decide whether you're using common design patterns (for example, a navigation at the top near a logo). Can you approximate the amount of text and content to be added? Where is the call-to-action within that content? It's important to note here that you don't want to start overly specifying visual direction—that's the domain of the UI designer. Consistency of basic layout, an implied grid, and a unified sense of negative space can help build user confidence in your design. Predictability of navigation and calls-to-action go a long way in establishing this.

Task hierarchy

For multistep functionality, considering the end-uses for each experience is helpful. For instance, interaction on a mobile device can create frustration. Breaking down steps into bite-sized actions can ease this, while also minimizing user frustration. Reducing visual clutter is also important in removing any friction. Again, you need to ask, what's the primary goal of this screen or experience? Everything else becomes secondary. Sometimes, designers get a bit overzealous with this challenge. They may end up hiding important functionality behind accordion menus or navigation. These should be easily accessed by a single interaction. A great example is the process of purchasing something digitally, reviewing a cart, and confirming payment and shipping. Many online retailers entice customers who already have accounts and details saved in their databases with the ability to streamline this process.

Cognitive load

Because we're often multitasking while interacting with digital experiences, our attention is already half-present. The ability to complete a task suffers if the information required to do so is overwhelming. This amount of attention needed to complete a task is referred to as "cognitive load." While this term is rooted in psychology, it applies quite directly to digital design. If the cognitive load is too high, users will often abandon the task. This means, closing your app or website or walking away from your digital kiosk. Ways to minimize cognitive load include:

- avoiding redundant content (visual, text, or functional)
- using familiar design patterns (navigation menus, grids, buttons)
- reducing the number of tasks (shortening a checkout process).

HACK

Many apps have user-registration components as one of the first screens that greet a potential user. While this is helpful if you need to capture their name and email address, people are sometimes hesitant to sign up for yet another service. You might ask yourself: Do I really need access to that information straight away? And will it create a choke point for users? Designing an experience where that information can be collected later, when the user feels a sense of trust, might be smart. Removing barriers in the user flow is key in helping them to work through a digital product and complete actions.

Streamlined methods

There are several tried-and-true methods of quickly iterating a concept through agile development cycles. Lean UX is one such method, outlined in a book bearing the same name by author and information architect Jeff Gothelf. At its core: getting user feedback early, making decisions based on that data, and iterating quickly to arrive at a minimum viable product (MVP). Along the way, any changes that increase progress toward user goals are kept. Changes that don't are scrapped. What this method lacks is a level of detail in terms of visual design. The idea is to just "get the thing to work first" and then add fidelity afterwards. Major steps in the process include developing a user hypothesis, building rough wireframes, testing and analyzing them, and ideating until a basic working version of the product has been made.

HACK

If you're interested in testing out the Lean UX method, search for "The Lean UX Canvas" to get a free downloadable template developed by Jeff Gothelf. It will allow you to quickly jump into the process.

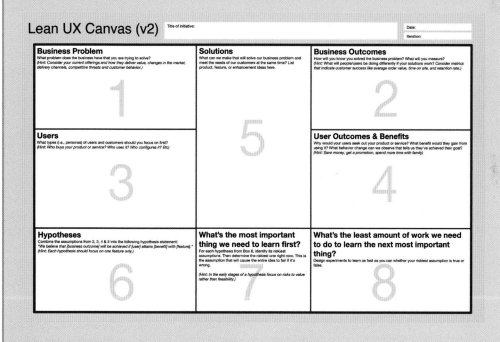

Developed at Google Ventures, a Design Sprint is another agile method that's comprised of a five-day process for mapping a challenge and arriving at a solution. A unique feature of this method is that it ultimately relies on one decider to push ideas forward each day. While this seems very non-democratic, in some sense it mimics the top-down actions of a CEO.

Figure 2.9
The Lean UX Canvas features prompts that assist with rapid iteration, which is part of the Lean UX process.

It also ensures the schedule is honored, and participants are given the opportunity to weigh-in along the way. The general outline is broken down as such:

- Monday: Start with a long-term goal, identify involved parties, and choose an area of focus based on that goal.
- Tuesday: Ideation of competing solutions in groups and individually, and sketch out rough ideas.
- Wednesday: Critique of ideas, discussion and decision, and storyboarding.
- Thursday: Prototyping, preliminary testing, creation of script, and recruiting users.
- Friday: Test, gather feedback from users, record interviews, and compile data.

Methods like these have been widely used in developing start-up companies and in "hackathon" competitions. Many successful products and partnerships have emerged through agile methods, and it's an exciting way to test UX principles.

Evaluation and validation

Testing the wireframes before adding high-level visual details is crucial to designing something that functions well. The first step is for the design team to walk through the user's process themselves, testing the user journey, user flow, and wireframes. Questions to ask during this process include:

- How easy is this to use? Consider the personas in play when doing so.
- Is there anything blocking goals that was missed in the user flow?
- If a user encounters a mistake, are there affordances like an undo function?
- Are user goals able to be easily achieved?
- Does the experience provide overall positive emotional feedback?
- Would the user likely use it again?

Mood boards

You're probably already familiar with mood boards if you're involved with any traditional methods of graphic design. They're a staple in helping determine the look and feel of a project through showcasing images, typefaces, colors, and even borrowed quotes. For the uninitiated, a mood board is basically a collage to share inspiration with a team or stakeholder. In some disciplines (web design, for instance), they can verge into very specific presentations of buttons, menus, and the like. My suggestion is to leave this for the UI stage if it deals with an interface, whether that will remain your responsibility or someone else's. But more holistic mood boards can complement the UX process and connect it back to something more visual. Some of the inspiration will come from stakeholder interviews, specifically things that will align with any brand guidelines. Additionally, it will come from the insight gleaned through user interviews.

Making clear statements to work from can be a good start to collecting images. Identify how users should feel while engaged with a digital project or product. Here's an example: As an interior designer, Jadyn feels confident when ordering fabric swatches through the Fabric Co mobile app. The statement is carefully constructed.

MOODBOARD

Start with a noun: a user developed as a persona. Then identify the personal or emotional connection. Finally, connect a real action from the user flow and tie it to the project. After developing these for each persona, make a list of adjectives that will help you begin searching for images. "Contemporary, clean, and muted" are three examples that can visually drive your search. After you begin searching for images, there are no less than a dozen ways to arrange and present them. Using layout software that you already know and exporting a PDF is a no-nonsense method.

Adding details

As the scope of the project increases, the fidelity of the wireframing process may follow suit. At the highest levels, wireframes for large-scale projects might include grayscale photos and art, fleshed-out content, and many more fine-grain details. To further add to this, an additional stage is to render the wireframe interactive with touch or click functionality. This eliminates narrating the functionality during a presentation. Instead of saying, "when this button is clicked, the user is taken to this screen," you can show it. There are dozens of tools used to create functional wireframes, and their complexity ranges from drawing hotspots around content to dictating complex functionality.

Usability report

One of the things I mentioned earlier is the fact that almost every aspect of digital design can be tracked in some way. While this might make people increasingly uncomfortable—large corporations tracking our every move and behavior in an effort to use that data for profit—it's likely only going to get increasingly sophisticated. A usability report lets you know exactly how your audience is interacting with your product. It allows you to receive feedback based on usage and goals achieved. One method to capture data is by using analytics software built for this purpose (this is useful for apps and websites, and some are even free). Another is by video recording the user to study their experience from an "over the shoulder" perspective.

Identifying problems at this point is much more fine-grain than at any other step. If there are major realizations or issues, it means that something failed along the way and steps need to be retraced. You might also find that a certain action is more valuable or successful than originally expected. The report will state how the participants were recruited, including the details of testing environment, etc.

HACK

Search for "usability report template" to download a free editable template from usability.gov. After a digital product is released in final form, these methods can be performed again to further dial-in performance by making small adjustments. Data analytics can glean a lot of insight about your users: everything from the geographic area they're in to what kind of device they're using.

Figure 2.10
Mood boards are a great way to bridge the connection between UX and UI disciplines.

Dark user patterns

Sometimes, a company's profit-driven desire to increase goal conversion can lead to using what's known as dark patterns. These are design choices applied to the user interface in a way that's designed to trick the user in some way or obscure choices in the user flow. It's ultimately the purview of the UX designer to address any problems or issues in this area. Some examples include:

- check boxes that automatically default to an opt-in email
- interrupting tasks to prompt a user for personal information
- giving extreme visual weight to premium options while hiding free options
- using a modal window to completely fill a screen, and obscuring the close feature
- advertisement disguised to look like a navigation component
- forcing login via social media to continue.

Unfortunately, many of these practices are commonplace on websites and apps. In recent years, there's been a backlash against them as users are experiencing a tipping point. Federal agencies are involved in investigating many of these practices, and legal standards might be the only thing left to stop them. As a designer, what can you do to prevent the use of dark patterns in your digital experience? Simply going through the assets and asking if you would object to anything presented is a first step. Paying clear attention to user feedback when concerning anything relating to capturing personal data is important. Sometimes, stakeholders may try to add an additional feature midway through the UX process, in effect ducking any testing safeguards. It's important to question these kinds of practices and do your best to mitigate any additions that compromise the experience. You won't always have the power to veto, but calling them out is an important first step.

Information architecture map

One of the final UX deliverables (before the final touches are implemented by a UI designer) is the information architecture map. This shows the entire hierarchy of the experience, including how many possible outcomes are available from each interaction. The site map or mind map and the user flow have obvious implications here, but the entirety of the project should be connected through a web of lines and diagrams. An IA map often ends up looking like a schematic. Many important features or major goals might have several points of connection (the ability to access a user dashboard from every screen, for instance). Others might only be connected through a single interaction (like confirmation of a purchase).

Figure 2.11
An information architecture map shows deep-level connections throughout the experience.

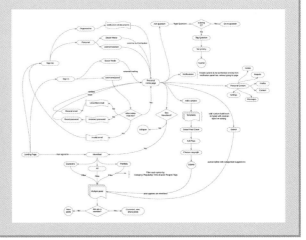

HACK

There are several paid tools that are purpose-built for creating information architecture maps, but any low-level design software is capable of doing it. Use as many letter-size artboards as you need to create it, so it's easily printed.

Context is key

If the functionality for a particular project is very straightforward and the visual design follows that simplicity, then the processes I've mentioned so far might be streamlined. For instance, if we're talking about a web page with a form field to enter an email address and a subscribe button, we can likely go from sketch to wireframe to finished design. If the stakes, cost, and value are all very high, then the process would logically be extended. If we're designing a new digital experience for a multinational corporation, the process would start with sketching, paper prototyping, wireframing, functional wireframing, visual mock-ups, high-fidelity mock-ups, and finally a finished product.

Connecting with UI

After wireframes and mock-ups have been tested and content layout has been established, it's time to dial-in the interface design and overall graphics. This is when UX design directly connects with UI design. I mentioned in Chapter 1 that UI design is informed by the UX process, and it should now be apparent as to how all of the research up to this point has helped to establish the tone, functionality, and layout of the user interface. It's a reminder that, while the intuitive spark is important to experimentation and innovation, most aspects of design are approached from an objective framework. "Shooting from the hip" rarely works for anything substantive, and it can be disastrous when applied to digital product design. Sometimes, the UX lead works directly with a visual designer to create the UI design. Increasingly, though, these two roles are becoming one job. Whichever the case, translating the visual design onto the rough layouts is the next step. The research has hopefully helped identify what content and functionality is most important to users, and the visual design will help emphasize this through contrast, hierarchy, and use of color. It's likely that the content will continue to evolve as the interface is developed and fidelity added. We all dream of clients and stakeholders approving final copy and content before the design stage, but that's simply not true. While you should question excessive changes to what's already been decided, expect some finessing to happen as you push the project ahead.

Case studies

After a project is finished, it's helpful to summarize the process through a case study. You might already be familiar with creating these for graphic design projects and extending one to the UX realm is pretty straightforward. Essentially, it's re-presenting the steps leading up to a successful project in bite-size form, and preferably with accompanying visuals. These are the major items to consider:

Title: Specific yet succinct. Describe the specific task(s) if applicable and the end use, for example, a customer onboarding process for a flight check-in kiosk.

Perspective: The initial discovery phase will help you form this. Who is the client, what do they do, and how did you get involved in the project?

The challenge: Use the project brief and *vision statement* to summarize. What was the overarching goal? One sentence is ideal.

Audience: This will be determined by the user research. Distilling data from the personas will keep this short and sweet (for example, 18–25 year olds who are digitally proficient and frustrated with traditional banks).

Your role. How were you involved in the project? What were your specific responsibilities? List them quickly and in order, for example: UX Lead, worked directly with company stakeholders and UI designers. Tasks included user research, wireframing and prototyping, evaluating and iterating based on user tests, and final handoff to product development team.

Parameters. What kinds of constraints were you bound by? What specifications formed the backbone of the project? For example, the client wanted to create an offshoot of their core brand to appeal to a young audience, while not alienating their longstanding client base.

Process. Briefly explain the timeline through major milestones, highlighting anything that changed direction through research, prototyping, and testing.

Results. What happened afterwards? This is the most important step, because it encapsulates how effective you were in your role and communicates the success of the project at large. Use specific data here. For example, the website saw a 140 percent increase in overall traffic, and purchasing of individual products jumped to as much as 190 percent.

Takeaways

UX design is confusing to a lot of visual designers because so much of its output is non-visual. For many of us, this is new and intimidating territory. But understanding the value of research and data is paramount because compensation for UX design can be very lucrative. Understanding how UX integrates and differentiates with UI is key to doing both well, especially if you need to juggle simultaneous roles. Finally, know what the scope of your project requires: designing a website landing page will certainly warrant skipping much of the user testing that you would want to conduct for a full-blown consumer app. Keeping ultimate goals in mind at each step will curb unnecessary ones.

UX DESIGN EXERCISE

Design a public transportation app—a digital tool that allows users to interact with public transportation in your town or city.

DESCRIPTION

Design assets for an app where public transport modes, routes, schedules, and fares can be easily viewed, sorted, saved, and purchased. The client might be a local government, municipality, or transportation authority. It could also be a private company seeking to partner with local government, or it could be a firm just looking to use public data to make a profitable product. Include UX assets for a smartphone-based experience.

RESEARCH AND METHODOLOGY

Search out public transportation information for your city or town. What modes are used? Bus transport is quite common, but see if it extends to rail, trolley, subway, and bike or car share. What kind of features would potential users value? In order to make a compelling experience, you might have to specify a direction through the app. For instance, commuting vs. exploring. Assessing the general needs of your community will help dictate that direction. Is

Figure 2.12
This app concept explores transportation options in Lahore, Pakistan.

tourism popular in your area? Is there a large commuting workforce? Are there any colleges or universities nearby? These will have wide-ranging implications on the user experience.

INTENT

What would motivate a client to create such an experience? What kind of information could be gleaned from users, and how would this impact their bottom line? For example, users who purchase tickets digitally could help free up space at physical ticket machines and kiosks. Identify key performance indicators that are tailored to your client selection.

DEMOGRAPHIC

Your initial research might have yielded some initial insight. Does your product cater to travelers, or mostly locals? Apps supported by municipalities generally tend to have an older demographic, while private companies skew towards a younger one. The "cool factor" is partially at play here: local governments don't usually advertise their products using any emotional strategies. Their brand aesthetic is likely toned down, while an individual company might tug the heartstrings of their users and seem visually exciting by contrast.

CONTENT

Using routes and timetables for existing public transportation is the easiest way to begin. Creating this kind of content from scratch is time-consuming and wouldn't yield any real advantages. However, don't import an entire bus system schedule since you just need one or two routes to show as a proof of concept. Bringing in more general content (like text copy) is fine for now, because you can finesse it later.

Figure 2.13
This is an example of market research that summarizes both overarching and business goals.

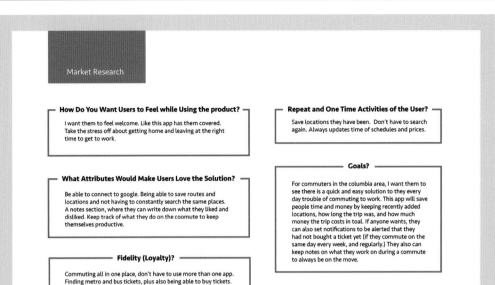

Market Research

How Do You Want Users to Feel while Using the product?

I want them to feel welcome. Like this app has them covered. Take the stress off about getting home and leaving at the right time to get to work.

What Attributes Would Make Users Love the Solution?

Be able to connect to google. Being able to save routes and locations and not having to constantly search the same places. A notes section, where they can write down what they liked and disliked. Keep track of what they do on the coomute to keep themselves productive.

Fidelity (Loyalty)?

Commuting all in one place, don't have to use more than one app. Finding metro and bus tickets, plus also being able to buy tickets. Keeping themselves accountable for working while on the commute.

Repeat and One Time Activities of the User?

Save locations they have been. Don't have to search again. Always updates time of schedules and prices.

Goals?

For commuters in the columbia area, I want them to see there is a quick and easy solution to they every day trouble of commuting to work. This app will save people time and money by keeping recently added locations, how long the trip was, and how much money the trip costs in toal. If anyone wants, they can also set notifications to be alerted that they had not bought a ticket yet (if they commute on the same day every week, and regularly.) They also can keep notes on what they work on during a commute to always be on the move.

PROJECT BRIEF

Starting with the vision statement, begin outlining the problem or opportunity. The specifications are known: this will be an app-based experience. The design strategy will take the shape of what kind of client you've chosen. Tone and visual goals might be more accommodating for a public entity, while a private company might opt for a wit-based approach and more defined visual style.

USER RESEARCH

Dig a bit deeper into the demographic. You might start by asking friends and family if they use public transportation apps. Setting up a poll that you can conduct through a larger network is even more helpful. Conducting real user interviews for a spec project might be overkill, but a thoughtfully written questionnaire that someone can fill out digitally might just do the trick.

PERSONAS

After enough research has been gleaned, craft two to three personas based on it. Design a basic template so that each one fits on a single page. Make sure to write a sample bio, noting their tech abilities, the user goals related to this project, sticking points, and wants and needs. A sample bio photo makes everything feel more real. Search for "headshot photo" on royalty-free photo websites such as unsplash.com.

USER FLOW

After you've identified some basic end goals, tasks and functionality that create a user flow are the next step. Start with the most basic task (such as login or signup) and continue through to the end of each piece of functionality. Remember, there will be places where actions or decisions split the flow into separate directions. The end result will look like a schematic. Make this look nice and neat visually, but don't feel the need to overdesign it.

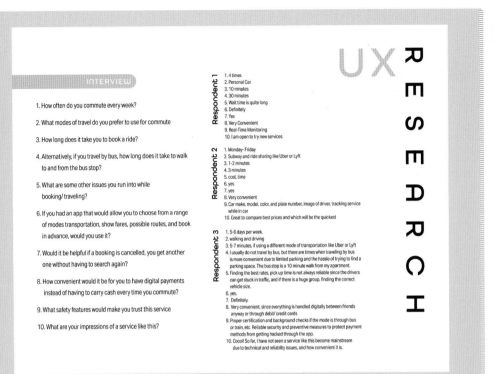

INTERVIEW

1. How often do you commute every week?

2. What modes of travel do you prefer to use for commute

3. How long does it take you to book a ride?

4. Alternatively, if you travel by bus, how long does it take to walk to and from the bus stop?

5. What are some other issues you run into while booking/ traveling?

6. If you had an app that would allow you to choose from a range of modes transportation, show fares, possible routes, and book in advance, would you use it?

7. Would it be helpful if a booking is cancelled, you get another one without having to search again?

8. How convenient would it be for you to have digital payments instead of having to carry cash every time you commute?

9. What safety features would make you trust this service?

10. What are your impressions of a service like this?

Respondent 1
1. 4 times
2. Personal Car
3. 10 minutes
4. 30 minutes
5. Wait time is quite long
6. Definitely
7. Yes
8. Very Convenient
9. Real-Time Monitoring
10. I am open to try new services

Respondent 2
1. Monday- Friday
2. Subway and ride sharing like Uber or Lyft
3. 1-2 minutes
4. 3 minutes
5. cost, time
6. yes
7. yes
8. Very convenient
9. Car make, model, color, and plate number, image of driver, tracking service while in car
10. Great to compare best prices and which will be the quickest

Respondent 3
1. 5-6 days per week.
2. walking and driving
3. 5-7 minutes, if using a different mode of transportation like Uber or Lyft
4. I usually do not travel by bus, but there are times when traveling by bus is more convenient due to limited parking and the hassle of trying to find a parking space. The bus stop is a 10 minute walk from my apartment.
5. Finding the best rates, pick up time is not always reliable since the drivers can get stuck in traffic, and if there is a huge group, finding the correct vehicle size.
6. yes.
7. Definitely.
8. Very convenient, since everything is handled digitally between friends anyway or through debit/ credit cards
9. Proper certification and background checks if the mode is through bus or train, etc. Reliable security and preventive measures to protect payment methods from getting hacked through the app.
10. Coool! So far, I have not seen a service like this become mainstream due to technical and reliability issues, and how convenient it is.

UX RESEARCH

Figure 2.14
Three user interviews are clearly presented in context with the specific questions asked.

PERSONAL

AMNA

DESCRIPTION
Amna is a 32 year old married lady and has a son. Professionally, she is a pharmacist, therefore, she has to commute to work 4 times a week. Amna is sociable, outgoing, generous, and loves to spend quality time with her loved ones.

BEHAVIORS
○ Independent
○ Hard working
○ Social
○ Generous

PAINPOINTS
○ Amna does not like the long wait times to get a ride
○ Going through different apps and services to find a ride is stressful

GOALS
○ Getting to work on time
○ Getting her work done in a timely fashion
○ Making time for her family

"She was unstoppable and she took anything she wanted with a smile."
-R.M. Drake

Image: "Designed by katemangostar / Freepik"

Figure 2.15
Personas should include both general and specific information to create a convincing user portrait.

Figure 2.16
A user flow should clearly communicate the linear path of an action.

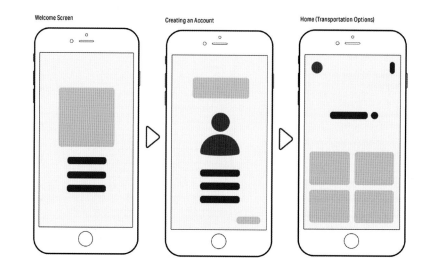

USER JOURNEY

With the user flow in place, begin creating the user journey by writing scenarios based on the linear steps. Groups of actions will form a single scenario such as signing up for an account. The user journey should show these groups in singular screens or pages. List the scenario at the top, along with goals. The steps from the user flow run horizontally across the middle in a linear fashion. Feedback noting frustrations, opportunities, and surprises goes below this.

CONTENT INVENTORY AND AUDIT

You've likely already brought in general copy with your more detailed transportation route information. Now is the time to rewrite that copy and craft it so that it resonates with both the entity that you've chosen and your persona. This will mean that your content will feel either official and formal, or a bit more casual and third-party. This isn't to say that a government entity can't be perceived as a bit fun, but consider the demographic and research in taking leaps of faith.

MARKET RESEARCH

This is where you'll look at any existing apps concerning public transportation. It's likely that your town or city won't have one, but try and find municipalities of the same size that might. Download several and compare them to any apps that have been developed by private companies. Think about the branding (or lack of) and how it contributes to the user experience. Compare

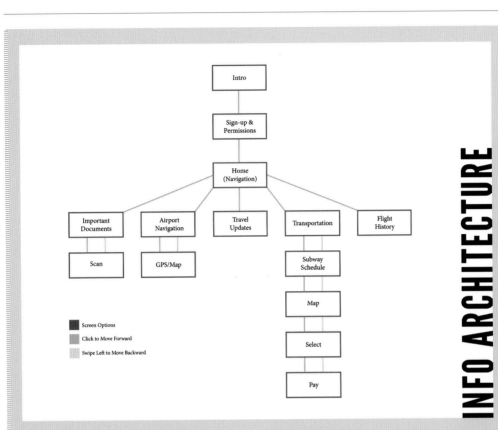

INFO ARCHITECTURE

Figure 2.17
This site map includes a key that gives additional insight into the flow between screens.

functionality and take notes about which actions are easier to complete between them. Assess what's essential, useful, unnecessary, or missing. Is there any part of the experience that's made to be fun? If so, how? And how could any confusion about a particular action be smoothed out and made easier?

INFORMATION ARCHITECTURE

Creating some site maps will help frame out the experience if you have a grasp on how functionality will connect with content. If you've prioritized functions but aren't sure how they'll be featured, a mind map might be a good option. Design the information architecture that fits on one page. These should be neatly presented, but don't spend too much time designing these documents.

SKETCHES

Quickly drawing some sketches that bookend the information architecture will give you a chance to "walk through" the functionality before going digital. If there are any dead ends at this point, it's easier to sort them out at this stage.

UX COPY

The research you've done should inform how serious or how casual the UX copy flows. Will it be clear and authoritative, or will it whimsically carry you along? The decisions you've made up to this point will determine that. With the paper prototypes in hand, go through each screen and address copy needs. Make sure the tone is consistent before moving on.

Figure 2.18
Wireframes need
to strike a balance
between
efficiency and
fidelity. This
example is spare,
but it looks neat
and ordered.

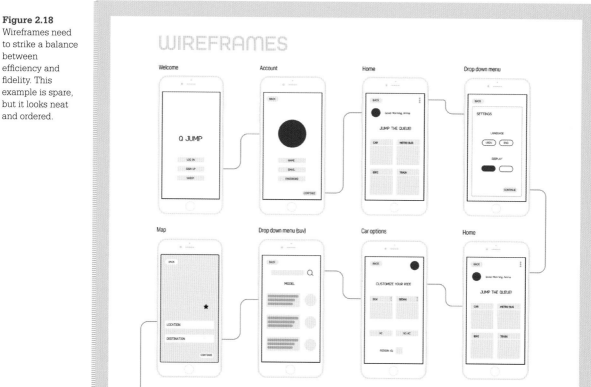

WIREFRAMES

You can then use your sketches and copy to create some low-fidelity wireframes that present the screens a bit more clearly. Remember to consider the most important functions per screen, the copy you've written, and to leave space for imagery (you can specify notes about this too).

MOOD BOARDS

An informative set of mood boards is the cherry on top of the complete UX package. Refer back to your personas, write a list of adjectives (for example, efficient, friendly, reliable, etc.) and use these to search out some images that capture the attitude of the app. The UI designer will thank you for giving some direction but not overstepping the visual direction. Then again, there's a chance you might be performing both roles!

REFLECTION AND REVISION

Looking back at the research and intent that you framed earlier, has that been expressed through the entire user experience? Does the path through the app feel consistent? What about the tone and UX copy? Does it seem appropriate? Interjecting a bit of wit could work well for a privately backed app, but it could be a faux pas for a public-facing organization or government. Revisit the user flow and user journey, and make sure that there aren't any snags in the process. Confirm this by testing the wireframes again. In comparing this to your market research, does it hold up well? Or are there places where the flow gets a bit muddy? Are there any moments where this app really shines? Can they be further highlighted as a feature?

GOALS AND OUTCOMES

Completing this exercise successfully means that you have a lot of documentation, likely more than any design project you've ever engaged with. Looking back at everything, it's like constructing a building. Starting with the project brief and moving through user research and personas, you have the framing and scaffolding. The user flow, user journey, and information architecture are like installing the electrical circuits. The wireframes and mood boards become the interior design. All of these separate documents can be neatly packaged together as one deliverable. This is a chance to flex your layout design chops, as this often looks best in the form of a small book or manual. Take it a step further by printing and binding it. As odd as it sounds, flipping through a physical book is a nice way to view and discuss a digital product.

Figure 2.19
Printing the finished project as a book is a useful companion to the PDF, especially if you're showing it in person.

Animation and
Motion Graphics

In traditional graphic design, the concept of movement has to be implied. This is shown through the use of diagonals, repetition, rhythm, cropping, and other visual devices. In animation, movement can be represented literally, shown through a timeline. Digital animation has evolved with technology, and it's now easier than ever to animate graphics for screens. As a designer, understanding elements such as pacing, audio cues, and synchronization is key to being well-versed in one of the most popular ways we consume media. Grasping these principles and concepts allows designers to present work that engages in storytelling, one of the things video and film do quite well. When I talk about animation in this chapter, I'm specifically referring to design expressed through animation. Anything to do with character animation is outside that scope and is a separate profession. Motion graphics rely on a combination of basic design forms like line shape and texture, with a range of content such as photos, illustration, and typography. The pre-production methods and initial conceptualizing of an animation are software-agnostic and can largely be done without a computer.

Medium and message

In his vanguard 1964 book, *Understanding Media: The Extensions of Man*, Marshall McLuhan coined the phrase "the medium is the message" when referring to how content is shaped by the medium it's delivered through, and how the characteristics of the medium can be equally influential. The 45rpm "single" record was that medium for early rock 'n' roll and pop music. The iPod was the same several generations later. Motion is the medium of the contemporary digital culture, and it has the power to communicate in a way that cuts through the noise. There are several benefits of using it across different disciplines:

- For a complicated interface, simple animation can help call attention to key functionality.
- When viewing a website, a subtle animated button instantly captures your attention. It can look quite sophisticated as well.
- Motion on a VR interface lets the user know an object has been selected. It's a response that feels intuitive and needs little else to support it.

Creating a sense of unity across multiple devices is easily done through motion. In fact, most major brands have incorporated a "signature sequence" of graphic animation that consistently presents their logos and marks. It becomes the thing that ties all of these digital experiences together. Consider the Netflix bumper that plays before every video and includes dramatic audio cues that are synchronized to the simple animation. It's short, dynamic, impactful, and reminds you of their brand every time you press play. The ability to drive a concept with a combination of graphics, video, and language is effective in a way that traditional media struggles to match. So much of our lives are set to music, and this has been reinforced by its proliferation as a backdrop in motion graphic videos. Media organizations across the world have embraced digital storytelling to deliver compelling content.

Tools and end uses

Most professional-grade animation software is capable of highly detailed two-dimensional (and some three-dimensional) rendering, everything from a short three-second looping graphic to a title sequence for a film. Because of this potential, the learning curve varies from accessible to fairly steep. After Effects has been the tool of choice for its versatility in creating both simple and very complex animations. Most of what we discuss in this chapter will focus on it as a production tool because of its wide popularity and history as the industry standard. While we'll cover basic 3D methods, most compositing for true three-dimensional space is also a field of its own. There are additional software tools that now focus on animation of user interfaces, which is a sub-field called "motion design."

Here's why After Effects is my tool of choice for most animation applications:

- Its fidelity and output for motion graphics and 2D animation is second to none.
- Though it's not a true 3D application, it has some built-in affordances.

- Cinema 4D Lite is built into After Effects, allowing basic 3D modeling, texturing, lighting, and shading.

In teaching my own students, I tend to use After Effects for just about everything. That includes designing a basic animated logo and traditional motion graphics, which it's fantastic for. But I also use it to teach how to prototype interactive components and gestures, and even create an app prototype. The big caveat is that it isn't necessarily the best end-production tool for those two things. However, it's familiar to students by that point and a powerful tool to continue working in.

HACK

There are several applications that can help quickly prototype and animate UI components. I won't confuse you by listing several competing options here, but most of them are good for creating simple interactions. Some of these might be preferred when designing projects that will ultimately be built with code. This is a relatively new shift, and designers working strictly in this space tend to use the term "Motion UI Designer" to describe their jobs. It's distinct from animation in that the end product is animation for a user interface or digital product.

Figure 3.1
The many layers in this After Effects timeline hint at the power and flexibility of the program.

Key concepts of animation

Directional space

The graphic qualities of simple elements—such as rectangular shapes and lines—can be very powerful even within static design. A horizontal line implies rest. A vertical line is stable but has the potential for movement. And diagonal lines are a designer's secret weapon because they represent active movement. Diagonal lines are so effective because they are rare in nature. A look back at the Constructivist and De Stijl design movements of the twentieth century easily proves how we're drawn to diagonals. The ability to animate in directional space allows us to create something even more convincing and complex. Line and shape can create a force within the composition that guides our eyes through it. This can be as obvious as a moving line or rectangle, or as subtle as creating a path through the use of negative space. When elements move on and off the composition, they emphasize this directional force. Using these as devices to

control hierarchy requires intentional thinking, but the payoff is great.

Timeline and keyframes

One of the most essential things to realize about animation is that it's a *time-based* medium. This is at once painfully obvious but also an advantage if you know how to manipulate it. For print-based media, creating a feeling of quickness or slowness is shown through principles such as rhythm and repetition, or proximity and physical space. It must be very deliberate and dialed-in to work well. Animation is much more immediate: you just show it in real time. Expressing emotion and mood is easily done on a timeline by manipulating classic graphic design principles. It's so simple but worth thinking about. You can emphasize scale in a dynamic and powerful way by transforming an object's size, very extremely or quickly. Or you can show it in a way that's brooding and introspective by doing the opposite: transforming it moderately and slowly. Constantly thinking about how these decisions create the overall tone of a motion graphic composition will make you a better designer.

Closely associated with the timeline are keyframes. This term comes from the early days of cartoon animation with hand-drawing techniques: an experienced artist would draw frames where major movements took place. Entry-level artists would then draw all the frames in-between the major movements. The job title "inbetweener" was given to this role, and luckily modern animation software does it for you. Setting the major points of movement (keyframes) is *everything* in motion design, whether you're animating an icon, interface, or graphic composition. Keyframes are spread across the timeline at different distances to show something at varying speeds. The space between them dictates how fast or slow the animation appears.

Figure 3.2
Theo van Doesburg's Simultaneous Counter-Composition (1930) is an iconic example of how De Stijl art expressed motion.

HACK

The first keyframe to start a movement is known as the "outgoing keyframe," and the following keyframe is the "incoming" one. If an animation features more than two keyframes, the additional ones can be both incoming and outgoing. This will make more sense when we discuss timing in detail.

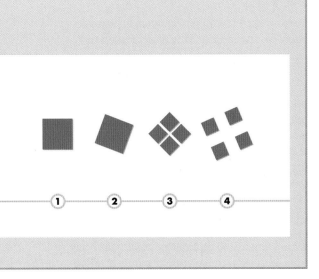

Figure 3.3
This shows a square being animated across four keyframes. It rotates and breaks apart as it moves through.

Composition size

In animation, we continue to work in pixels in terms of composition size, and we retain 72ppi in terms of resolution. There are many typical presets to work from, with 1920 × 1080 as a standard 16:9 ratio. For output that's motion graphics related, the final measurements will likely be dictated by various video specifications. Projects that veer into motion UI design for interfaces or apps will likely follow popular devices sizes for both iOS and Android.

HACK

If you need to export for a variety of sizes, always start with the biggest first. A video conversion application can easily scale down to create a smaller version, but you can't scale up. Adobe Media Encoder is the best option, and it's included with Creative Cloud. If you have a target size you need to aim for (say 5mb for example), you can tweak output settings like quality and bitrate until you get to that number.

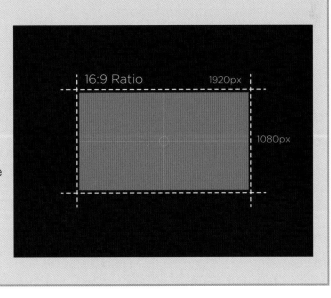

Figure 3.4
A 1920 × 1080 composition is popular. It follows the 16:9 aspect ratio of most TVs and computer monitors.

Frame rate

For any kind of animation, we also need to consider the length. This is expressed in both individual frames and standard timecode (hours, minutes, seconds, frames). Which to use depends on the final application. A short UI button animation may only take a half-second, so you would use frames to have better control. A longer motion graphics piece is best measured in seconds. Before we get into that, we need to define frame rate. That simply means how many frames are shown over the course of one second to create the illusion of motion. Animation frame rates have largely been tied to film and video, because for a long time those were the only methods to view it. Pioneers in film discovered that the human eye stopped seeing individual images and started seeing motion somewhere around 16 frames per second. There's still a flicker effect at that rate though, so it needed to be bumped up to smooth out the animation. Because the actual film stock is expensive, it was decided somewhere along the way to cut the frame rate at 24fps (frames per second): good enough and affordable.

Video was introduced as a medium in the 1950s. Instead of images progressively shown to create motion, it used interlaced lines of data to form an image. The underlying math is too much to get into here, but based on the technology, the frame rate for video became 29.97 frames per second. It's realistically 29fps since the last bit can't be seen on a timeline. Progressive scan video became common in the mid-2000s and tended to look more like film because images are shown sequentially instead of interlaced. Video data storage also made the jump to digital hard drives. This allowed for a greater frame rate, which was an impediment in the days of storage on magnetic tape.

Sixty frames per second is a common frame rate for smooth animation delivered on modern devices, and After Effects is capable of 120fps for slow-motion video. Depending on factors such as the age of source footage and graphics, you may find yourself working with 29.97fps or 24fps. If you're working with UI animation, 60fps is standard. So, each second will be expressed as sixty frames across the timeline. Depending on the needs of the project, you might be animating across several seconds or be "zoomed-in" to the timeline to manipulate keyframes within a single second. Motion UI design for interaction tends to be tighter and quicker, while motion graphics a bit looser. In After Effects, command-clicking the timecode at the top of the layers will switch the display between timecode and individual frames.

Figure 3.5
Progressive video is more akin to classic film in that it utilizes single frames versus combining interlaced lines.

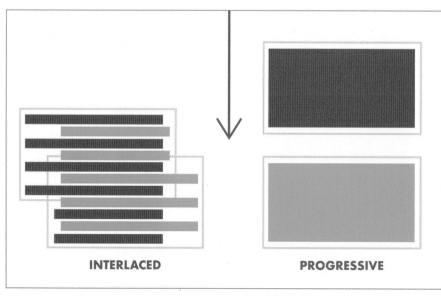

INTERLACED   PROGRESSIVE

HACK

Moving through the timeline is easy with keyboard shortcuts: shift-command-arrow advances ten frames at a time, while command-arrow advances a single frame.

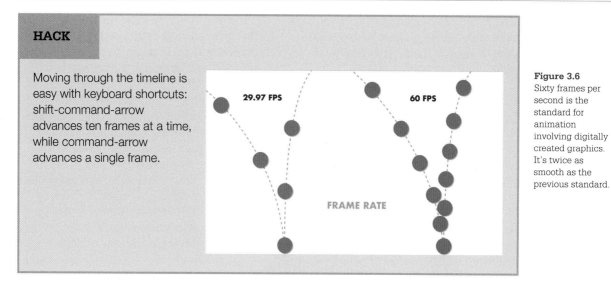

29.97 FPS   60 FPS

FRAME RATE

Figure 3.6
Sixty frames per second is the standard for animation involving digitally created graphics. It's twice as smooth as the previous standard.

Resolution

Since we're operating at a now-familiar 72ppi, one bit of advice remains the same as in UI design: work with vector graphics as a rule, and start with the largest raster images possible when you must use them. This is critical when scaling. You can't resize an image or graphic past 100 percent of its original size without pixilation. It's also helpful to realize the size at which you're viewing the composition. Most software will allow you to zoom in to the canvas at up to 800 percent, and all graphics (vector or not) will look pixilated past 100 percent of the final composition size. In After Effects, there's a box that needs to be ticked for vectors to appear crisp. It's called the "continuously rasterize switch," and it's among the toggles seen in each layer. If your animation doesn't look sharp consider any source raster images first, the overall composition zoom level next, and the rasterize switch for each layer.

Transformations

Opening a piece of animation software for the first time can be daunting. After Effects crams a lot of functionality into its workspace, and it doesn't sport the most intuitive interface. There are a lot of buttons, switches, and submenus that aren't labeled in an effort to save space. I find that in a class of twenty design students, maybe two or three will have had any prior experience with this software. It has a reputation of being a dense program to use and most people are a bit circumspect about jumping in and giving it a go. But what if you do want to animate something quite simple, with an eye on learning the rest of the program later? Well, there's a great method for that. You'll find that fairly impressive animations can be designed using five basic transformations. These are position, anchor point, rotation, transparency, and scale (the acronym is PARTS). In fact, when teaching students how to begin animating motion graphics, I start with a simple assignment: animate a logo for over five seconds. The specifications of this project are limited to using these five basic transformations. When selecting a

Figure 3.7
The "continuously rasterize switch" should always be checked to keep vector graphics crisp in After Effects.

layer in the After Effects timeline, you have immediate access to these with a single click. To explain them, let's consider a rectangular composition space:

Position

This refers to the movement of elements both within the composition and off-composition. An element might move off-screen from within the composition or vice versa. Often, after an initial animation of related elements, the next sequence can be set up with a screen wipe. This is easily done with a large solid layer, moving from on-screen to off-screen. A group of layers can move independently or as a group to reinforce unity. A third option that can be particularly effective is when the position of objects in different layers are staggered to create a cascading effect. This kind of effect feels very dynamic and creates a sense of dimension in the animation.

Anchor point

This is the position from which a transformation happens. Think about a windmill rotating from a fulcrum versus something that's swiveling from a hinge. In the first instance, the anchor point is in the center of the object. In the latter, it's moved to a corner. When combined with other transformations, this can serve to build complexity or subtlety, depending on what's required.

Rotation

This can be thought of as the number of full rotations, or within 360 degrees. Usually, you'll want to be conservative with it. Rotations at more than 360 degrees will seem overly flashy for most applications and immediately distract the eye.

Transparency (or opacity)

This is a design principle that doesn't get as much attention because it's subtle. It becomes an active design element when used at a value between zero (completely transparent) and one hundred (completely opaque). This can serve to build depth in a 2D composition, allowing other layers to mix and merge. Think about some of the lushest film title sequences you've seen, where the composition exudes a sense of layering and depth. It's likely because of the active use of transparency. Transparency is also very helpful in smoothing out other transformations.

Scale

This is such an important part of design generally, and this extends to animation and motion graphics. Quite often, amateur design fails to exploit the use of scale, which makes it difficult to control emphasis and focal point. Scale can also serve to create depth and perspective. In the animation of user interfaces, scale can quickly identify a call-to-action. In motion graphics, it can become a device to transition between vignettes or groupings of smaller animations. Imagine a square in the center of a composition with a series of transformations applied (let's say rotation and opacity) over two to three seconds. After these, we can then animate the scale of the square so that it fills the entire composition. This is another way of "wiping" the screen to set up a new scene.

HACK

If you're animating an element from off-screen to the center of the composition, that amount of movement might look awkward. Why? Because it's long and excessive. A solution is to start animating the position from halfway inside the composition. The dilemma here is that you don't want the element to instantly show up on screen, which would be equally amateur. By adding a quick transparency fade-in to the position animation, it adds a bit of finesse while solving the problem. Transparency also allows for rich layering when it's an active design element. Allowing other layers to be seen underneath can enhance graphics, giving them a sense of sophistication. This kind of treatment also brings back a sense of tactility into what's often a completely digital process.

For simple animation projects, most of what you'll want to achieve can be done by following this process:

- Select a layer in the timeline, and click the small arrow to the left labeled transform.
- Choose from the five transformation properties (shift or command-click to select several).
- Set a keyframe with the stopwatch icon next to each transformation.
- Move forward (or backward) in the timeline.
- Automatically create a second keyframe by changing a value (i.e., from 100 percent scale to 50 percent).
- Test it out by pressing the spacebar to play back the animation.

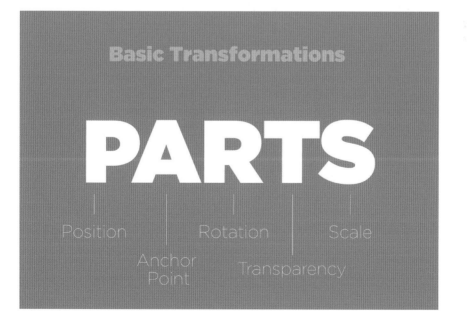

Figure 3.8
The five basic transformation properties are easy to remember using the PARTS acronym.

HACK

To save space and confusion when looking at the timeline, press the letter of the acronym that corresponds to the transformation ("R" for rotation, for instance). You'll then only see that transformation property displayed instead of all of them. Add the option key as a modifier to create a keyframe for that property without clicking anything. Manipulating objects in the composition window will probably be intuitive for the most part, but you can also change transformation properties directly in the layers panel. For any value that shows up highlighted in blue, click, hold, and drag left or right to move the value in either direction. I find that this method offers a bit more precision.

Figure 3.9
This tiny slider bar at the bottom of the timeline can zoom in to the single-frame-level, or out to show longer time.

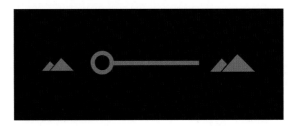

Classic animation principles

In the physical world, very few things start or stop instantly. Most respond to physical forces such as gravity and atmosphere. Let us refer back to Disney's "twelve basic principles of animation." They were first made public by the animators Ollie Johnston and Frank Thomas in their 1981 book *The Illusion of Life: Disney Animation*. In the text, they deconstruct the methods used by the studio dating to the 1930s. These methods are helpful in bringing life to digital animation, and they are worth exploring in detail.

Squash and stretch

This is the role that perceived materiality plays in animation. If you drop something hard and rigid from a certain height, it doesn't have much "give." It may even shatter, break, or damage the receiving surface. Drop something more flexible from the same height—say a rubber ball—and there's some resiliency just after the moment of impact. The ball compresses a

bit before rebounding back. That elasticity is what helps us reconcile the material. On the rebound, the ball might stretch a bit vertically. This is because it's reacting to the "squash." If you're trying to convey some organic qualities in your animation, squash and stretch can be appropriate. They might translate to fun, jubilant, or youthful. Scale is the key transformation in making it work, and by default it is proportionally locked. That's to say, if you increase the scale in an animation program, the X and Y values change the same amount. You'll need to unlock the proportions to manipulate the scale independently. This just means clicking on the lock icon. Let's visualize the mechanics of a circular shape:

- Starting point: set a scale keyframe.
- Half a second: move the shape to the floor of the composition; set the horizontal scale to 120 percent—this gives an implied squash.

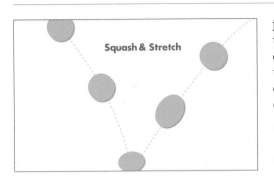

One second: move the shape halfway back to the start; set the horizontal scale to 80 percent—this would mimic the stretch.

This technique is best served in moderate doses unless it's something designed for children. In that case, a more liberal effect can be appropriate.

Anticipation

If there's a slight ebb before an object begins moving, it creates a sense of anticipation. Think about getting ready to twist a cap off a bottle. Most likely, you'll cock your wrist a bit in the opposite direction before twisting, and over-rotate it

just slightly as you finish. Using this technique in animation can help to emphasize a particular element or area of the composition. It can also convey a sense of force or power. Consider rotation of an object to demonstrate:

- Starting point: set a keyframe for the rotation property.
- Half a second: set a rotation keyframe to –10 degrees.
- One second: set a third keyframe to 190 degrees.
- One-and-a-half seconds: set a fourth keyframe to 180 degrees.

Staging

Less of a principle and more of a best practice, staging states that every keyframe or movement should convey clear intention. This is a very smart way to think about animation holistically because a secondary goal is to use as few keyframes as possible. When you inevitably need to make edits to a sequence, changing values and moving around individual keyframes can be time-consuming. And when you just need to perform a quick redo, fewer keyframes

Figure 3.10
Squash and stretch is an easy way to give digital objects some perceived material qualities.

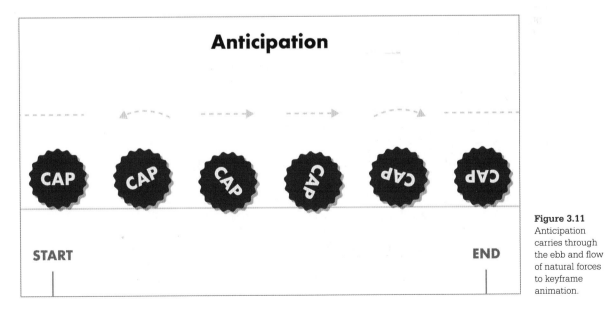

Figure 3.11
Anticipation carries through the ebb and flow of natural forces to keyframe animation.

are better. With that in mind, it's good policy to give a quick inspection of your keyframed layer after you have dialed-in most of your movements. Look through and see if there are any redundant keyframes. Then, give it another playback with a bit more scrutiny. Are there any movements that are weak or don't really contribute anything? Conversely, do they muddle the intention of the animation? Time to start deleting, if so. The fact is, most things that we animate—whether something as simple as a logo, or something as complex as an entire interface—are rarely seen in a vacuum. They're usually placed in a layout of some kind, where they'll be competing with other design elements. So, it's only logical to make sure your final exports are clear and concise to begin with.

Straight ahead action

This essentially describes the two basic methods of animation. Straight ahead action would be designing the animation progressively, like the way you'd draw in an old school flipbook. For organic-style animations, using this method gives you good results. It allows you to be as meticulous as you want or need to be. Pose-to-pose animation refers to the way most animation software allows you to set keyframes. For instance, set a keyframe for any property at any point in the timeline. Then, move forward or backward in the timeline, and change the value of that property. Doing so will automatically interpolate all the frames between them. This is the core principle of keyframe animation. It not only can save you time, but sometimes animating backwards is even more intuitive. In the case of separate elements animating to create a unified form, it's likely that you already have the *finished* art. It's much easier to start at the end, and

deconstruct the form backwards, than it is to rebuild something that's already complete. Most logos are animated this way, because the finished art is usually in-hand before any animation starts.

Follow through

This can reinforce an area of the composition by using elasticity to briefly overstep a position. When you see follow through in something that's moving, it creates a sense of tactility in your brain. That is to say, it obeys the forces of gravity and nature, and feels more believable. Think about some of those golden-age cartoon animations and how there's some elasticity in the way that characters come to a stop on-screen. In this example, you'll have a desired position endpoint in mind as you animate:

- Starting point: set position keyframe of object.
- Half a second: set the object's path to be slightly skewed backwards.
- Three-quarters of a second: straighten out the path and advance the object's position forward.
- Set position keyframe slightly past the endpoint.
- One second: set the object's path to be slightly skewed forwards.
- One-and-a-half seconds: straighten out the path and position keyframe to the desired endpoint.

Figure 3.12
Follow through employs a bit of elasticity to seem more respective of the force of gravity.

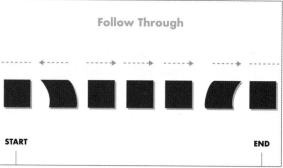

Slow in and slow out

This is the principle that's at the core of blocking out your animations. It's the idea that gravity affects the beginning and ending of any transformation, giving it weight. Think about riding a bike from a stopped position. It takes you a bit of effort to gain some momentum. After a while, you're pedaling along at top speed, and you need a bit of distance to come to a stop again. In digital animation, this kind of even-smoothing of speed from two fixed points in time is called "easing-in-and-out." In After Effects, it's specifically called "easy-ease." If you charted position and time on a graph, *no easing* between two points would look like a diagonal line. This is called "linear animation" and has no sense of visual finesse. Easing would produce a smooth S-curve.

HACK

Start all animations with easy-ease, and dial-in custom easing curves from there. Select the keyframes you want to apply it to, and press F9. You may need to also press a modifier key (like "fn" on a Mac) to access the function keys.

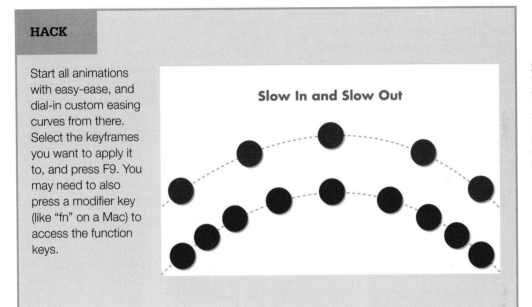

Slow In and Slow Out

Figure 3.13
Slow in and slow out relates to "easy-ease" in After Effects, which makes animation timing seem more natural.

Timing

You'll get a lot of mileage from timing because it's applied holistically to all animations. It deals with how spirit and character develop from the time between transformations. It's also concerned with the speed or velocity between each transformation. These work together in synchrony. The implied form of an object has a lot of input on timing. When I say this, I'm speaking in relative terms. A small sphere bouncing around four sides of a composition, slowly losing energy over a duration of five seconds? We think of a light and forgiving implied material: maybe a ping-pong ball. Conversely, a large rectangle dropping vertically, taking one short rebound and landing back again full stop? That suggests a dense, rigid material. The viewer isn't actually *thinking* this, but if the timing *feels* wrong, they'll react to it. The speed, which suggests gravity, is also crucial. In either case mentioned above, the speed of the object should be fastest when it is closest to the next keyframe. Just like if you're jumping on a trampoline, you're fastest immediately before and just after the next bounce.

Timing relies on a bit more than just placing keyframes closer and further apart from each other on a timeline. Magnitude or perceived force is necessary for the timing to feel weighty and natural. So how do we give our timing weight? The easy-ease method I mentioned gives us a good starting point to begin customizing our motion curves. The graph editor in After Effects is the top-right icon in the layers panel, just to the left of the timeline. When clicked, the timeline switches to show a two-axes graph. The vertical Y-axis shows the rate of change for a transformation, like scale. Time is represented on the X-horizontal axis. An un-eased set of keyframes starts and stops in diagonal lines on the X and Y coordinates, and we know that an ease-in-out set displays as a smooth S-curve. But what about something that starts out slow and then ramps up in speed before quickly stopping again? That would look like a gradual curve upwards leading to a steep climb. How about something that starts quite fast and then slows down gradually? That would be the exact opposite: a steep climb followed by a smooth horizontal taper, which is called an "ease-out."

Arc

This applies more discretely to conventionally drawn animation, though it still has use in the digital world. It suggests that natural moments don't follow a perfectly straight path. Animation software attempts to reconcile this with spatial interpolation. If you set up an object with three object keyframes that create a triangular position of movements, the object will "round the corner" on the second keyframe. This is known as "Bezier keyframe interpolation." If you want to intentionally zig and zag, you'd choose a linear interpolation. Depending on the aesthetic, this is something you may want—you'll find case uses for both. To access these options, control click the keyframe(s), choose "keyframe interpolation," and then "spatial interpolation."

Secondary action

Here, we're referring to any animation that supports the primary action. I mentioned that transparency often used to "smooth out" another transformation. That's a classic example of secondary action: something that adds to the overall realistic complexity of an animation. In that case, it adds some subtlety and finesse, acting behind the scenes. Another example of a

Figure 3.14
Three timing methods are shown here: default linear, easy-eased, and ease-in.

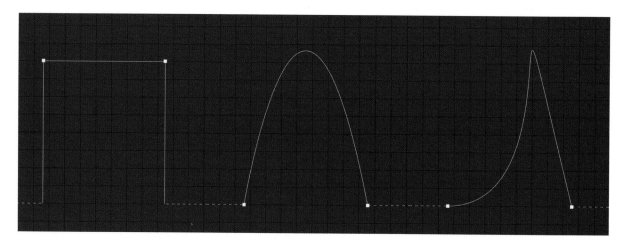

secondary animation might be a contoured line drawn around a form as it's animating. The quality of the secondary action should always be supporting the main one. This is an important distinction, because it can be difficult to rein in animation when you're first learning. It's in our nature to get excited about a new discovery or skill.

Solid drawing

This is perhaps the most mysterious of the twelve principles, but it refers to drawings having weight, depth, and dimension. This principle applies most specifically to cartoons but is also quite extensible to 2D animation and motion graphics. For instance, a scene or series of scenes should have a strong line of action and a hierarchy in terms of depth. Objects should move in a way that feels very natural, even if they're abstract. If they're in the foreground, they need to be crisply rendered. They should be sharp in contrast, fully saturated in color, and large in scale.

HACK

A reliable method for giving an element depth—even something as simple as a rectangle—is to add a subtle drop shadow. Something as small as one or two pixels offset right, and three or four pixels offset below, with between 10 and 20 percent opacity will give perceived elevation without drawing attention to the effect itself. For two-dimensional compositions where you're trying to achieve a three-dimensional feel, blurring and scaling down background objects will offer a sense of depth and perspective.

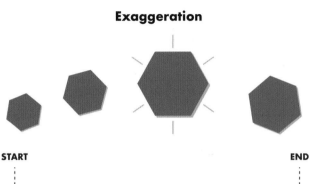

Exaggeration

START   END

Exaggeration

Ollie Johnston and Frank Thomas explained exaggeration as a way of pushing movement and expression in animation, enhancing the mood of a scene. In bringing characters to life, this concept magnifies their real-life movements to reinforce a feeling. By channeling a bit of the dramatic, we can more easily express an idea or action to a viewer. So, how do we extend this method to motion graphics and basic two-dimensional animation? By pushing the top end of our transformations, we can reinforce them. That just means increasing the transformation value of the penultimate keyframe and pulling back a bit on the last one. This is related to follow through but focuses on the dramatic effect of the higher transformation value. Obviously, this doesn't convey subtlety, so save it for when you really need some impact.

Appeal

The last principle is the most difficult to articulate. Since it's such a subjective term, one could argue that appeal is tied to personal taste. At the time these principles were penned, this probably referred to a charismatic cartoon character. Since we're talking about design, we can wrap it up by digging back into classic principles of organization. Hierarchy, focal point,

Figure 3.15
Exaggeration is all about pushing the value of the transformation to make it pop, and then pulling back slightly at the end.

balance, proximity, alignment, and contrast are important to consider. If your animation or motion graphic employs these well, chances are it will be appealing. Know when and where to stand out. If it's prominently displayed as a video on a website, it should be dynamic. If it's supporting animation as part of an interface, it should blend in and not distract. Context will inform what's needed.

Prototyping animation

Sketches

When starting a new project, it's best to begin with rough sketches. This allows you to think about the amount of information you're presenting and to consider what kind of graphics will support it. During initial brainstorming, rough ideas about visual elements, movement, and composition are important. This is the first chance to think about what kind of imagery and art you will use. Will it be illustrated? What about photos or video clips? Maybe a combination of media? Will typography play a large role or be minimal? These are all questions to ask yourself as you quickly iterate through concepts in this stage. I tell my students to use written notes in the margins and/or draw directional lines to indicate movement in rough sketches.

HACK

After some very basic directions are worked out, tracing paper or vellum pages can be stapled together, with a frame drawn on each. Loosely drawn animated forms can be sketched out on each sheet. This is an easy way to see exactly how elements will interact with each other in the composition. In the days of early animation, this method was used in combination with backlit worktables. It may seem counterintuitive to work in such an analog process, but I guarantee that the most proficient software user is still faster with a rough pencil sketch.

Figure 3.16
These sketches for a five-second animated logo provide a visual roadmap for what needs to be created in After Effects.

Storyboards

The most recognized form of storyboarding was pioneered at Walt Disney Studios in the 1930s. Staff animator Webb Smith thought to sketch out individual cartoon scenes on sheets of paper and tack them to the wall. By adding to the story sequentially, animators could plan out the entire project before the laborious task of creating it by hand. Storyboards are very useful in presenting the arc of a project at a glance. This makes sense, because animation and motion graphics can take a long time to design and produce. Since they bookend the idea, they're also used to communicate the concept to various stakeholders. The number of storyboards per page can vary from two to twenty. This depends on the length of the composition and the complexity of the project. In any case, they should be made to represent key points of action, so that your mind can fill in the parts in-between. If you have four storyboards representing twenty seconds of animation, they should communicate the entire duration.

Style frames

At the beginning of a commercial motion graphics project, there's usually a visual pitch to sell the concept to a client. This is done through a series of style frames, which are full-color images that represent the visual aesthetic of the project. A style frame is essentially a stand-in for a single frame within a longer animation. The amount to create varies, but they're distinctly "quality over quantity." In creating style frames, a high level of finish is important. They should look as though someone has paused a motion graphics video on playback. The style that emerges from the artwork is presented here: Is it clean and crisp, rough and textured, or lush and layered? The quality of images, color palette, and typography are all expressed in this step. Concepts of motion can be implied through blurring or transparency to further add to the realism. In high-level production, there is much effort and time spent at this stage since it likely means getting the job or not.

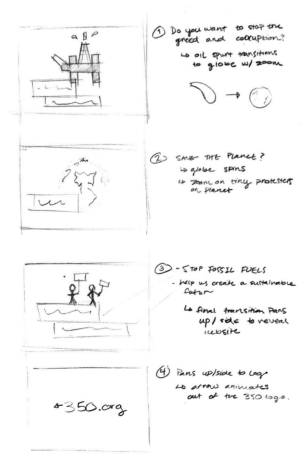

Figure 3.17
A basic storyboard can serve to guide the narrative and pacing for a motion graphics piece.

HACK

In judging just how much fidelity or time to put into a style frame, you might consider using a "swipe file" for a personal project or small gig. Simply said, it's a series of folders or files that you've collected and curated for future use. Examples include stock photos and unused work from previous projects. By quickly collecting sources from existing material as you go, you'll save significant time when you need to start a new project. You might even create a preliminary style frame from swipe file material for a rough idea before diving into it. This helps art direct any imagery that needs to be sourced, whether it's photography, video, or illustration. Showing an existing image to a photographer and adding notes about what you like and what you'd change is extremely helpful in getting the shot you want and staying on budget. Many motion graphic sequences for films and video series have started from a collection of stock images that were cobbled together for reference.

Figure 3.18
Style frames are a high-fidelity method of setting the tone and overall aesthetic of a piece before any animating has started.

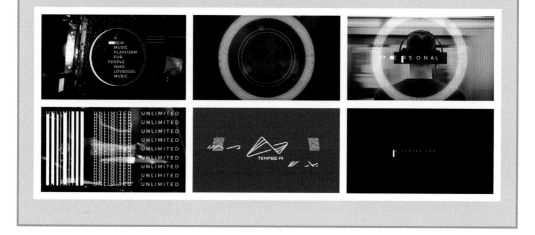

Animation workflow

Pacing

The timing of an animation can manifest itself in several ways: the time it takes for a transformation to start, or for the user to initiate one. We'll address the second one when we talk about animating user interfaces, but a general rule for motion graphics is to move in a half-second on the timeline before starting. It gives your eyes a chance to process and begin focusing. Starting at the zero mark on the timeline can be distracting if there are transformations shown right away. Another consideration is pacing, or the overall flow. This is determined by several things: namely, the length of the animation and the complexity of the composition. In the case of the five-second animated logo mentioned earlier, you're creating a simplified experience. Many of the design elements coming together will be formed from abstract shapes. The goal at the five-second mark is to see a fully formed logo, having been visually pleased in the process. For a longer motion graphics piece, both length and complexity demand a different approach to pacing. If you're delivering several ideas across an animation, these need to mesh well with each other. They progressively add to the overall message and finish with a strong call-to-action. The concepts can be both thematic and text based. If you're using copy, it needs to be delivered in small enough chunks to be read in the amount of time you have available.

Audio

Combining sound with motion graphics brings the composition to life by creating a sensory experience. This is especially true when animation and sound events are synchronized. When basic transformations are tied to audio cues, it raises the level of sophistication, making either seem more complex. There are several ways to combine the two. One is by looking at the visual waveforms of an audio file in a timeline. Not all software will display the waveform by default. In After Effects, for example, you must opt to show it from within a layer. Once accessed, it should resemble looking at a distant mountain range. The peaks (high points) and the valleys (low points) show us the overall range of volume. They coincide with loud or percussive moments, and quiet or ambient ones, respectively. Now, if you're looking at a waveform where the peaks are flattened at the top, you're seeing a file where the overall levels are set too high. While playing back the audio in real time, take note of where levels are registering in the audio meter. Again, depending on your software, this menu might also have to be initialized. It may take a few cycles through to get an idea of where the levels are peaking (the loudest, highest points). For primary audio—whether it's music, narration, or sound effects—your peaks should hit around –6db. Any higher and you risk digital clipping or distortion. However, the value that the signal should normalize at is around –12db.

For secondary sources, the level should rest around –20db. This will be easier to see in an audio signal that is constant, and more difficult to see in one that's varied. To help, most software audio meters have corresponding colors alongside the values. Green indicates a safe level, yellow warrants more scrutiny, and orange/red indicates the signal is clipping. The combined audio level of your mix (all sources) should be normalized between –10db and –20db. The second way to sync audio to an animation is by listening along in real time and setting audio markers as you go. If you're rhythmically inclined, this might be the most intuitive method. I'm someone who's constantly drumming my fingers on the desk, so it feels very natural. A second benefit is that if you're off by a few milliseconds, you can adjust the individual markers manually or delete them altogether and try again.

HACK

The keyboard command to create a marker in After Effects is an asterisk (shift-8 on a laptop). Have your finger on the key and be ready to tap it during audio playback. You may need a few tries to get it, but you can always control-click any frame and select "delete all" from the submenu. Another thing to note: After Effects does not like compressed audio, so convert any MP3 files to WAV format before importing. Adobe Media Encoder can easily handle this.

Transitions

Depending on the length of your animation, you may need to transition to another scene (for motion graphics) or to another screen (for interfaces). It's good to consider the kinds of transitions that are available and which you'll want to use:

Straight cut

This is just how it sounds: an instant cut from one frame to the next. This technique is used extensively in television and film. In contrast with other techniques, there's no visual meaning implied by using it. It simply carries the narrative along quickly and efficiently.

Fade in/out

This is useful at the beginning and end of a motion graphic piece. Fading from black signals the beginning of a story, and fading to black means the end. Fading in and out of a white background is useful when communicating something in past tense. The length of the fade is instrumental in dictating perceived time. A quick half-second could serve to imply a shorter lapse of time (minutes, hours). A long fade that lasts three to five seconds could signal significant change.

Wipe

One clever method for clearing all the elements or objects on a composition is to wipe the screen clear. It allows you to start fresh with a clean slate. Doing so communicates the end of a concept or thought, so make sure this is the case before using it. Another side benefit is that all of the layers used for a particular scene can be grouped together on the timeline and toggled easily. A wipe is usually animated with some gusto on the incoming keyframes, so be sure to tweak your easing curves accordingly.

Dissolve

A dissolve can communicate the passage of time in motion graphics. As a classic film-editing technique, it's different from a fade because you're seeing the passage of time through superimposed images. Again, the length of the transition has a direct effect on perceived time. Using a dissolve as a reoccurring transition in a scene can have a dreamy or whimsical quality. You're seeing vignettes or snippets instead of a full flashback. In digital layouts, dissolves are a convenient way of showing a montage of images such as a photo carousel on a website. It's useful because it allows you to swap content in a sophisticated way without distraction of background or movement.

Sequencing animation

When sorting out the role of the primary and secondary animation of any one composition, think about how they're going to affect each other. This is very important in motion UI design for interfaces, where several transformations might happen in a second or less. A call-to-action button might animate in stages, where the first part might signal the functionality and the second part shows confirmation. Getting the timing right between these begins to verge into interaction design, which we'll discuss in the next chapter. The speed of easing and the importance of both parts to be seen as one smooth action falls within motion UI design, though. Breaking up long blocks of text is common when you need a gap for the viewer to process a longer thought.

HACK

Make sure to playback in real time, early and often. There's nothing worse than spending an hour focusing on a five-second animated segment only to find out that the pacing is way too fast. There are some basic ways to sequence multiple stages of an animation, whether it's made up of several or a single changing component(s):

Smooth offset

This is a tried-and-tested trick in moving a series of elements in and out; it is one fluid cascading motion that looks and feels elastic. Groupings of images and text work well with this method. Don't make this painfully long. It should be snappy and slightly expressive but not gimmicky. Tweaking the easing curves is a must for this not to feel robotic.

Figure 3.19
Groups of elements can be moved together using an offset, which gives them a playful quality.

Morphing

Bridging the content can be done effectively through morphing elements together. This can work well in changing out a shape to a logo or illustration, or by combining or splitting elements.

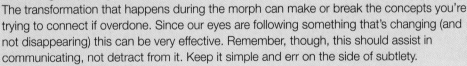

START   END

The transformation that happens during the morph can make or break the concepts you're trying to connect if overdone. Since our eyes are following something that's changing (and not disappearing) this can be very effective. Remember, though, this should assist in communicating, not detract from it. Keep it simple and err on the side of subtlety.

Figure 3.20
Morphing shapes is easily done through changing the outer shape of an element across the timeline.

Blur and transparency

To make sequences look more cinematic, you might want to apply a blur to them as a sequence is animating in or out. This has the same effect as a lens coming into focus in a scene, softening the interstitial space. If you want a more drastic focus, you can try a motion blur, which is somewhat like whipping your head around to look at something. You can apply this in After Effects using the double-circled icon switch to the right of each layer. Simply toggle it on or off. When shifting groups of content in and out of the frame, their overall opacity can play an active role in creating layered depth. Combining that with scale, position, and blurring can create a mood that's both dynamic and elegant.

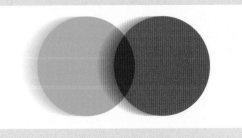

Figure 3.21
Blurring moving objects gives the composition a more human perspective. Transparency further enhances that depth.

Figure 3.22
Animated layers
can become rich
and complex
through parallax
motion, where
different speeds
create density.

Parallax motion

Creating a parallax effect is a
good technique for building
movement across layers. This is
where the foreground layers
move faster than the background
layers, creating a sense of depth
while placing the viewer in the
scene. This is what you

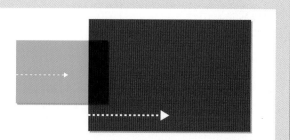

experience when you're riding in a car and looking out the window. Objects on the side of
the road whoosh by quickly and objects in the vast distance move at a glacial pace. This
can be made even more realistic by scaling down and slightly blurring the background
layers. The crisp and fully saturated foreground becomes the focal point, while the
background serves to add depth.

Regarding these methods, using them once or twice is probably the limit. Any more than
that and people will begin focusing on the effect itself. The last thing you want to do is build
something custom that ends up feeling like a generic preset from overuse.

Precomposing, parenting, and null objects

A typical After Effects motion graphics
project will start to quickly accumulate
layers as you add more elements,
transformations, and dimensionality. For
all but the simplest of animations, you'll
quickly find yourself scrolling up and down
in the layers panel. If you're on a laptop,
this problem is exacerbated. Naming the
layers is one trick to making sense of
everything as they start to add up: simply
select one, press return on the keyboard,
and start typing. Another way to start
grouping them into manageable chunks is
called "precomposing." To start, select a
bunch of layers that make up a part of an
animation. Use the Layer > Precompose

menu command (command-shift-C) to
group them. Select "move all attributes
into the new composition" when prompted,
and you'll see a new composition with just
those layers appear. Don't panic: your
previous composition isn't gone. It should
be in its own composition tab to the left of
the one you're currently working in. If you
click that tab, you'll see your old layers
again. The only difference is that the ones
you precomposed are shown as a comp
icon as one layer. I can't stress enough
how much time this will save you. Here's
the best part: you can go back and edit the
layers you combined anytime, and you can
now treat the grouped layer as its own
transformable layer. This is key to building
complexity in motion graphics.

HACK

If you still find yourself scrolling after using this method, select the layers panel so it's outlined in a blue stroke, and hit the tilde key (just under the esc key at the top left). Your layers are now full screen. Un-toggle them by hitting the same key again.

Parenting is another phenomenon that opens up a world of possibilities in After Effects. This is a way of associating one or more "child" layers to a "parent" layer's animated properties. For instance, you have two layers in your composition, each with a shape. The first layer only has a position animation applied to its shape. The second has scale and opacity applied to its own. If you select the second layer and look in the modes and switches columns to the right, you'll see one labeled "parent" with the value set to "none." Change the value to the name of the first layer, and the second layer will now be parented to it. This means that the scale and opacity transformations are still applied, but now so is position. You can parent as many child layers as you want to a parent layer.

A "null object" is an advanced form of parenting. It really should be called an invisible layer because that's what it is. Create one by choosing the Layer menu and New > Null object. It's only marked by a small red square when selected and isn't visible otherwise. You can apply any normal transformation to it and parent other layers to it. You can even parent a layer that's already controlling other child layers to it. Meaning, you can control layers at multiple depths in one fell swoop. It's also essential when using features such as camera tracking or creating augmented reality prototypes. We will look at this in more detail in Chapter 6.

2D animation in 3D space

As mentioned before, After Effects is capable of some basic 3D but lacks a true purpose-built engine for it. The combination of two-dimensional elements in 3D space is described by many as "two-and-a-half dimensional animation." Still, basic shapes and text can be extruded to appear as 3D. This looks quite convincing when lights and a camera are added, as we'll discuss next. Moving 2D objects around in three dimensions can be tricky to wrap your head around at first: it's like holding two pieces of paper in front of you with your arms extended at different lengths. Once you get the hang of it, you can add dynamic depth and effects to still photos and backgrounds. It's also valuable for motion UI design, letting you animate elements that draw attention to functionality. The basic gist is that you now have access to the Z-axis, which is depth in the composition. Positioning elements at different Z values, or rotating them on the X or Y values, adds to the dimensionality.

Dimension

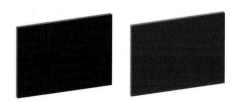

Figure 3.23
Though After Effects isn't a true 3D application, layers can be shown in perspective and manipulated within 3D space.

HACK

Switch from active view to one of the three custom views at the bottom of the composition window; they'll help you see and manipulate 3D space from different angles. You'll notice that more values become available when you tick the 3D box to the right of the layer name. Position, scale, and rotation now have three values. A new property—orientation—also appears. It's valuable in moving objects in an angular fashion around the anchor point.

It's tough to use restraint when animating 2D objects dimensionally, mostly because of the "swinging door effect" you get when they are rotated in ninety-degree increments on the X, Y, or Z axis. Although that effect can be useful in interaction design, it can be annoying to watch in a more passive way. Try shifting by ten degrees or less when combined with other sequencing methods to give it a sense of space.

Lights

A variety of lights let objects cast and receive shadows with on/off values in the layer settings, and can serve to build depth

and ambiance in a composition. You can make a new light layer by selecting Layer > New > Light. There are four types of lights, but "ambient" and "spot" are the two that you'll use most. The first offers lighting control over the entire composition, and the second can illuminate parts of it. You can move lights around to add dramatic effect, and they really expand much of the possibilities of camera layers by adding light depth in the Z-space. Spotlights can be manipulated by changing the overall intensity (brightness), size (cone angle), and softness (cone feather). It's easy to change from a hard-edged circular light to a softened moody one.

HACK

Figure 3.24
Adding spotlights to a basic extruded 3D text layer gives it more dramatic dimension.

To see how lights work with extruded shapes, hit "command-K" to open the composition settings, click the 3D renderer tab, and choose Cinema 4D. Then create a basic shape, convert it to a 3D object, open up the layer to find geometry options, and increase the extrusion depth. Now, create a new spotlight layer and move it around your shape. You should see shadows, gradients, and real dimension.

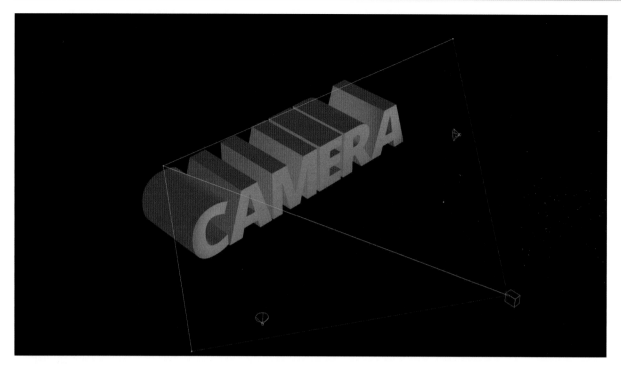

Cameras

The final part of jumping into 3D in After Effects is working with camera layers. They allow you to view 3D objects from different angles and lengths. Instead of moving an entire composition around in space, the camera can move in, out and around the composition. This really opens up a lot of creative freedom and extends the dynamic possibilities of basic objects.

Figure 3.25
A camera layer allows you to move around the content, versus moving the content in and out of the composition.

HACK

To create a camera layer, choose: Layer > New > Camera. The modal window that follows offers the ability to dial-in advanced camera settings, but choose a one-node type at the default 35mm size for an easier introduction. Specific camera tools (unified, orbit, and track) become available to help move it through the composition, as do settings like depth of field. Opening the camera in layer panel and click-dragging those values may offer more precise control over positioning.

Adding tactile qualities

One result of a fully digital workflow is that you must intentionally plan for organic qualities in your composition. Your project specifications might call for transforming vectors, photographs, and video. If so, you're in luck because digital software does that well. If you need to bring some more depth and texture into the work, though, there are some other methods to consider.

Layer stack

The first thing to understand is how the layer stack works. Essentially, layers at the top of the panel show up as the top layer in the composition. You can obviously edit the

opacity of that layer to reveal more of the images below it, but there are many other ways to combine layers and elements to create depth and tactility.

Masking textures

If a shape or closed path is drawn over a layer already selected, it creates a mask instead of a new layer. The mask can be switched from additive to subtractive once it's a part of the layer, and further softened with opacity and feathering. This is very easy to do and is the go-to method for creating everything from punched-out patterns to vignettes.

Figure 3.26
Masking a layer against a textured background gives it a cutout look when combined with a few subtle effects.

HACK

A simple "paper cutout" effect can be achieved by creating a mask over a textured background photo and applying a drop shadow (Layer styles > Drop shadow) and distressing it a bit (Effect > Stylize > Roughen edges).

Track mattes

You can also use layers below the one you're trying to target and affect them with a track matte. Use an "alpha matte" that borrows the transparency of the adjacent layer, or "luma matte" that takes its luminance. By combining vector layers with textured photographs or scans, you can bring some texture into your workflow. This looks fantastic when pairing text with an image in the layer below. Select the alpha matte in the "TrkMat" dropdown menu on the right side of the bottom layer.

Blending modes

There are several After Effects blending modes that work similarly to those in Photoshop. You need to select two layers to start: the topmost layer will be affected by mixing the image from the one underneath. Select whichever you would like to try in the "Mode" dropdown to the right of the top layer. There are a lot to choose from, and they use different properties to achieve the results (additive, subtractive, and luminance, for example), meaning there's a broad range of possible outcomes.

HACK

Frankly, some of the blending modes are pretty useless unless you're looking for extremely harsh effects. There are a few that I've found most useful across a range of applications:

- "Multiply" knocks out the lighter parts from the top image, allowing textures to come through from the bottom one. The overall image is darker, and it's good for adding distressed effects.
- "Screen" is useful for lightening and smoothing out images. Use it for softening the overall top layer and punching up light details that you want to appear over the darker parts of the composition.
- "Overlay" lets you retain the extreme light and dark contrast in your top layer, while replacing the color of the mid-tones with the color of the bottom layer. It's a great way to add pronounced accent colors to the image.

Figure 3.27
An alpha track matte allows you to use the adjacent layer to create lush fills.

Wiggle expression

After Effects includes coding capabilities for further customization and automation. They're called "expressions," and most of them are beyond the scope of this text. But there's one expression that's easy to implement and can give elements a sense of randomness. It's called "wiggle," and you can apply it to any transformation property. Simply option-click the stopwatch icon for that transformation, and a new text field will appear in the timeline. You'll also see some red numbers next to the property values; this just lets you know that an expression is being used. Delete the text already in the field and replace it with: wiggle (5,5). The first number controls frequency (how fast you want it to work). The second number controls amplitude (how far you want it to shift). Experiment with different pairs of values. A low first and high second number would result in "slow and far," while the opposite would be "fast and short." Use restraint with this effect; it can get tedious very quickly if overdone.

Figure 3.28
Kuntzel + Deygas used a tactile approach to bring warmth into the digital title sequence for *Catch Me If You Can*.

Incorporating analog methods

Sometimes the best way to bring a bit of grit into your digital workflow is simply to create things by hand. No number of digital effects can compete with the random imperfection of tactile methods if you're after a handwrought look. Scanning and importing marker or watercolor elements can add the warmth of traditional compositing qualities into digital animation. Combining these with blending modes or mattes can make them even richer with depth. A great example of analog craft in a digital workflow can be seen in the title sequence for the film *Catch Me If You Can*. Parisian duo Kuntzel + Deygas were tasked with designing a visual narrative that was set in the 1960s and realized that an overly polished aesthetic would feel out of place. They took a cue from the plot—the film's protagonist is a master forger and mysterious figure—and hand cut silhouetted body parts, which were then stamped to create stylized textured figures. These stamped images were then brought into a digital composition and animated over a highly detailed vector composition. The result feels both vintage and contemporary at the same time: flickering rough-edged characters juxtaposed against flat bright colors. Try to think of different mediums that might lend themselves to whatever concept you're working with. Paint, textiles, crayon, or ripped paper could all extend different moods in tangible ways.

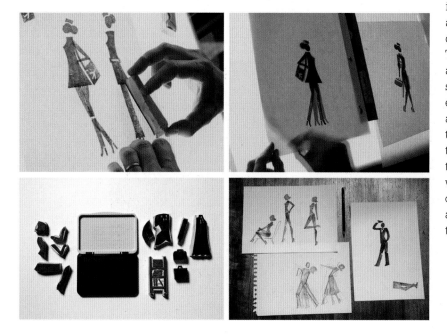

Final output and sharing

Most animation outputs as various video formats. The ability for very high-quality files to be created stems from use in high-end film production. As an example, a twenty-second motion graphics clip with sound exported at the highest quality can be several gigabytes in size and not easily playable online. Most animation files will be prepped for digital distribution, so further compressing the files is the last step before use. Adobe Media Encoder can reduce file size with the use of codecs, which are customizable sets of data. Using and modifying a codec by further crunching the bitrate can give you a video export with a much smaller size. An .mp4 file is typically the preferred format for viewing those files online.

HACK

After Effects can render directly to Media Encoder and you can keep working while it exports in the background. When it's time to share the video, there are several options to consider:

YouTube is, of course, the market leader of this platform, and using it is free. There's a cost to consider though: advertisements. If you're sending off a project for approvals and it's preceded by a long ad, it can be an instant buzzkill. There are settings available to turn off ads, but Google doesn't exactly make it intuitive to do so. The related videos that show up after a video has played can also be inappropriate. There are ways to alter this when embedding videos: just search for "YouTube player parameters."

Vimeo is one of the oldest video sharing platforms, and their growth has been sustained by creatives. Most professionals working in film and video prefer it because of the lack of excessive advertising. There are banner ads displayed on videos for free accounts, but all others require a subscription and are ad-free. There are similar parameters you can tweak for showing embedding videos through Vimeo, including making them password-protected. This is great when showing a work-in-progress that you don't want the world to see. In terms of hosted video services for creatives, Vimeo is the gold standard.

Native HTML Video is a platform-free method of hosting and sharing videos. It requires you to upload the files directly to your website via file-transfer protocol (FTP). We briefly discuss this in Chapter 5. This option offers the most complete control and oversight of your work. Make sure your web hosting plan is large enough to accommodate large video files (the most basic of tiers usually aren't).

Offline video embedding

If your final video files need to be shared via other methods, it's good to know that video files are easily embedded in popular software such as Acrobat and design-friendly programs like InDesign. Note that embedding videos this way progressively adds to the file size, so it's important to encode and reduce them to a reasonable size. Even PowerPoint has the ability for video embedding, and in certain cases it might be the path of least resistance in sharing your work. I can't tell you how many times I've relied on a patchy Wi-Fi connection in presenting to a large group and later regretted it.

Exporting for interfaces

If the final product of your animation is motion UI design for the Web or an app, there are methods that can facilitate this. Bodymovin is an After Effects script that allows AE files to be exported for use on the Web. They can be extended with a tool called Lottie, which is a library that allows animations to play natively on iOS and Android. This is a pretty huge step forward because, before this, any motion UI design that had been mocked up had to be recreated with code using video exports as a reference. The ability to export something as working code eliminates that bottleneck in the workflow. The intermediary steps involved in this process are likely to become simplified as the demand for UI animation increases.

Takeaways

Controlling classic graphic design principles in a time-based medium, and making them feel responsive to natural forces, remains important for all motion graphics applications. We will discuss motion UI design a bit further in the next chapter, but the core skills with respect to animation are consistent with everything we've discussed here. Considering how popular video formats are, the careers in these disciplines are likely to grow. Their basic workflows should be part of every contemporary digital designer's skill set.

ANIMATION DESIGN EXERCISE

Create a twenty-second motion graphic video spot serving as an advertisement or public service announcement.

DESCRIPTION

Design and produce a twenty-second motion graphic video spot using imagery, text, audio, and motion graphics. The advertisement can promote a physical or digital product, a service, cause, organization, or an event. Over the course of the video, a central concept or plea needs to be introduced, supported by additional content, and followed through with a strong call-to-action. The client can be a company, nonprofit or cultural institution, general cause, or event-based organization.

SPECIFICATIONS

Go with a 1280 × 720px composition size, 24 or 30fps, exactly twenty seconds in length. The final video output should be an .mp4 file. The reason we're not specifying a full 1920px frame is because you might want to manipulate position or scale in a background video. This slightly smaller size gives you a bit of room to do so.

INTENT

This motion graphics piece is an advertisement or public service announcement. The big takeaway for this exercise is the call-to-action at the end. What kind of client or concept would lend itself well to this format? Consider a cause that you could easily support, or a product or service that you understand. The client

doesn't have to be a real entity, and you can create a fictitious product or service as well. Because the final video will live online, it may be more advantageous to create the brand from scratch (because of copyright issues).

RESEARCH AND METHODOLOGY

When animating something simple like a logo, you're trying to distill the essence of a brand or organization into a short visual expression. For this longer-form animation, you're appealing to the viewer to do something. You can already see the need for text to be read on-screen and engaging graphics. Both need time to be processed, and pacing becomes even more important at this stage. In a twenty-second piece, you might ask: How can this be broken down into five-second chunks? You'll introduce the idea within the first five seconds, use the following ten seconds to support that, and end with the call-to-action.

CONTENT

What kind of visuals might work well with your concept? Photos, illustrations, video? Maybe some combination of these? There are inherent aesthetic associations with how each are used. Contemporary photography or video can convey a forward-facing business, while whimsical illustrations might suggest something more casual. Just know that these meanings can be juxtaposed to create contrast or embrace wit.

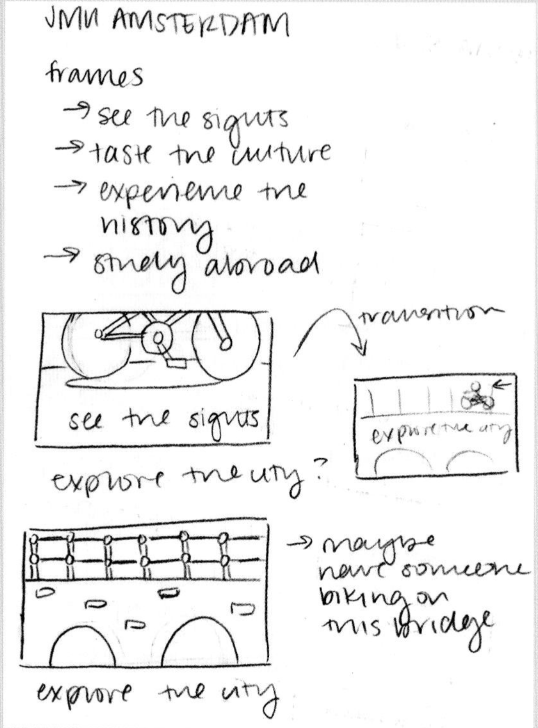

Figure 3.29
These preliminary sketches capture initial themes and visual concepts for a twenty-second motion graphic video.

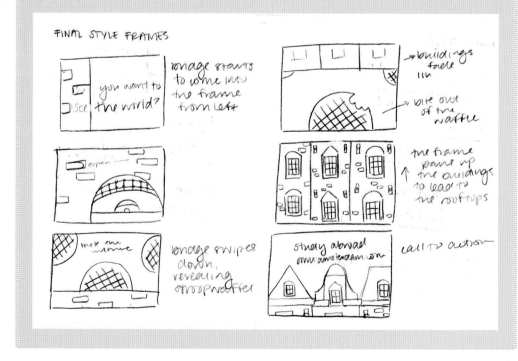

The copy used should be succinct, but it also needs to be emotionally captivating and memorable. What's the question or proposition? This will be what grabs the user's attention. What are the main ideas you want to convey? What is the call-to-action? Everything leading up to this has set up what you're asking the user to do. That might be purchasing something (product or service), donating time or resources, attending an event, or participating in an experience.

SKETCHES

A quick sketch of each chunk of action will help you start animating with intent. These should quickly communicate the scene, animations happening in that time frame, text that appears on-screen, background audio, and the transition to the next scene.

Figure 3.30
Additional sketches capture individual scenes in smaller chunks of time, and they serve as tools to animate efficiently.

MOOD BOARDS

Assembling some visual content can be done quickly after you've decided on some basics. There are many websites that feature 100 percent free photography and video (they make money through advertising and partnerships). A few noteworthy ones are Gratisography, Unsplash, and Pexels. Arranging these on a basic mood board will allow you to see them in context with each other, as well as typefaces and colors. Take screenshots of video clips to show them as well.

Figure 3.31
A mood board can capture the visual aesthetic of a motion graphic piece, showing typography, colors, and sample imagery.

AUDIO

Acquiring audio for this exercise is a bit more difficult than visuals. In short: don't use popular music, period. There are algorithms built to find this in videos across social media, where it's flagged and removed. Specifically searching for "copyright safe music" on social media will paradoxically yield good results because there are individuals that upload their own music for pure exposure. Other places to look online are the Free Music Archive and FreeSound. If you're musically inclined, creating your own ambient track might actually be quicker than searching out what you have in mind.

STYLE FRAMES

Using some of the content you've collected, design four to eight style frames. Remember, these are highly polished compositions that should communicate a level of detail, which looks like a finished product. You can use these to showcase typography, color schemes, and the overall look and feel.

Figure 3.32
Style frames are the last visual step in the pre-production process, and they ensure that no time is wasted during animation.

COMPOSITIONS

With your sketches and style frames in hand, it's time to begin assembling your composition in the timeline. Import the content that comprises the first five seconds or so, and reference what you've designed on your first style frame. After keyframing your initial animation and tweaking their velocity in the graph editor, test it by playing back in RAM preview. After the first few scenes have been designed, you can work out the transitions between them. Bring in your audio files, set their levels, and be sure to fade them in and out.

RENDER AND EXPORT

After viewing the entire composition and adjusting for timing and pacing, it's time to export. Use the command Composition > Add to render queue to create a lossless video file. This will be very large and can be used to compare quality against. Open Media Encoder, add the video file to the queue, and choose the h.264 preset. You can further tweak settings here, but adjusting the bitrate will make the most difference. Keep lowering the bitrate and exporting until you can see a noticeable difference between this and the original file. That's the sweet spot. The resulting .mp4 file can be uploaded to Vimeo for easy sharing and embedding.

Figure 3.33
Pacing is important to consider: you can only really communicate two to three ideas within twenty seconds.

REFLECTION AND REVISION

Looking at your final video, how have you addressed the intent outlined earlier? Does the overall aesthetic and presentation fit well against the client (real or imagined) or cause? How is the imagery drawing emotional ties to the concept being presented? What's the tone of the copy and call-to-action? Is it easily scanned and integrated with the imagery? Are there dynamic motion graphics driving and enhancing the concept? There should be much more at play than just photos and videos with text overlays. Answering these questions and confirming effectiveness is key to reflecting on your approach. If you pursue any revisions, remember to save a copy before doing so.

GOALS AND OUTCOMES

A strong portfolio piece is the most obvious evidence of completing this exercise effectively. We've addressed some basic questions above about what a successful project looks like in this category, but the true test is to compare it to real examples. Find two to three examples of motion-graphic advertisements or public service announcements, and rate them against yours. Better yet, have someone else do it. It needs to be "on-brand" with the client you've chosen or created. The final imagery should feel "created" rather than chosen. Viewers should feel compelled by the call-to-action, and it should all look seamless.

Figure 3.34
Silhouetted photos, bold colors, strong typography, and whimsical details all contribute to this strong motion graphics piece.

Interaction Design

Interaction design was borne out of user interface design but slowly diverged into its own discipline. Swiping, clicking, and tapping our various devices and experiencing the designed response (usually in the form of an animated function) are core examples of interaction design. Think about the significant aesthetic value an interactive experience provides. Whether it's a smartphone interface, digital kiosk, or website, interaction design is all about the connection between users and digital products and services. Sound familiar? While closely tied with user experience design, interaction design (IxD) focuses on balancing tasks with tactility, making sure they're intuitive, appropriate, and deliver a sense of surprise and delight. Because of this, IxD has an intrinsic relationship to UI, UX, and animation.

What exactly is IxD?

The term interaction design dates to the 1980s, though it took at least another decade to become widely known as a distinct discipline. In the mid 1990s, the wide adoption of Macromedia Flash allowed designers to experiment with animation and interaction for the Web and was capable of displaying rich media in a way that was extremely sophisticated. This was at a time when the Web was still in its infancy and browsers struggled to display interactive content. Flash opened a whole world for anyone wanting to embrace this new frontier and only required that the user have a plug-in installed. Most other interactivity within digital design required a closed system that had to be created from scratch. Digital kiosks certainly existed then, mainly in museums and cultural institutions. They were expensive to design and develop, requiring specialized skills in an emerging discipline.

The discrete Flash plug-in guaranteed that the content would perform consistently, regardless of the browser or computer. Flash continued to be an asset to designers until it was dealt a death blow in 2010, when Apple prevented it from running on the then-new iPad. The popular iPhone allowed for native apps to run on Apple's iOS operating system. Suddenly, the Web wasn't the only place for designers to flex interaction skills. The success of the smartphone, in general, and the subsequent hunger for new apps drove the appetite for interaction design. Around the same time, HTML5 was gaining popularity and was capable of complex interactions on the Web without the need for a plug-in. The discipline was firmly cemented by this point and has seen significant growth since.

Relationship to UI and UX

IxD has clear ties to UI design, extending menus, toggles, and buttons through animation. That animation is distinct from what we've largely discussed in the previous chapter, though. It provides feedback during an interactive experience, showing cause and effect. It can also help to visualize sequencing and errors. We've come to rely on this feedback when using digital products, from seeing a "sent" pop up after typing an email, to confirmation of "liking" something on social media. Goal-driven design and research inform these interactions, and the animations support performance. Because of this functional aspect, it becomes clear that UX design also has a role to play in continuing to shape interaction design.

User interface and implied action

The relationship between an element's properties and its capabilities is known as "affordance." In other words, its appearance might suggest how to interact with it. Leaning on some UI principles can be useful to help explain. For instance: Does the button or menu have a drop shadow or slight gradient? That could contribute to a sense that it could be clicked or tapped. Visible qualities give us an immediate clue in filtering what is static and what is interactive. Using design patterns that are commonly understood can help us quickly do so. These are called "signifiers," and they're clues about how to engage with a digital layout. Push experimentation too hard on a user interface, and you're likely to confuse the user. A white triangle icon pointed to the right and overlaid on a photo suggests that there's a video to be played, right? But what if you replaced the triangle with something abstract, like an asterisk? The user would have to decipher its implied action on their own.

HACK

Go through your top three favorite apps. Note the icons used for various functions and jot down how you think you made the connection as to what they did. Now, download three random apps, and go through the same process cold: Did your intuition work as well for the new ones? Was there any kind of in-app instruction? Did you make some initial mistakes? These kinds of observations are important to realize as you're building functionality into the UI.

Figure 4.1
This app features a blue vertical bar as a menu signifier, which is both very creative and unconventional.

Figure 4.2
Blur and
transparency work
together to
de-emphasize the
background while
an icon animates.

Extending UI with animation

Confirmation that an interaction has been made is not only beneficial for the user but also increasingly expected. A great way to extend the UI and design is by leveraging animation for clarity. This can accomplish several things. First, it can enhance the interface design. When elements start moving, they can showcase some of the decisions that went into the creative process. Of course, if the animation principles we discussed in Chapter 3 are thrown out the window, the result can take the experience down a notch. But more than that, animations make what's essentially a flat layout seem more real. And fidelity of craft is the thing that's becoming consistently expected for showing portfolio pieces. You're demonstrating that it looks visually appropriate and that you understand how important functions should work and provide feedback to the user. Here are some of the ways that animations enhance user interface design:

Masking content load
When an app or website is loading content in the background, a convenient way to distract the user from leaving the experience is to play a quick animation. This can exist as several things: a bouncing logo, a progress bar showing how much time is left, or even a short scene. Another popular function is the "lazy load," which pulls in content as it's scrolled with a slight delay. As it's loading in the background, you're likely to see an animated placeholder of some kind to visually provide a signal. Perhaps, a circle (to suggest a profile photo) and three lines (representing lines of text) that are subtly animated through transparency.

Enhancing scrolling
The devices that we view digital content with are increasingly smaller. Applications made specifically for smartphones may present content in individual screens, but websites present a scroll issue. Savvy designers have embraced this limitation by creating a layered experience. As the user scrolls, supporting elements move at a different speed than the content layer, creating a parallax effect like that we discussed in Chapter 3. Not limited to websites, the offset speed of the different layers scrolling creates an experience that feels multidimensional.

Transitions

The binary visual changes in digital design were one of the issues that Flash solved so well. Buttons could segue smoothly when interacted with. Images could softly appear. Type could move on screen with transparency. As designers, we prefer finesse over simply flipping a light switch. Modern digital design extends this lineage, and users have come to expect snappy timing. A transition is one of the most useful pieces of animation in an interaction designer's tool kit. They're subtle, but very effective when used to reinforce hierarchy. Transitions can be applied to most elements in varying ways; the trick is considering what way would enhance them the best for that situation. For instance, movement usually serves smaller elements well, and transparency and color shifts can be easy on the eyes for larger elements. As with anything, transitions can be overdone, so take a step back and look at everything in context before you add them to everything.

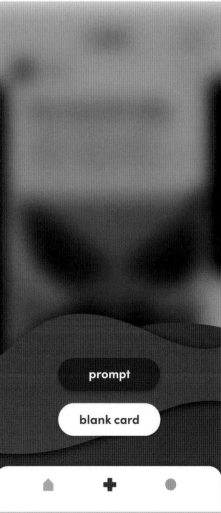

Figure 4.3
The "add card" function shown in this app prompts a dynamic animated transition to the next choice of actions.

Focal point

If a viewer needs to be alerted, a subtle animation is a way to draw their attention to any part of the screen or composition. It can be as simple as an email alert or as complex as showing what part of a form needs to be completed. Sometimes, helper icons will appear and animate in a subtle way (pulsing, changing opacity, etc.) to help shift focus to a part of the layout that needs attention. We mentioned "dark patterns" in Chapter 1; animating large overlays on screen that attempt to force a call-to-action should be avoided. This is especially true if the function to close them is obscured, very small, or not visible to most users.

Logo drops in

Torch's glow pulsates

Microinteractions

Short, prescriptive moments where the user can interact with the UI are what define microinteractions. When they're done well, they have the potential to elevate the user's experience. When ill-considered or overused, they can detract from it. There are physical examples, like setting a smartphone to vibrate, or waving your hand under an electric hand dryer. In digital design, though, most microinteractions feature a bit of animation. The interface design is greatly enhanced by this because unlike designing a poster, we're interacting with the layout. An app design concept is a popular portfolio piece covered in many university programs. A way to show your skills holistically across the UX, UI, and IxD spectrum is to extend that app layout into a full case study that reveals UX implications, annotations that describe functionality, and microinteractions that highlight the experience.

Embedding animations

Showing your animations as stills or a succession of screen grabs is better than nothing, but it's far more useful to show the actual animations. On a website, that's easy: you can just embed the videos on the page. But what if you want to show a case study as a PDF? You can hyperlink directly from the file. Here's the process:

1. Design your microinteractions in After Effects.
2. Upload them online using Vimeo (they have a free account available), and then copy the corresponding URLs.
3. If putting together a layout with annotations in InDesign, you can create a button that's labeled and linked to the appropriate videos; add the URLs you just copied.
4. When you export the PDF, check the "include hyperlinks" box.
5. When someone views the document and clicks those buttons, it will open a browser linked to those videos.

Prompts

The microinteraction starts with a prompt. This can be something initiated by the user, a timed sequence, or some other conditional event. Interacting with a user interface by tapping or clicking would be considered an intentional prompt. This might in turn activate an animation that confirms the interaction. Again, these aren't long drawn-out affairs. They're just short snippets that validate our actions, giving us immediate feedback. And when done well, they should add something to the experience. If you're using an app and complete an action, you might see a modal "pop-up" with additional details. That's a user-triggered prompt, but there are others that are triggered by time (i.e., Stay logged in?) and so on. If you spend a minute thinking about it, you can probably recall a half dozen conditional microinteractions you've experienced. And that's an important takeaway—thinking

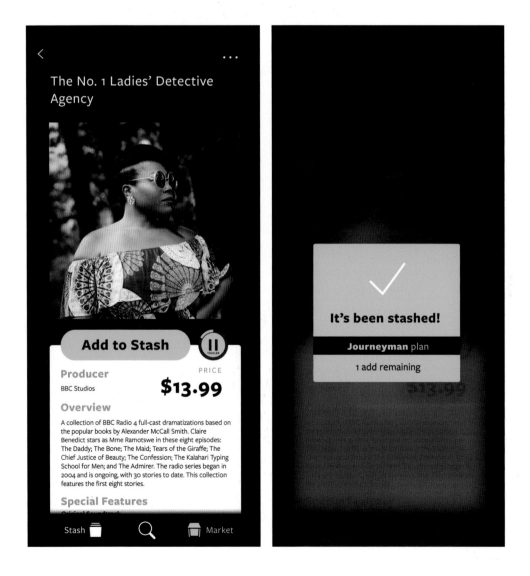

Figure 4.5
A modal window opens as an overlay prompt, and provides details about the choice made.

about it. Because, for the designer, the goal is for the user to engage with the prompt as a seamless extension of the overall experience. It's a tricky line to negotiate: inspiring interaction for the user but also not becoming tedious.

Parameters

A microinteraction needs to have a set of rules by which it functions. How does it animate? How long does it last? What are the user's options? This is probably a good time to talk about speed. Your goal should be about a half-second at the top end. That includes any velocity curves and easing within the animation. In fact, thinking about them as bursts will help you mentally separate them from traditional animation or motion graphics. Imagine tapping a button on your smartphone and then waiting for a five-second animation to finish. Then imagine that every function on the device used that same interaction. You'd be livid within a few minutes. When designing, consider how transformations will affect the rest of the interface. How much negative space is around an element slated for microinteraction? If there's motion, you don't want it "hitting" other elements. The same applies for rotation and scale.

Visual narrative

While designing, make sure that you're considering the visual narrative of the task. When viewing a microinteraction, our minds preload what we already see on-screen. A mental model of what is about to happen helps us make sense of everything: the overall composition, the task at hand, and the expected result. Your microinteractions should animate in a way that builds on a visual narrative of what's about to happen. For instance, in the Torch app example, we see an "add" button at the bottom right. Interacting with this button initiates a microinteraction that transforms the plus sign into a check mark. It's a smooth animation that only relies on scale, aside from the morphing of the symbol. It's quick, responsive, and assists in confirmation. It takes advantage of a visual narrative that we might expect in some way, because we're used to buttons behaving in a similar fashion. Imagine instead if it rotated three times, faded out in opacity, and faded back in again as another shape. Our expectation is suddenly paused. The overall flow and perceived narrative of the interaction is broken, and we must re-evaluate the visual layout. When effect is

Figure 4.6
The Torch app features a subtle microinteraction that adds to the visual narrative of the experience.

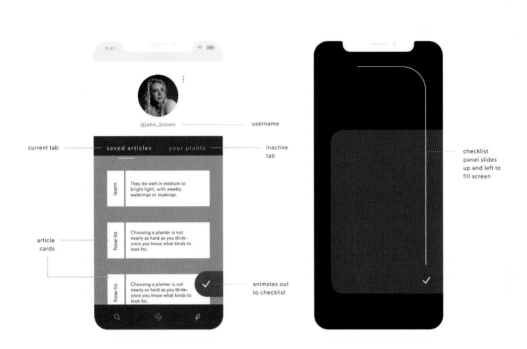

Figure 4.7
This check mark button initiates an animation that moves upward and fills the screen with a new background.

overemphasized, the interaction itself suffers. A good microinteraction supports a core task with subtle details rather than detracting with something flashy.

Cognitive load

Our expectation of a familiar visual narrative helps us compartmentalize information. When something strays too far from our mental map, it takes a bit longer for our brain to process and understand. We can get overwhelmed, gloss over information, or even give up. This happens in a fraction of a second, but on a larger scale it detracts from completing the task at hand. Think about it like this: you're bicycling down a stretch of road where you cross three intersections; as you approach each intersection, you look both ways but cautiously proceed without stopping. That's like completing a set of tasks with microinteractions reinforcing your expected narrative. Now think about biking along the same stretch of road, where there's a stop sign at each intersection. That's akin to a set of microinteractions that are visually jarring, forcing you to stop the bike and start pedaling again.

Reward

Delighting users through perceived tactile experiences is the core of contemporary interaction design. Especially where handheld devices are concerned. Ensuring that velocity curves are animated in a way that feels snappy and responsive is important. It all adds up to what's called "user delight." I know that term seems a bit exaggerated, but that's essentially what's happening in our brains. Completing an interaction that features some sort of visual feedback releases a microdose of dopamine, acting as a reward. It's the same chemical release that makes you want to instantly check your email when you hear that familiar "ding." You're designing something that's interacted with in a purely digital way, but you want the user to feel a sense of implied tactility. Their actions can initiate mental responses that feel physical in our brains.

The topic of user delight is quite controversial, as interaction design is actively being used and manipulated to keep us addicted to social media. The concept of using this kind of pseudo-psychology in IxD has been pushed to the extreme, causing us to check for that mental reward again and again. I'm not going to get into ethical and social implications of overusing these kinds of techniques. Just know that we've reached the tipping point and exercising judgment and restraint with respect to "addictive interactions" is key. For instance, rewarding a user for completing a task necessary to the experience is one thing. Doing the same to keep them mindlessly engaged is quite another.

Motion and movement

We talked about cascading animation in Chapter 3, but it has value here as well. Combining animation movements into a fluid single motion is the key to a successful microinteraction. This relates to visual narrative but is specifically concerned with streamlining motion. If your microinteraction plays out in starts and stops, you run into the same issue with cognitive load. Complexity of motion contributes to complexity of task. The movement should be swift and focused, helping confirm that the task is complete. When possible, take advantage of ways to combine transformations: rotation and scale, transparency, position, etc.

Sweat the details

When planning a microinteraction, consider which UI elements represent the most important functions. Focus on those few and look for opportunities to finesse without adding filler. Tacking on an interaction to an ill-considered design is a losing battle. If an element is already distracting or overbearing, animation will only make it more so. Take a step back to fine-tune your static layout before designing microinteractions. Since motion will command a strong focal point, you might think about the hierarchy of your composition before animating. The interaction stage isn't the time to test out experimental layout ideas. Otherwise, you're increasing your workload. The details you build into the interaction should serve to enhance the UI. And by that, I'm not saying "pack in as much punch as possible." Quite the opposite. Less is more, but the "less" should be fine-tuned and focused.

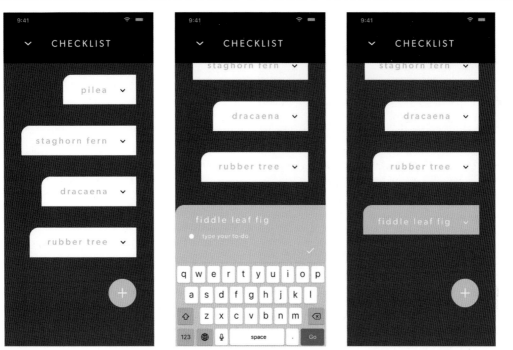

Figure 4.8
The color and
contrast assists in
creating a new list
item, contributing
to a smooth
interaction.

Staying on-brand

That's one detail we might not immediately associate with animation, but it's an extension of the identity through movement. Consider an "add to cart" action for a luxury watchmaker's website. It should echo the product being sold, moving smoothly and effortlessly. Perhaps a subtle use of scale and maybe a pop of transparency? It's not too difficult to visualize how we can communicate a distinct tone with a microanimation. Here's a quick mental exercise: consider another UI button. This one is for a fitness app on your smartphone. Contextually, you might be using it while exercising, so it would call for something big and bold. Maybe a snappy color change, and a movement that quickly communicates. It's sometimes easy for us to forget about the qualities that interaction design can contribute. Folding UI, UX, and motion design in one fluid approach is tough to negotiate. It's

combining classic design principles, research, and the intuitive spark that makes something work well. Like the other UI components, interactions should stem from and reflect the visual message of whatever it is you're designing.

Input mechanics

As design for mobile devices becomes more intentional, interactive elements are naturally getting bigger. Current digital design trends skew toward a minimum of fifty pixels for touch targets. That's about the size of a typical check box. As you've probably experienced, everything seems to be getting larger on mobile devices. This is a product of a couple things: the way that we multitask while on our phones, and the intentionality of design to accommodate that.

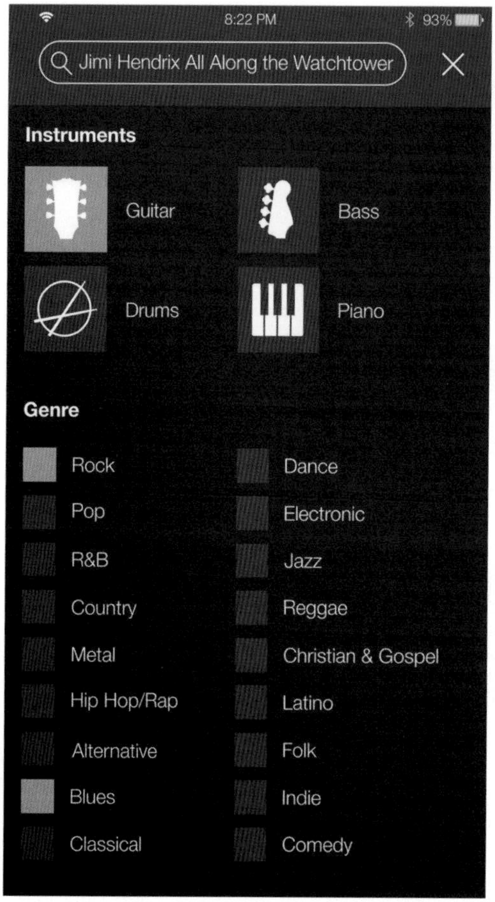

Figure 4.9
The check boxes here offer granular control at the smallest recommended size for a mobile experience.

There are a variety of methods used to interact with devices, from a traditional computer to a mobile phone. These are the most widely used:

The mouse

Since the advent of the first Macintosh computer in 1984, designers have had the benefit of designing for mouse interaction. It's the Cadillac of device peripherals because of wide adoption and allows for delicate high-end interaction. It's easy to manipulate a mouse to interact with a small element, pretty much anywhere on a screen. But the increased portability of devices and screens has made a large dent in overall mouse usage. Smartphones and tablets don't promote mouse usage. And most laptop users don't carry a mouse with them, so they're mainly used in workspaces.

The trackpad

It's been around since we've been using laptops, and in theory it mimics the capabilities of a mouse. Studies by the Nielsen Norman Group—a leading firm in UX research—have shown that the trackpad is actually *easier* for children in the overall arc of device learning. It feels a bit blunter than using a mouse, and long-term use contributes to wrist fatigue. Younger users are likely to use it to queue up media, play games, and interact in a more general way, so the fact that it's easier for them makes sense. In users that seek fine-grain control, its lack of precision is a slight hindrance. This is especially true when you need to interact with a small button or component on a screen.

Index finger

Since smartphones eclipsed phones with physical buttons, the index finger is one of the most effective ways to use smaller screens. Especially when completing a form, toggling settings, or interacting with any content that requires a bit of touch precision. The act of doing so requires both hands, though. Because of this, it requires a bit of concentration and focus. That simple fact probably clues you in to a few things: it's used far more often on tablets because of the form factor, and elsewhere it's used far less often than you might first imagine.

The thumb

We've seen devices shrink in size, then become larger. The size that seems to be most effective is one that can still fit (if barely) in a back pocket. This size seems ideally suited for holding in your palm and interacting via the thumb. The intentionality in design for devices has led to an increase in thumb usage. There's a physical factor at play. Maybe you're holding a latté in one hand, for instance. But there's also some psychological considerations. It's a more casual and inconspicuous way of using a smartphone. You may be waiting for a train, at an appointment, or even walking. It's easy to just grab a phone one-handed, interact via the thumb, and smoothly put it away again after your task is completed. As openly using devices in public became more accepted, thumb usage was part of that negotiation. The easiest-to-use thumb interaction zone varies by device size, but it's anchored to the bottom of the screen and mostly centered. Make sure important elements are easily accessible via the thumb.

Device-specific challenges

The fact that most people hold a smartphone with one hand affects where UI elements are placed on a mobile screen. While many of the most common menus are housed in the corners of a mobile screen, the most accurate thumb interaction zone is anywhere *but* there. Hitting the bottom right corner seems easiest in the way that most people hold devices, with their pinky finger flush against the bottom edge. The bottom left corner is possible with a bit of a stretch, but both top corners require you to shift the phone further down in your hand. This challenge can be easily solved by using your other hand to hold the device. From what I've observed, users are slowly skewing towards a one-handed grip for most

interactions. There are a few important points to consider, knowing this. Luckily, most principal content naturally lands near the center of the screen as we scroll (also with our thumbs). Experiences that use dynamically loaded content as a primary form of delivery take advantage of this.

The primary menus, however, still tend to live at the top corners of the screen even though it's obvious to see they're more difficult to reach. This is likely a holdover from web pages, where the navigation is historically at the top.

Social sharing buttons usually end up at the bottom corners, which is important to know if that kind of functionality is important to you.

Figure 4.10
This illustration shows the thumb dexterity required to interact with areas of a typical screen (right-handed).

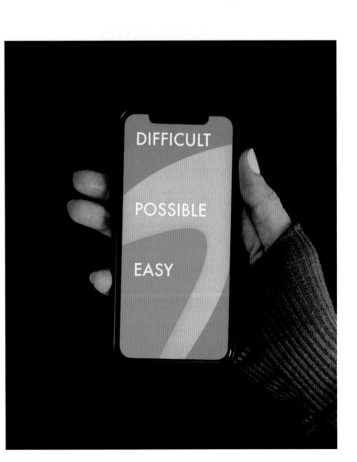

Figure 4.11
This is a
real-estate app
designed for a
laptop experience.
There is enough
space to highlight
specific data.

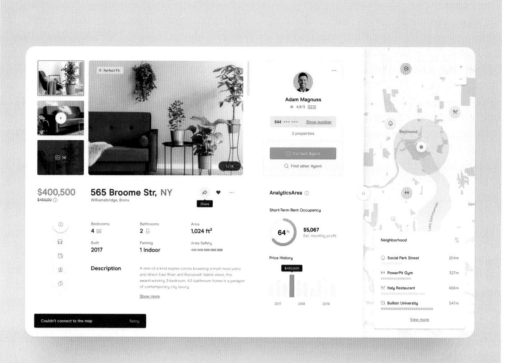

Figure 4.12
The same
experience is
imagined as an
app, which
condenses
information and
increases
contrast.

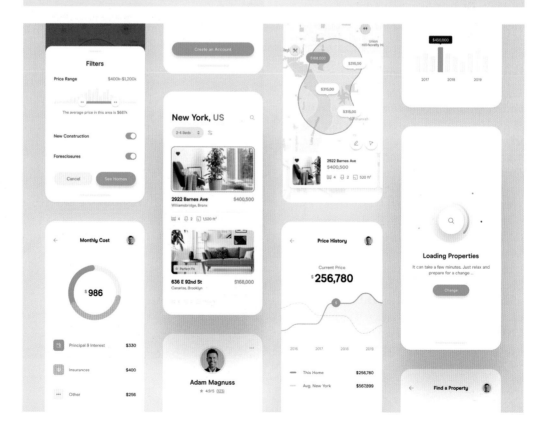

Demographics, case uses, and methods

Understanding your audience is obviously a huge part of UX design, but after discussing the four main methods of device mechanics, it becomes obvious how it bleeds into interaction design. What are you designing? And for whom? And what devices will they use? Is it a real-estate dashboard that a forty-five-year-old adult is using with a laptop and trackpad? Interactions linked to key functions—such as viewing a property—will be important in this case, and they'll need to be easily manipulated. What about that same experience for someone in their mid-twenties, viewed on a smartphone? Short bits of information are prioritized, and color becomes more crucial for call-to-action items. This is an audience that's on the move, interacting with the experience whenever they have a free moment. The touch target needs to be foolproof. Whether to use fine-grain or blunt controls will be initially decided by your audience and necessary functionality.

Menus and patterns

The hamburger menu

Interaction patterns have been around since the dawn of the personal computer, but they've only enjoyed public awareness since the iPhone era. The three-line "hamburger menu" mentioned in Chapter 1 was first designed by Norm Cox while working for Xerox PARC in 1982. Of all the various menus used in interaction design, this one has become the most ubiquitous because of its simplicity and flexibility. It's been heavily used since the introduction of the smartphone and has interestingly made the jump from smaller screens to larger ones. You may have even noticed it being used on a website at a laptop size, and this follows a general trend of simplicity in design. As more interfaces and apps have been designed for a device-based experience, the spare layouts—including their design patterns—have migrated to larger screens. While this isn't always appropriate, the return to a liberal use of negative space has enjoyed popularity among designers. The hamburger menu was created for the Xerox Star workstation, which featured the first graphical user interface in a commercial product. Mr. Cox describes exactly how it came about:

> We considered using an asterisk (*), a plus (+) symbol, and an ellipsis (…) to connote more options, but they all seemed to be too abstract, and a conceptual stretch for users unfamiliar with this new computer concept. We eventually settled on the three-line image, representing the look of the stacked command buttons in the drop-down menu. This symbol was visually simple, easily explained to users, and functionally memorable. There was never a question as to how many lines, since two lines looked like an "equal" sign, and four lines were visually too many. Three lines were the perfect number. The only other design consideration was whether to have the lines vary in length, to further mimic the varying width of the stacked buttons. We decided that the consistent length lines were less distracting, and a more purposeful design.

Norm Cox (2015)

Figure 4.13
If you look closely at this early user interface, you can see the original "hamburger menu" used in several instances.

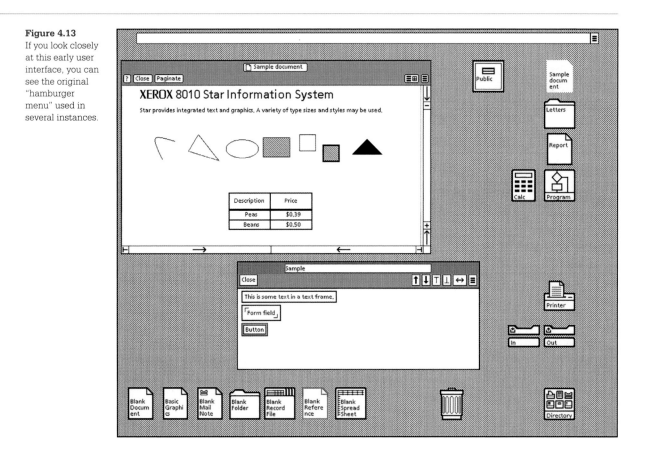

In the original Xerox Star interface, the hamburger menu initiated a layer to appear above the content, instantly. This is a binary animation, and it operates like a light switch: on and off. It's easy to implement because it doesn't require any sort of animation to function. In 1982, the concept of an animated menu function was abstract. Most people had not even seen or used a computer at that point; they had previously comprised entire rooms of bulky hardware. When the hamburger menu enjoyed a comeback in the late 2000s, scripting languages had slowly become the purview of the front-end designer (someone who does a bit of coding for layout as well). The menu reveal became more fluidly animated, and designers began to use motion to design menu content that springs down and back up like a slinky. In contemporary digital design, animated hamburger menus have become a familiar form.

borders, to give it separation and weight. It's become almost de rigueur designing for mobile devices since it allows users to scan for content and expand details with interaction. This is known as "progressive disclosure." Accordion menus can work with both binary (instantly showing and hiding) and transitional (animated reveal) functions.

Off-canvas menu

The off-canvas menu became a popular variant of the animated accordion menu, with menu content sliding in from the left or right edge of the screen. Moving content horizontally like this also gives a bit of visual impact, because so much of the expected motion is vertical. This is especially true when designing for content that scrolls. One benefit of an off-canvas menu is that it displays content with many categories very well in its full-screen vertical fashion. They're valuable if your menus have several categories and subcategories because you can use negative space to visually separate the groups.

Figure 4.14
This is the hamburger menu used in a modern layout. Its ability to blend into the UI is a testament to its longevity.

Figure 4.15
Accordion menus have become a common method to show many options in a mobile layout.

Accordion menu

As a design pattern, the accordion menu has earned a reputation as a reliable technique. Simply put, it shows and hides additional information through a click or touch interaction with a title or category name. It's similar to the hamburger menu in terms of function, but it's common to place accordion menus within the main content of a digital experience. They extend well beyond navigational schemes and are useful for revealing any kind of content with heading and detailed content pairs. Clicking or touching on the heading opens or closes the rest of the content associated with it. This might look like headline text and associated content. Visually, an accordion menu is often paired with icons (arrows, for example), and top and bottom

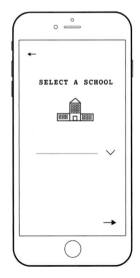

HACK

Figure 4.16
This is an off-canvas menu with icons and a screened background. Both can help increase focus.

Although I've seen plenty of binary accordion menus, I've never seen an off-canvas version that didn't rely on an animated transition. It's just a bit too awkward to do without smoothing it out. There are two main ways to implement them: the first is to "push" the main screen content to the side as the menu appears. This allows the user to see that they're still at the same place that they were when the menu was activated. If they had scrolled to a particular place in the content, this is useful because it keeps everything in context. The second way is to lock the main content in place and animate-in the menu as an overlay. Personally, I find that this method is preferable since the horizontal movement is a bit less jarring. The popularity of this menu pattern shouldn't be the reason for its use, though. It can look a bit silly when you have only two menu items, so make sure you need at least 50 percent of the screen height before using it.

Hamburger menu as secondary navigation

As the ubiquity of the hamburger menu has given way to these other options, it's found new life as a secondary menu for many digital experiences. This allows the designer to highlight the three or four most important functions more prominently as buttons, while folding additional features within a hamburger menu. As device experiences become more customized, there seems to be plenty of life left for this little three-line wonder. The fact is, it's still an effective way of freeing up real estate on a screen or device. Prioritizing calls-to-action while still giving users access to secondary functionality is the perfect evolution, as it can fade into the background when contrasted against icons that better represent their distinct functions. In a pinch, it still works across most experiences, and we'll likely see it living on for years to come.

Floating menu

Occasionally, you might encounter a menu that sits directly on top of the layout, almost like another layer. If the content is scrollable, this menu might stay fixed in place as the content scrolls behind it. That's specifically called a "sticky" floating menu. Not all floating menus are sticky though, and the visual separation between it and the content layer helps define it. On mobile screens, a floating action menu is usually found at the bottom of the screen to alleviate any thumb reach issues. On larger devices, they may move to the top corners. The "floating hamburger" is a popular version of this, although other icons and graphic treatments are common. A floating menu can grab attention, especially when set in a contrasting color. There is one downside: just like the more typical hamburger menu, the content is still hidden.

HACK

A subtle drop shadow is a nice way of separating floating menus from the content layer and adds depth and dimension to the layout. A good specification for this is to use a three-pixel offset (down and right), a six-pixel blur, and about 15 percent opacity.

button floats
above list;
stays in place

Figure 4.17
This sticky floating menu provides a good level of contrast against the user interface.

Dotted or soft menu

There are several kinds of menus denoted with three dots, expressed horizontally or vertically. What generally separates them from the hamburger menu is that they're used to show additional options. I refer to this as a "soft menu" since these kinds of options tend to be used for non-navigational content or settings. The best placement for a soft menu is therefore not in the same position as the main menu, hamburger or not. The soft menu can also feature destructive actions such as reverting or deleting. So, what's the difference between horizontal and vertical dots? There's not a definitive answer. For instance, Apple tends to use horizontal dots, and Google displays them vertically. A rationale for using one over the other is to follow the content. Will the menu content expand top-to-bottom? Use vertical dots. Does it slide out from off-canvas? Then you may want to show them horizontally.

Labeled menu

Adding text to an existing icon can increase user engagement. This is especially true when designing for a demographic not familiar with complex design patterns. For digital experiences that serve an older audience, this is an important consideration since these patterns are still not that old in popular usage. An icon with the word "menu" nearby is a common find. Occasionally, you'll see the labeled text without any additional iconography or just a solid rectangular border around it. If the experience is minimalist to begin with, this approach might be fine. A portfolio site or online CV comes to mind. Context is key here.

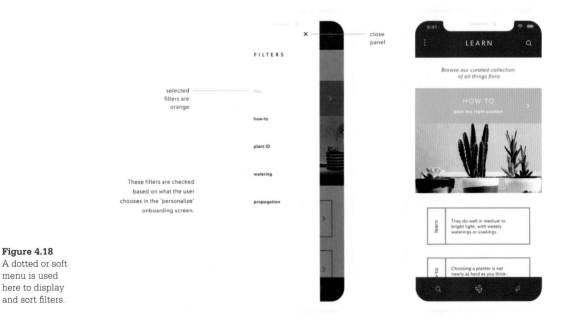

Figure 4.18
A dotted or soft menu is used here to display and sort filters.

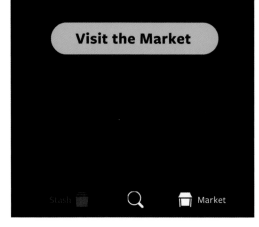

to engage with. The number of options should be limited when possible. The activated menu shouldn't be taller than the amount of screen size you have available. Google adds some light and shadow to these menus to "lift" it off the UI a bit. Early iOS interface designers reimagined the dropdown as a scrollable list, and it instantly became a well-used design pattern (though users didn't actually have a choice). Apple refers to this pattern as a "picker" and sports unselected options that are slightly grayed-out and curve slightly inwards as they get farther away. The result looks a bit dimensional and cylindrical as it's being used; a tactile-feeling interaction that's achieved through subtle details. That particular treatment is specific to iOS, but it highlights some creativity that might be injected into the most banal of menus.

Figure 4.19
Labels extend and enhance the usability of the icons shown in this bottom tray menu.

Select menu

The select menu is an ancestor of the version long seen on the Web, commonly referred to as the "dropdown menu" by most people. There are several predetermined options to choose from (like a list of countries or states). They aren't loved by designers because they can be quite unwieldy when there is a lot of content to deal with. The size of the menu tab itself can be made larger, so it's easier

Figure 4.20
A select menu is a good choice when sorting through a long list of options. Transparency helps to add focus.

Figure 4.21
Radial menus are highly usable with a thumb interaction, and they are an interesting option for limited menu items.

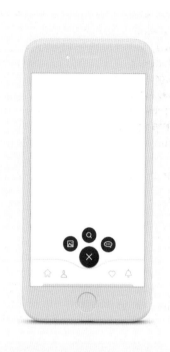

Grid menu

Grid menus naturally filtered their way into interaction design patterns as icons started to fill our smartphone screens. There are a few benefits, and they're surprisingly on opposite ends of the spectrum. For larger widths, this lends itself quite well to mouse usage since you can spread out across the screen. Gridded items can be designed in an asymmetrical layout if there's enough space. If you're looking to break the expectation that everything needs to fit in a tight grid, this can look refreshing. For smaller screens, more defined grids tend to be the norm for this method. Breaking up the space in a vertical layout is a bit more

Radial menu

Although not nearly as popular, the radial menu warrants some mention. A radial menu is one that's initiated by tapping or clicking a singular icon to reveal a ring of additional icons. Usually, these appear using a combination of transparency and rotation. According to a 2004 paper by Autodesk Research[1], its first known use was in 1969. This would predate all other menus we've discussed thus far, and it's surprising that we haven't seen more of it. What makes the radial menu attractive is that it's quite easy to open with a thumb. Because you're limited to a handful of menu items, it also forces you to be succinct. Since keeping options concise can be a challenge with menus, this limitation might easily be an asset.

Figure 4.22
Grid-based menus work seamlessly in the rectangular confines of modern devices.

---

[1] https://www.autodeskresearch.com/publications/menuhistory

difficult to pull off in practice, and all smartphones fall into this category. There's still room for creativity within a rectangular grid, though, and this is one of the few menus that allow for background images. That might be in the form of a photo or illustration. It also adapts well to the flat-design aesthetic where simple icons are shown against a contrasting background.

Tray menu

Many mobile apps feature a menu fixed to the top or bottom of the screen. This model offers a lot of consistency if you're willing to limit the menu items. The issue is that you're short on space, so you'll need to use icons or very succinct text. For popular apps, this has been a viable method in moving beyond the hamburger menu. A big feature is the ability to directly access the menu at all times, from any screen. A downside, however, is the fact that it takes up valuable real estate. For the smallest mobile screens, this could be a deal-breaker. The bottom tray version is the one most easily accessed via the thumb. If immediate access to a limited number of functions is paramount, look no further.

HACK

You might be tempted to use stock icons for tray menus, but there might be an opportunity to streamline them, or tie them into your brand. Tweak them when possible, so that they all look unified in their design, and be careful about using particular designs. Instagram pretty much owns the "heart" icon at this point.

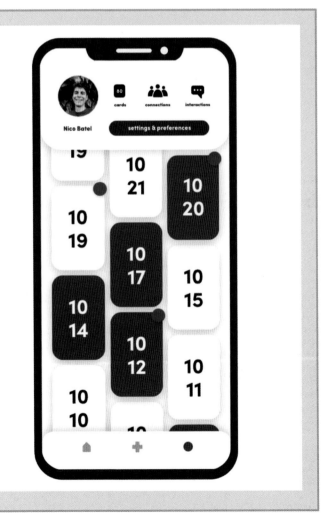

Figure 4.23
This bottom tray menu contains three options and presents the UI with clean minimalism.

Touch gestures

Tying a microinteraction to a touch gesture can be valuable for mobile experiences, but they also require the user to be familiar with it. Some, like using your fingers to "zoom" closer into an image, are now commonly understood. But how many people know what a "three-finger drag" does on a trackpad? Proficient app users are likely to be familiar with some of the more esoteric gestures, but basic users will need to learn advanced variations. This can be done through a set of initial onboarding screens that's shown the first time a user is introduced to the experience. It's become a common way of segueing into more complex or custom gestures, up to a point. There can be a pitfall in trying to match the same fidelity of mouse-based movements though; gestures with fingers are inherently blunt. And the small size of many device screens prevents any complexity that requires more than a few inches of distance.

Swiping

The Tinder app popularized the swipe interaction in 2012, and it's been actively used by designers since. In fact, image sliders—that often use left and right arrows on traditional devices—work even better on touch devices. The swipe gives the user a more intuitive way to control image carousels. This is helpful because sliders and carousels have been critiqued for their usability on traditional devices (users don't often click through them). Interestingly, popular video streaming services, such as Netflix and Amazon, have doubled down on them. In those two cases, the swipe is the major point of interaction in browsing titles.

Tap and double tap

Tapping has become increasingly complex in the wake of IxD as a proper discipline. While touching a button or link is a tried-and-true result of a single tap, there are other situations to consider. One common example is opening a modal window, where the content appears as a new layer. This is initiated by a single tap, opening the potential to interact with the content in this new layer. Aside from directly selecting content, the single tap is fast becoming a "setup interaction." For example, when a text message is received on a smartphone while it's in standby mode, a single tap on the text alert will prompt an option to open it.

Double tapping has become synonymous with Instagram, and for that reason it's difficult to think of any other app that utilizes it. If you experiment, you'll find quite a few that use it as a means of accidental discovery. The YouTube mobile app allows you to double tap the left or right sides of the screen to rewind or fast forward in ten second increments. Doing so on an image in the iOS Photos app zooms to the specific area tapped. In referring to Instagram, the heart icon is already implemented in the UI. So, why the double tap? There seem to be several reasons, depending on who you ask. For one, the resulting animated heart microinteraction is much more dramatic. Ease of use while quickly scrolling is another. How about rebelling against the fact that interaction design has become so dependent on acrobatic dexterity? The entire image is tappable and doing so allows us to flex some blunt behavior in an otherwise buttoned-up interface. The double tap reinforces the idea of play, something that goes against much of what's been said about learnable interfaces. It highlights the intuitive spark that transcends all principles of design and enhances them when used well.

The long press

The long press has been around for years as a product of iOS, though it's one of those gestures that still hasn't gained much footing because of its complexity. Its first use was to reorder or delete apps from a device home screen. It's since been commonly used to reorder content and reveal additional information for chunked content. The importance in implementing the long press gesture is the timing: too short and it's accidentally triggered. Too long and it becomes tedious to wait for. Another big consideration in using it is what will happen (or appear) after it's initiated? If content rearrangement can happen, there needs to be some clue for the user. Google's Material Design Language addresses this by increasing the drop shadow under the content being selected. It's subtle but very intuitive, which underscores the fact that users only need a hint to get started. If a long press results in a menu, consider the length and complexity of that too. Tricky interactions like this need to be easy on the information delivery side, because they're already a challenge to start.

Pinch and zoom

When smartphones first debuted, pinch and zoom was the de facto if you wanted to view a website. Responsive design for devices had not yet been invented, and websites were designed for a much larger screen. While the term name includes both motions, they are opposites; pinching a point on a screen with your thumb and index finger zooms out, making the view smaller. Spreading the same two fingers apart zooms closer, cropping from the point your fingers originate from. Thankfully, this isn't used as widely for viewing websites these days because of responsive design. It is, however, a common interaction for viewing maps and close-up details of images. If you're using it for either, make sure that there's enough screen space to manipulate your fingers. A tiny map that requires a user to pinch and zoom will be instantly annoying.

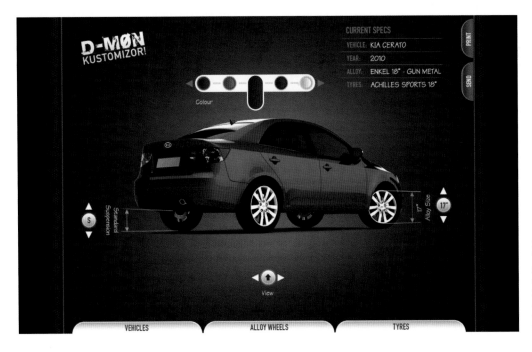

Figure 4.24
This kiosk-based interface is complex in functionality, and the ability to drag offers fine-grain control.

Drag, swipe, and flick

Using most toggle buttons in an app or website experience requires a touch or drag. That's a simple binary interaction, though. Dragging can have larger implications in situations where a user is dragging an object to initiate another action within the layout. This can include deleting something, moving an item into another folder, or navigating a dimensional experience like a 360-degree video. Swiping is common and familiar to most users. It has become the default way to advance photo slideshows and navigate multiscreen dashboards. A swipe can also be a setup interaction for a second one. Swipe and tap (to open, dismiss, or delete) is one method mobile notifications are engaged with. Flicking is very similar to swiping, but it takes velocity into account. It's a great interaction for scrolling through content very quickly or setting up a function that uses a select menu.

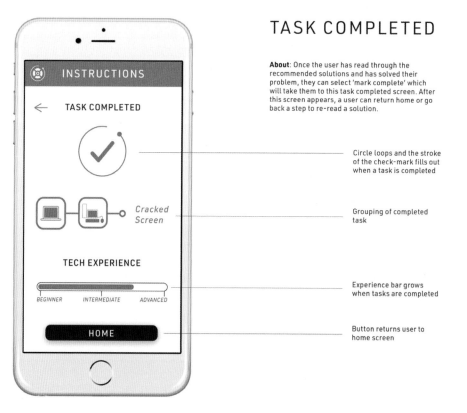

TASK COMPLETED

About: Once the user has read through the recommended solutions and has solved their problem, they can select 'mark complete' which will take them to this task completed screen. After this screen appears, a user can return home or go back a step to re-read a solution.

Circle loops and the stroke of the check-mark fills out when a task is completed

Grouping of completed task

Experience bar grows when tasks are completed

Button returns user to home screen

Figure 4.25
Annotations quickly describe the actions on this screen, and they are of value to stakeholders.

Prototyping workflow

Static designs with annotations

An interactive experience may feature a dozen or more screens, and they need to be considered holistically. Dividing functions into categories before interactions are created and applying them to digital layouts is the key to keeping track of everything. The easiest way to do this is to design a document that features your static designs, along with annotations. Clearly describing what parts of the digital layout users can interact with, and how functions work, will make production much easier. Labeling what a button might do, and the next screen seen after it's tapped or clicked, creates a user journey through the digital experience. This is clearly connected to UX at a high level but also forces you to think about things like consistency. Are all the functions in a certain category using the same microinteraction? If not, why? This is a useful step, and one that I suggest anyone complete before applying movement to any functionality. Just like the user flow is a roadmap for functionality at a core level, static designs with annotations help you quickly see how they work in your digital layout.

Interaction prototyping on paper

Most of my students are quite comfortable with jumping straight to the computer after (very) rough sketches. They're digital natives. And for logos and other simple layouts, that kind of workflow has become the norm. You might not expect me to argue for a tactile process in developing an interaction design, but hear me out. As we discussed in Chapter 3, moving from static design to animation can be like opening Pandora's box. You could easily spend half a day mocking-up twenty versions of a half-second interaction. "What if I tried rotation? How about a transparency fade?" Still not convinced? How many times have you approached a design project without considering a typeface, scrolling through an endless list? Odds are, you spent more time vacillating between random choices than you would have if you'd done some research.

HACK

I've developed a process over years of teaching that helps you sketch out an interaction:

- Draw the user interface on a sheet of paper. It's easier if you have a device template or outline to work from.
- Add the "normal" state of the action to this sketch: how that part of the interface looks before any interaction starts.
- Staple a sheet of tracing paper on top of the page you've just sketched.
- Now, without an endless array of effects to distract you, think about what kind of interaction would really work best.
- Draw the animation on the tracing paper, noting the movement and transformations that happen. You can use text, lines, textures—whatever you need—to help visualize what happens during the interaction.

The advantage of using tracing paper is that you can easily see both the normal and animated states of the interaction. It doesn't have to be a work of art, but some degree of legibility can be worthwhile—you can present this to a stakeholder before going digital. In fact, people tend to think more objectively about function when there's an absence of extraneous details. When it's ready to be animated, you have a clear set of instructions to execute.

Figure 4.26
These vellum overlay paper prototypes are a great way to design interactions without the distractions of software.

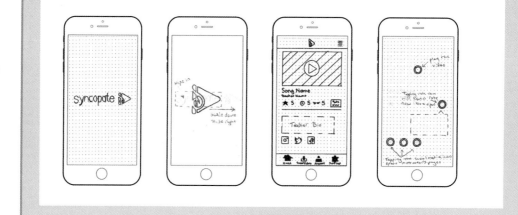

Hi-fi prototyping and animation

The last step in designing interaction for digital experiences is hi-fi prototyping. This stage combines everything we've discussed so far in this chapter: considering UI and UX implications, sketching, static designs with annotations, and designing microinteractions and menus. The goal is to deliver a prototype with all the visual resources needed to build the final product. That might be an app, a website, a digital kiosk, or a smart appliance. These various deliverables have very different production paths. And, while many digital designers can code a basic website themselves, I don't know any who could tackle programming for the others mentioned. Even iOS and Android apps use vastly different back-end systems for development. These are heavily specialized jobs that are very separate from design. So, you can see how important it is to hand off exactly what's needed to produce a digital product in various forms.

Luckily, design software has finally caught up. Many applications allow designers to mix static and motion design in the same layout. This is huge, because it allows you to hand over a deliverable that shows your screen designs with the animated portions in place. As you can imagine, this is also valuable as a final review for clients. They get to see the experience in its finished form before moving into the laborious (and expensive) development phase. Many tools even allow you to dial-in custom easing curves that can be copied on the development end. This means that the microinteractions you've meticulously sweated over will look and feel exactly the same in their end product. As mentioned in Chapter 3, there are also methods that allow you to export interaction animation directly for end development. In that case, a developer wouldn't have to recreate it in code because it's a ready-to-use asset.

Takeaways

Interaction design has implications that are beyond simply adding to an already well-designed user interface. It *becomes* the design. Interactions that are carefully considered can make or break your user experience. They can confirm actions and provide valuable feedback to users, extend your brand's unique voice and character, and highlight your product or experience in a sea of visual clutter. If misused, they can also ruin something that's well intentioned, make it awkward to use, and turn off potential users. The expectation for high-fidelity prototypes that include animated interactions is only increasing, and digital designers should expect to include them in the design process before any final development begins.

INTERACTION DESIGN EXERCISE

Design an app concept that highlights interaction design within a seamless user interface, and includes motion to give context

DESCRIPTION

Create and design a concept for a smartphone app. In order to be as real as possible, several assets will be created including a user interface, content for all screens, branding, and—specific to this chapter—animated interactions. A layout that showcases an interface design is pretty common at this point, but adding animation to extend the UI can show a breadth and depth of understanding interaction design.

SPECIFICATIONS

At least twelve screens should be designed, though you might find the need to double that for it to feel complete. Overall dimensions should be sized to current smartphone specifications. The interface and layout should show a breadth of the overall experience. Final assets will include screens displayed in a PDF and printed book, an interactive prototype, and video files showing animated interactions.

Figure 4.27
An app concept with a dozen or more screens showcases the holistic approach to design throughout.

INTENT

Start with conceptualizing an idea for an app. Steer clear of generic and oversaturated categories (food, social media, productivity). Find a niche, but make sure there are more than five people that would actually use it. This is an example from one of my former students:

> Cartograph helps the user plan their ideal road trip through National Parks. It asks questions such as the length of the trip, key points, interests, and skill level in order to give the user a personalized itinerary.

RESEARCH AND METHODOLOGY

What would be useful to the world at large or a niche group? Consider the kinds of apps you use and what the purpose of that app is. You'll start with sketching the user interface. This preliminary research will help inform and guide your concept. Do not simply reiterate an existing app. Write a 100-word brief that outlines the following:

- What is the purpose?
- Who is your audience?
- What problem does it solve (or what ideas does it explore)?
- What kinds of actions might be associated with those? Pick a few that might be important and stick with them. Three concise functions visually expressed well are better than ten that are half-baked.
- What are the benefits of using it?

CONTENT

This project extends the fidelity of the ones we completed in Chapters 1 and 2. Here, we want the screens to look as finished as possible because animation will be applied in the form of interactions and screen transitions. Take time to create text copy that's real enough to look believable. Of course, this doesn't need to be created from scratch. That doesn't mean you should copy all the content wholesale, though. Looking back to the UX copy we discussed in Chapter 2, make sure that the tone fits the aesthetic. Dig into the details and avoid buttons that are labeled with overly generic text. The overall product needs to read like the branding you design for it.

NAMING

A strong name will help this project feel complete. Something sharp and succinct is good, but avoid the cliché of app names that end in "ify" or "ly" for longevity's sake. A witty approach is always smart, but avoid names that might challenge the merit of the concept.

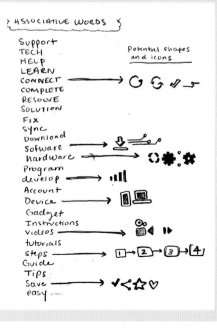

Figure 4.28
Developing an early connection between word and image is a great way to ensure a consistent visual language.

Figure 4.29
A sitemap will allow you to envision the amount of screens necessary for all actions within an experience.

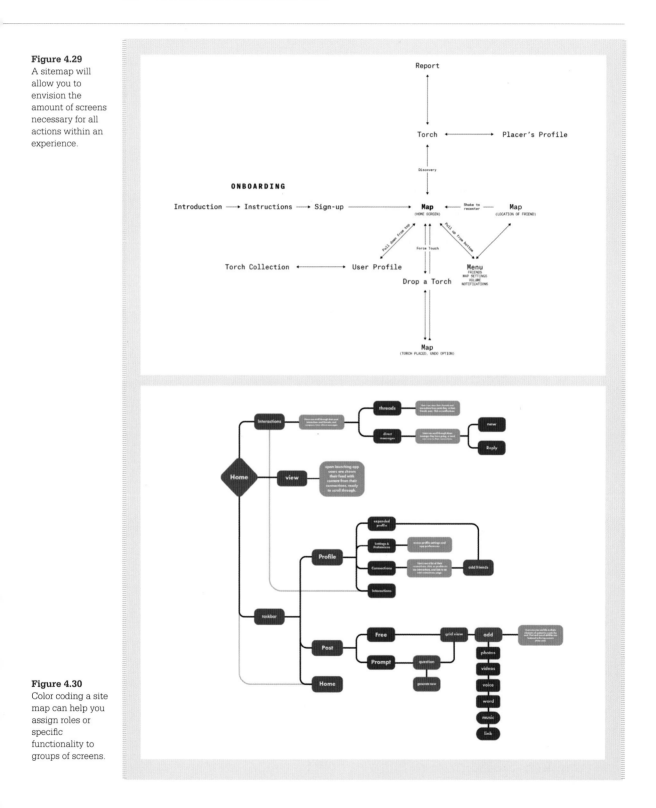

Figure 4.30
Color coding a site map can help you assign roles or specific functionality to groups of screens.

INFORMATION ARCHITECTURE

Creating a map to "bookend" the entire app is helpful to start. Otherwise, it's difficult to tell exactly how many screens you might need to complete the experience. Start with logging in or signing up (if that's needed) and work your way through completing tasks. As you work your way through what kinds of functions this app might entail, refer to your research. Don't try to fold too much into it, or you'll end up with clutter and confusion.

SKETCHES

Once you've figured out how many screens you might need, start with sketches. Design a first batch of six initial screens to see how various layouts might work together. Pick them from random places across the site map, so they're not just the first six. Include things like opening branding, screens with form fields, long-form copy (if needed), and placeholders for visual elements such as photos or illustrations.

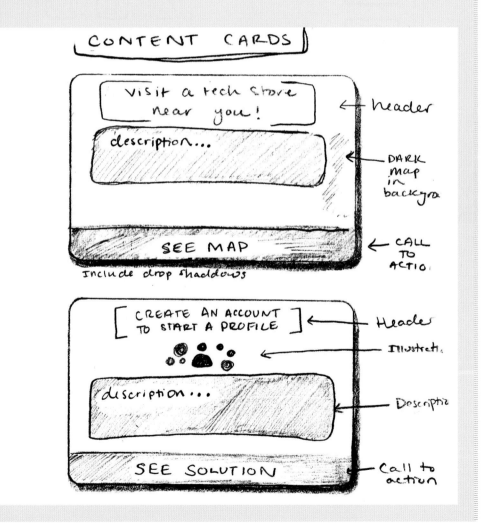

Figure 4.31
Sketches are an efficient way to start imagining layouts and interactions.

Figure 4.32
Adding fidelity to sketches can help explore the look and feel of a layout. They also look great when showing process work.

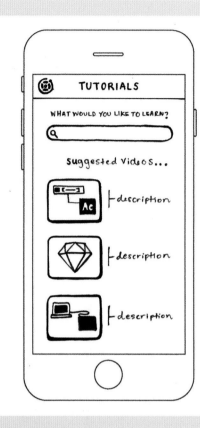

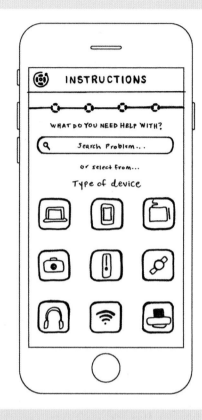

WIREFRAMES

Using your sketches as a guide, create wireframes that are sized for a current smartphone. This step might yield a confirmation about the amount of content you have on each screen. It also might help you realize that you need to reduce a bit to increase hierarchy. Instead of a separate stage, you might choose to create wireframes by designing the first few mock-ups without color, texture, and imagery.

BRANDING AND IMAGERY

A finished brand will separate portfolio quality work from visual experiments. Design a logo that's flexible enough to have impact on an opening screen but is also legible at very small sizes. Think about how other branding elements like typography, texture, and color might work their way into the layout. Select typefaces that pair nicely together, have multiple weights, and are legible on digital devices. Choose a strong dominant brand color with one or two subordinate colors to add depth and contrast (in limited doses). If your app requires photos, select public domain or creative commons imagery from websites such as unsplash.com, gratisography.com, pexels.com, or archive.org.

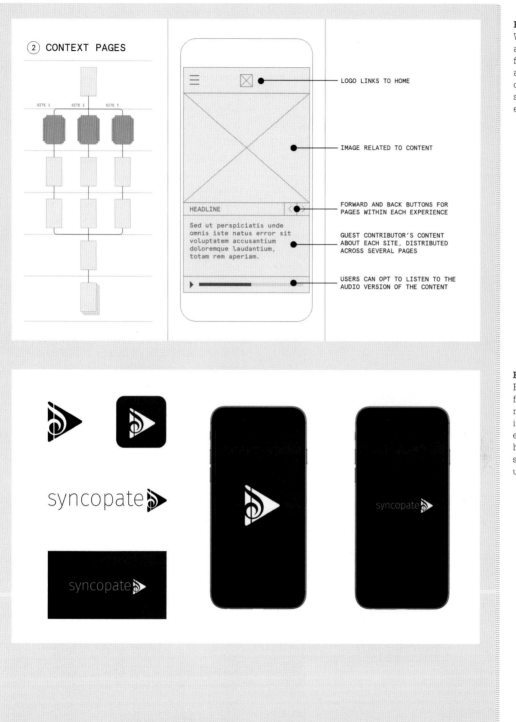

Figure 4.33
Wireframes force attention to functionality and allow you to consider the screen in its entirety.

Figure 4.34
Branding that's flexible and modular is important for experiences that have limited space and utilize motion.

MOCK-UPS

Extend the six sketches to twelve digital mock-ups. You should build using software that has the ability to easily prototype later. Keeping all the screens easily visible will let you compare them to each other as you design them. Don't try to completely finish each screen before moving on to the next, because you're likely going to make changes as you design for different scenarios and functions. Get to about 75 percent and come back for the final touches afterwards. Consider how adding size and color to action items, such as buttons, helps the user advance to the next step. Remember, not all content might fit vertically. Design content for a scroll if necessary.

PROTOTYPE

Link the mock-ups together through the interactive features of the software you've used. Make sure that there are no dead ends in the functionality (i.e., a user can't advance or go back). Test this out yourself, and have a volunteer do the same to confirm clarity in your UI design. As a last step in the prototype process, record yourself testing every screen at a pace that a first-time viewer can follow. Sometimes, this is the best way to easily show someone the entire experience in one go. Export the recording as a video file for later use.

INTERACTIVE ANIMATIONS

After the initial screens have been designed, choose six interactions to prototype and animate. They should vary in complexity: two can be simple feedback animations like loading screens or menu instances; two more should show interactions that animate directly with content, perhaps revealing new content or screens through the interaction; the last two should be complex, leveraging multistep functions across three or more screens. There are many digital tools that are capable of designing animations with simple to medium complexity. However, I find it easier to stick to After Effects because of its capability in designing complex animations. Make sure to apply easy-ease to your keyframes, and then tweak the velocity curves to make your interactions feel snappy and responsive. Export these six animations as video files and upload them to a video-hosting platform such as Vimeo (their free option is sufficient). Then, assemble all six animations in a new timeline, and introduce each one with a text description of the interaction. Export the compiled animations as a video, and upload that as well.

Figure 4.35
Color and contrast become an important part of creating hierarchy and focal point in an interactive UI.

Figure 4.36
Software such as
Adobe XD can
allow you to
quickly build a
linkable prototype
to digitally share
and test.

Figure 4.37
Placing links to
animated
interactions
within the PDF
file is a clever way
to extend the
breadth and depth
of an app concept.

PDF DOCUMENT

Images of various screens from this project will serve as project thumbnails when showing it in your portfolio, but a PDF documenting the complexities of the app you've conceived will really show your ability to dig into the details. Set up a new document in InDesign with at least as many pages as you have screens. A document size that's portable is recommended—we'll discuss why in a bit. The document should start with a description of the app, followed by branding and sketches. Then introduce one screen per page, with annotations and labels accompanying each. You can use hairline rules to "point" to parts of the UI, but don't let them dominate the layout. Interactive button states, loading screens, and interface animation can be shown and described as well. On a separate layer,

create buttons in the layout that will link to the six interactive functions you've animated. You can use the hyperlink function in InDesign to link these to the Vimeo URL for each respective video. Finally, at the end of the document, include links to the interactive prototype, video of the app walkthrough, and video of all six compiled animations. Be sure to test the links from the final PDF.

PRINTED BOOKLET

This may sound counterproductive in context with a digital app, but printing a version of the PDF you just designed can be valuable in face-to-face situations (i.e., an interview). It allows you to discuss design and functionality without crowding around a phone or screen. And if you've approached this project with creativity and craft, it *just*

Figure 4.38
A printed app process book is a nice final touch, and it helps when presenting the project in person.

looks good in a printed booklet. This is the reason I mentioned designing it as a portable size as well. Remember the links we placed in a separate layer? Hide that layer before sending the file to print, so that they don't display in the printed book. You can replace them with QR-codes that can be easily scanned with a smartphone.

REFLECTION AND REVISION

Compare the extensive list of deliverables in front of you to the questions you answered in your research brief. Does the app have a clear purpose? Can you easily describe the problem it helps solve, or the concept it explores? Is there a clear demographic that might use it, and does the visual approach appeal to that audience? Does the functionality make the app useful or interesting? Compare it to actual apps that you can download and use. How does it stack up visually? Spending a bit more time to reconcile any of these questions is a valuable investment in showcasing a large-scale project.

GOALS AND OUTCOMES

A successful finished product should really show the depth and breadth of the concept, and attention to detail at every level. The concept and content should feel realistic, and the visual design should be impactful. These both support the interaction design and provide a reason to go through the final step of animation. This has the potential to be a great portfolio project if done well, and it comprises skills from four disciplines: UI, UX, animation, and IxD. The final PDF should enhance the app screen designs with notes and annotations but not overwhelm it. The six animations should feel realistic and snappy. The prototype should allow a person to feel what it's like to use the app. The printed booklet is the icing on the cake. The deliverables from this project can be shown on your website, shared as videos, tested on a real device, and shown in person. That's a huge advantage in showcasing a portfolio piece.

Design for the Web

Nothing has changed the landscape of graphic design in the last twenty years more than the World Wide Web. Being able to translate two-dimensional design into code, and then receive it back in a dynamic medium is empowering for designers. There's always been some trepidation about learning HTML for those coming from an art-based approach to design. However—as I tell my students—it's not programming, it's simply markup. What does that mean? Well, when you purchase something online, for instance: adding an item to a cart, checking out with a credit card, adding shipping details, and completing the transaction. That entire process relies on heavy back-end programming. For most simple websites, however, content is "marked up" with fairly simple instructions on how it should look in the web browser.

Even if web design isn't your end goal, knowing a bit of markup will no doubt make your work easier for developers to execute. And, a skill set that includes the ability to create basic websites from scratch is increasingly in demand. Hundreds of books have been written on HTML alone, and many of them have become exhaustive doorstops. As a visual designer, you might want to make a simple one-page website. You don't need a comprehensive knowledge of the language to do that. Mistakes will be made, but the easiest way to learn markup is to figure out the basics and then break things along the way.

A brief history of web design

Origin story

When British engineer Tim Berners-Lee invented the medium in 1990, he was mostly concerned with being able to share research. By connecting hypertext files through servers, he created the way links work on the Web. In fact, HTML is an acronym for HyperText Markup Language. This feature proved crucial because it later became the way to link visual layouts. In 1993, the Mosaic web browser finally allowed images to be displayed on a web page, and designers quickly followed suit. Or at least they tried.

Tables

With the ability to include visual content, graphic designers took to figuring out how to make sense of the Web. By the mid 1990s, the first attempts were made using tables to control layouts. Imagine trying to design a composition using a spreadsheet. It's almost impossible to imagine now, but there wasn't any way to design print-like layouts before the use of tables. The markup used to create a tabular structure of text and images was overly complicated and tedious. At the time, the ability to style text on the Web was also limited. If you wanted anything other than a few default options, one had to render the text as an image. Imagine trying to do an internet search and not finding what you're looking for because there's no selectable text. Cascading Style Sheets (CSS) debuted in 1996, as a means of specifying visual properties of markup. However, its capabilities at this time were still pretty crude.

Flash

We've touched on the history of Flash in Chapter 4, but it's important to realize just how influential it was for web design. The program utilized a timeline and user interface that provided a way to get started with minimal HTML. The ability for interaction was the icing on the cake. Pioneers like Joshua Davis pushed the bleeding edge of contemporary design at the time. His personal website—praystation. com—was a playground for experiments, crowdsourcing ideas from the burgeoning digital community. The creative pace of this era was a major breakthrough in selling an unfamiliar technology to the general public. Flash sites were painstakingly laborious to update, and the ability for search engines to crawl Flash-designed sites was slim-to-none. That said, it was a powerful visual tool at the time, and served as an introduction to the medium for many a young designer (including myself).

Web standards

Part of the reason early websites were difficult to design and style was the lack of uniform standards by browsers. A site might look completely different from one browser to the next, and developers had to write very choppy code to present content consistently. By the mid-2000s, advocates for web standards had the ears of the design community. Early innovators, such as Jeffrey Zeldman and Dave Shea, moved the needle forward in showing what was possible with semantic HTML and CSS. By the end of the decade, the ability to use custom fonts online hit a high watermark for web design. For the first time, the level of craft and sophistication rivaled that of traditional print design. A typical workflow at the time started by designing the entire web layout in Photoshop, and then translating it pixel for pixel in working code. It was complicated, and subscribed to the "waterfall" process, where design and development existed in separate workflows and sequence.

Figure 5.1
Web design has finally come into its own during the last decade, capable of achieving a level of craft that rivals print.

Figure 5.2
The responsive era ushered in a sea change in the way layouts are approached for devices.

The responsive era

In 2010, Ethan Marcotte wrote an article for the popular web design blog *A List Apart* called "Responsive Web Design." It proved to be the tipping point for the medium. Utilizing the "media query," a feature built into CSS, Marcotte designed a proof-of-concept web page that adapted its layout depending on screen size. This just so happened to come at a time when smartphones were becoming ubiquitous, and the concepts that Responsive Web Design (RWD) offered were a perfect marriage for displaying content on them. Finally, design for the Web had graduated from simply trying to emulate print design. The inherent flexibility of screen sizes meant that the pixel-perfect layouts of the past were now obsolete.

Where are we now?

The modern Web is more like a fluid grid that adapts to different devices and screens. Because of that fluidity, some of the precision of print design is lost, but what is gained is the dynamic nature of web content. We've entered another fork in the road. As web design tools have become mature, they've also become increasingly difficult to grasp for entry-level designers who want to code. There are frameworks, style libraries, package managers, and dozens of complex tools aimed at automation. Many websites also rely on a lot of dynamic programming. Because of that, a good chunk of the Web actually verges into "web app" territory. The good news? There's still a need and place for standards-based static web design.

Foundations

The viewport

Before we get into the structure of markup, we should talk about the responsive part of RWD. That is, varying screen sizes. The term "viewport" is used to define the visible area of a website. This varies across devices—smartphones, tablets, laptops, and desktops. It's good to know that on smaller screens, the browser window isn't re-sizable like it is on a traditional computer. We measure the viewport in pixels, and style content with CSS for various size ranges. These are called "breakpoints." When designing content into layouts, you'll want to consider how many breakpoints to design for. Here are some general rules of thumb when considering layouts:

- small devices (mostly smartphones)—600px and under
- medium devices (smartphones and some tablets)—768px and under
- large devices (tablets and laptops)—1400px and under
- extra-large devices (desktops with large monitors, TVs)—1400px and up.

Scale is important; you don't want to spend the time required designing a four-breakpoint layout for a site that might get thirty visitors per month. On the flip side, large-scale websites may use half a dozen to serve a wide audience using a variety of devices. Use what the context calls for. When starting out, it's best to stick to two: one for mobile and one for everything else.

For instance, a common breakpoint is 768px, and most smartphones will fall under that size, even when turned sideways. Anything larger is likely going to be a true tablet. Why the random number? The original iPad set the standard, and it's 768 pixels wide in portrait mode. Another common breakpoint is 1400px. This accommodates a browser at full screen on an average laptop. Desktop users don't always have their screen maximized, so I tend to cap the width for all layouts at this size. This gives us a two-breakpoint layout to start sketching with.

Thinking about content

Once you have an idea of how many viewport widths you're going to design for, it's good to start thinking about what kind of content will be featured. After all, the strategy for the layout will need to support it. How much text will be used? Is it long form or short, with bullet points? What about media and imagery—photos, illustrations, videos? How many of each? Is there tertiary information that might be considered? Hierarchy, contrast, and rhythm are all important to consider. Of course, all these things get more difficult as the viewport size shrinks. Considering how much space the UI will need, planning for what the user will see first is key.

Mobile first

One way to get in front of the challenge of controlling hierarchy with so little screen space is to consider a "mobile first" perspective. Here's some backstory: I was working as a professional web designer when the responsive design movement began to take hold. At the time, it was common to design a full website as a "fixed width" layout. Then, we would try to redesign all the content to work on a mobile screen. This led to a lot of back-and-forth and scrapped directions in resolving the layout. We were trying to make a square fit in a circle. An article written by designer Luke Wroblewski in 2009 addressed this issue before responsive design was even a thing. His call for a mobile-first approach suggested prioritizing the most important content, forcing users to focus. The result of implementing mobile first is best described in his own words:

> ... the end result is an experience focused on the key tasks users want to accomplish without the extraneous detours and general interface debris that litter today's desktop-accessed websites.

All this is worth mentioning because although it may seem obvious, it's not. My students—digital natives who have largely grown up around smartphones—will still draw a sketch of a full-sized website when asked to start conceptualizing; that is, until I explicitly ask them to sketch mobile first. The visual representation of a website for most of us still tends to be what's seen on a large device.

So, what does content look like on a smartphone? A two-column grid might be acceptable to show thumbnail images, depending on the level of detail needed. For anything that features a decent amount of text, it's most likely shown as a single column. After the UI and branding are in place, you're lucky to have 500px to work with above the point where you must scroll. A single image, a headline, and a few lines of text are what's realistic.

Progressive enhancement

Once you've designed some layouts for mobile, it's time to consider what it might look like on a laptop. Instead of a single column to feature content, there's a bit more room to spread out. What about any tertiary content that didn't make the cut on a smartphone viewport but might be appropriate with more space? A sidebar, additional image, even a tool that might help users? Adding additional features when screen size allows for it is known as

"progressive enhancement." Here's an example: look at a website for a major news outlet on a smartphone, and then on a desktop. You might notice additional things at the desktop size: longer headlines and the addition of sub-headlines. The number of advertisements is likely to increase. Wide images, an expanded navigation menu, and an overall impression of layout shifting is apparent. Prioritizing content falls into a UX role, but know that some media types (video, for instance) tend to skew better towards mobile users.

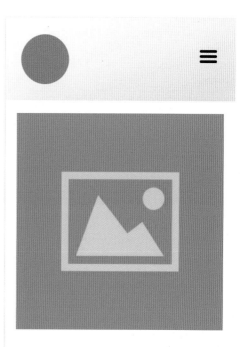

Suspendisse pellentesque fringilla libero sed vehicula. Etiam vitae nulla enim. Suspendisse ac justo purus. Integer scelerisque, sem vel varius tristique, mauris mi fringilla diam, sed laoreet lorem justo ut libero. Vestibulum ante ipsum primis in faucibus orci luctus et ultrices posuere cubilia curae; Maecenas

Figure 5.3
You can quickly build and test a mobile layout using some basic HTML elements.

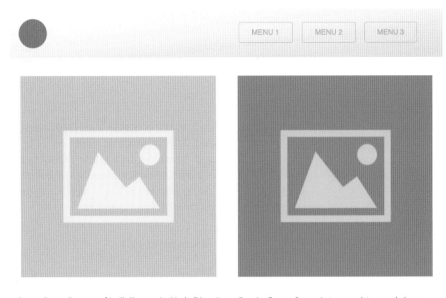

Figure 5.4
Expanding the layout to a laptop width offers room for progressive enhancement such as additional imagery.

Digging in

Now that you have a basic idea of how content works across screen sizes, it's time to try your hand at markup. You'll need a basic text editor to get started, and many are free. My own preference is Atom, an open-source editor. An FTP client is also helpful in getting files on the web. Cyberduck (ignore the silly name) is a popular one. Lastly, gathering some basic content to work with is helpful in getting started. I ask my students to collect information for a recipe when learning the basics. Don't forget to include a few images for variety.

The structure of HTML

HyperText Markup Language uses tags to surround specific parts of content. The browser uses those tags to determine how to interpret the content. For example, a paragraph in HTML looks like this:

`<p> This is a very basic paragraph. </p>`

Notice that there are two tags surrounding the paragraph: an opening and a closing tag. The second one also features a slash, which tells the browser that it's nearing the end. Most HTML tags are used in pairs, but a few are "self-terminating," which means that they only use one tag. A few include:

`<br>` a break tag that tells the browser to jump to the next line. It's like keying "shift-return" in a word processor.

<hr> horizontal rule that appears as a thin line across the page.

Tags are often nested—or sandwiched—within other tags as well. In fact, the outermost <html> tag surrounds everything else on the page. And the <body> tag defines all visible content. The <head> features non-visible content used for search engine optimization (SEO) purposes. The "doctype" tag is self-terminating and tells the browser which version of HTML to serve up. HTML5 is the current version, and the tag looks like this:

<!doctype html>

The doctype is always the first tag at the top of the document. It's important to include it since the way that tags are displayed depends on it. Immediately after the doctype comes the <html> tag. Everything else on the page will be sandwiched between the opening and closing tag:

<!doctype html>

<html>

   -- everything else --

</html>

The first thing inside the HTML tag is the head. Think of this as the brain of the web page. It will contain a few other tags that help with search engine optimization. The most important is the <title> tag (more on that in a bit).

<!doctype html>

<html>

<head>

<title>Title of the web page</title>

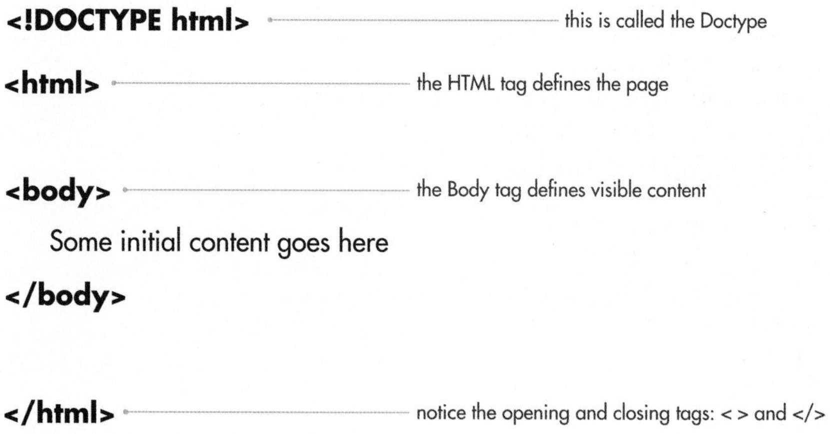

</head>

</html>

```
<!DOCTYPE html>          •——————————————— this is called the Doctype

<html>          •——————————— the HTML tag defines the page


<body>          •——————————— the Body tag defines visible content
    Some initial content goes here

</body>


</html>          •——————————— notice the opening and closing tags: < > and </>
```

Figure 5.5
Some basic tags are necessary to start building the most simple of web pages.

After the closing </head> tag, the <body> is where most of the additional content will live. It's the visible portion of the website, meaning what you see in a browser:

```
<!doctype html>

<html>

<head>

<title>Title of the webpage</title>

</head>

<body>

<p>My first website is live.</p>

</body>

</html>
```

Saving

Everything so far has been the shell of the website. If viewed in a browser, the result would be a page showing one sentence. Underwhelming, I know, but necessary. This is a good place to save the document before continuing. In doing so, it's important to save the document with an ".html" extension. Most text editors won't do this for you because they're capable of saving files with many other extensions. For this first page, save it exactly as: index.html. I'll explain why in a bit. Before you commit, also make sure you have no capital letters or spaces. Linux and Windows servers handle caps differently, but one result of using it could be a dead link. Spaces will render in a URL as "%20," so a file called "design portfolio" would output as: design%20portfolio. Use a dash or underscore in place of spaces. It might take you a while to get used to this, but it's crucial to prevent these kinds of errors.

Okay, back to the name. Why did I ask you to save it specifically as "index.html"? It's because all web browsers immediately look for a file with that name when accessing a website. Think of an entire website as a folder. Within that folder, you might have several files, such as: contact.html, about-us.html (remember, no spaces), portfolio.html. If someone types your URL into the browser bar, it will first look for a file called "index.html." Otherwise, a list of file names will be displayed in the most generic way possible. For that reason, the home page should always use that name. Seem reasonable? Let's make it a bit more complicated. On larger sites, you might have subfolders within the main directory. This is pretty similar to how you might have files stored on your computer: Desktop > Schoolwork > Graphic-design > Filenames. Imagine a site with the following folders: products, services, and contact. Each folder would also have its own index.html file. Test all of this by visiting your favorite website and adding "index.html" to the URL. You should see the exact same thing you saw before adding the extension. Go to another section of the website and do the same. You can now imagine how everything is set up behind the scenes. One thing about designing for the Web: it's paramount to stay organized. You could potentially overwrite files if not.

One thing you're probably realizing is that HTML isn't overly forgiving. My students will often spend an hour staring at a file, only for me to point out a missing tag, capitalized file name, or space used incorrectly. The big takeaway here: start your troubleshooting checklist with obvious things such as these. This will save you a lot of time in the long run.

Previewing

To view the web page, you need to open it in a browser. Several text editors allow you to preview the document by opening up a browser window directly from the interface. This is a feature that also saves time because it updates the browser window every time you save the HTML file.

HACK

If you have a big enough display or monitor to work with, keep the text editor and the browser window side by side so you can preview the outcome while you work. This cuts down on much of the back-and-forth between markup and preview.

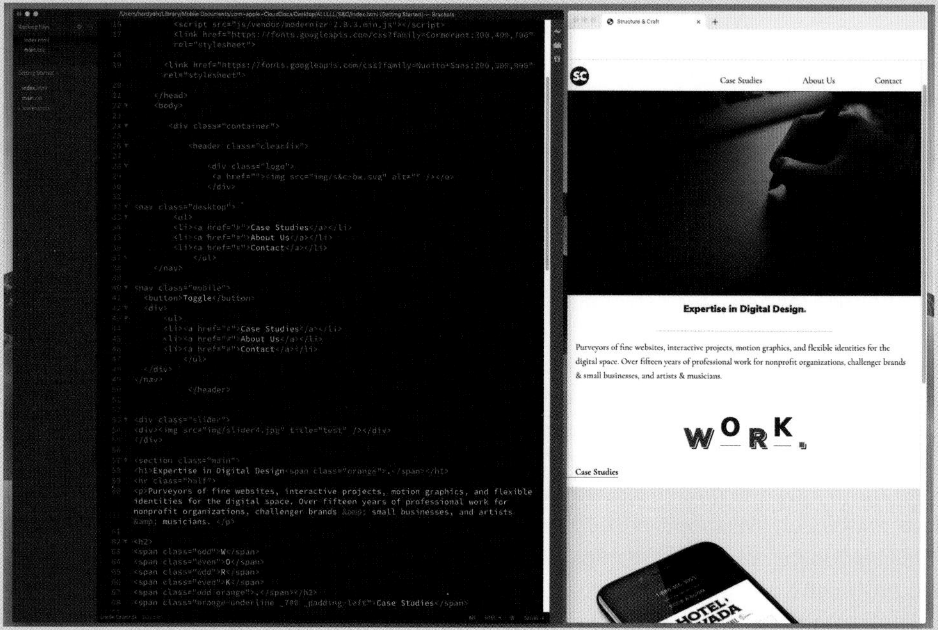

Figure 5.6
Keeping a browser test window open allows you to quickly preview your code in real time.

Headings

Just like a magazine layout will feature a heading, subheadings and body text, the Web depends on this as well. After your <title> tag, the <h1> tag (heading level one) is the most important piece of content in terms of SEO. Something generic like "welcome to my website" will certainly get lost in the shuffle. Since it's the title, it needs to stand out to grab attention. The <h2> subhead should then support that central concept. Heading levels go all the way to <h6>, but most people don't find the need to utilize them all. Here's an example:

<h1>Jane Doe, Digital Designer</h1>

<h2>Hand-crafted points and pixels</h2>

<h3>Serving Nonprofits and Community-based Institutions</h3>

Inline vs. block content

This simple concept carries a lot of visual weight in web design. Inline content flows next to other inline content. Block content breaks to the next line. Let's use the two tags for bold and italic text, <b> and <i>.

<p>Should designers <i>really</i> learn to code? <b>Find out</b> by reading this article.</p>

<p> More info...</p>

The above markup results in this:

--

Should designers *really* learn to code? **Find out** by reading this article.

More info ...

--

You can see that the <i> and <b> tags do make the text italic and bold, but they stay within the sentence. However, the second <p> tag results in a new paragraph with visible space between. The first two are "inline elements," and the last is a "block" element. All headings and paragraphs are block-level by default. Other inline elements include images and links. These default ways of display can be changed by using CSS. More on that to come.

Menu

SPEKTR is a film production company based in Amsterdam.

We tell grounded stories for brands, agencies and platforms.

Read more

Figure 5.7
This website juxtaposes high-contrast video introductions against no-nonsense headings.

Figure 5.8
Reversing text on a background image is a classic way to incorporate headings within a layout.

Links

These are what make the Web connected. They're what allow you to start on one page and end up on another, whether on the same site or a completely different one. Links are the "web" in the "World Wide Web." We see links in menus, around images, and in the vintage blue underlined text that is the default on all browsers. Link tags are officially referred to as "hyperlinks" if you want to embrace mid-1990s lingo. Here's how they're written:

```
<a href="http://www.somewebsite.com">
link to website</a>
```

There's a bit more to this tag than we've seen before. The additional part is called an "attribute" and its function is to provide more meaning to tag. You'll see attributes used in tons of other elements. Usually, they're seen in name="value" pairs like you see above. In this case, the name is the "href" part (hypertext reference if you're dying to know) and the value is a URL between the quotes. What's essentially being said is: "Send the browser to this website when a user touches or clicks this bit of text." Whatever is sandwiched between the opening and closing tag becomes the visible link.

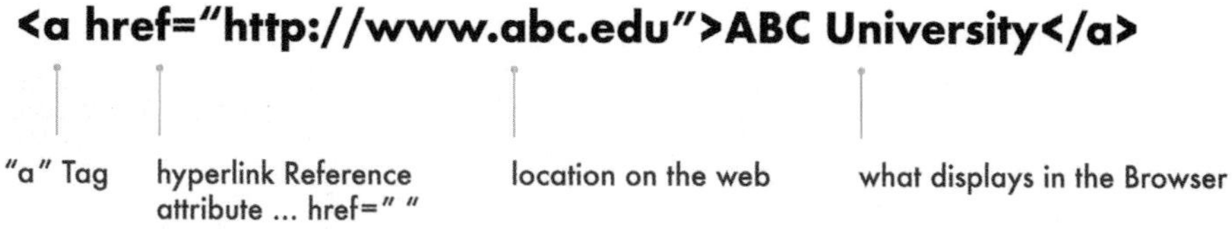

<a href="http://www.abc.edu">ABC University</a>

"a" Tag   hyperlink Reference   location on the web   what displays in the Browser
           attribute ... href=" "

Figure 5.9
Attributes provide context and specificity to basic HTML tags.

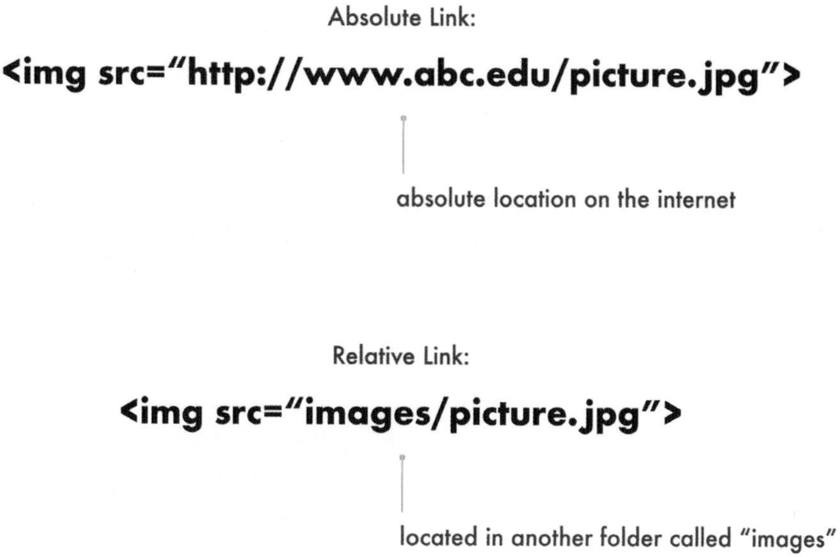

Absolute Link:

<img src="http://www.abc.edu/picture.jpg">

absolute location on the internet

Figure 5.10
While absolute URLs are easy to link to, relative URLs give more control over your content.

Relative Link:

<img src="images/picture.jpg">

located in another folder called "images"

Absolute and relative

In the example above, the link would go to a specific website somewhere on the internet. This is called an "absolute link" because it's so clearly instructive. Sometimes, though, you might want to link to another page on your own site. Then you wouldn't need to type the entire URL in the *href*. Let's assume that all web pages on your site are together in one folder; you can just link using the file name. Links are inline by default, and here's an example of one within a paragraph:

<p>Here's a relative

<a href="contact.html">link to a page</a>

as an example of how they work.</p>

Here's a relative <u>link to a page</u> as an example of how they work.

Images

We've experimented with just text so far. And for the first few years of the internet, that's all that existed. In 1993, Mosaic became the first browser to allow images on a web page. Since then, they've become ubiquitous on the Web. Just think: When was the last time you saw a website without them? The image tag is another tag that is self-terminating. Here's how it looks:

```
<img src="name-of-image.jpg"
alt="description of image" />
```

The beginning of the tag lets the browser know that it's an image. The first attribute is just telling the browser where to find an image. The second one is giving users a text description of the image. This "alt attribute" is required in HTML5 and helps with accessibility.

Resolution and images

To view images on the Web, they should be saved at a resolution of 72dpi. This is similar to the resolution for other digital formats, such as video. A warning: linking a 300dpi image (the resolution for print) on a website will result in a slow load time, not to mention the fact that it will look huge. There are four types of file extensions for images on the Web:

.jpg

Most photos you see online are JPG files. They're used for highly detailed images. Since its debut in 1992, it's been pretty much standard. JPG images use "lossy" compression, which means it degrades image quality when saving.

.png

This is a good choice if the image contains transparency. If you want any irregular-shaped image, using a PNG is the easiest method. Clip out anything you don't want to see, and the background of the web page will show through.

.gif

This is great for animated logos or images with a very limited color pallet. If you want the smallest image size possible, this is the way to go. There are preset amounts of colors (32, 64, etc.) to choose from when saving.

.svg

The "scalable vector graphic" is the best extension for non-photographic imagery that needs to be scalable. Increasingly, this is becoming the best option for logos and simple graphics to appear crisp across many layouts and widths

HACK

If you are creating a logo as an animated GIF, tick the box that will enable it to play just once when exporting from Photoshop. There's nothing more distracting than a repeating animated logo.

Content and mobile data

In the early days of the Web, saving images with file sizes as small as possible (while still retaining visual quality) was an art form. This was necessary because internet speeds were slow. In the age of fast Wi-Fi, that art has been somewhat lost. It's worth revisiting for one specific reason, though: mobile data. Many mobile phone plans charge for data, and serving up a high-quality image straight from your smartphone camera to a website will crush your viewers' bandwidth. Remember when we were talking viewports a while ago? We know that 1400px is a common stopping point for the width of a full-size web page, so it's a good idea to cap your image widths there as well. Anything larger is just adding extra load time.

HACK

When preparing to export images from your favorite image editor, experiment with the quality before saving. The difference between the highest quality and a medium quality isn't always that noticeable in an image. Reduce the quality from 100 percent downward until the image visually suffers. You'll notice "blockiness" in the form of JPG artifacts. Bump up the quality just a bit and save. Doing this could reduce the file size by half or more.

Figure 5.11
CSS gives the designer freedom to move beyond the default appearance of HTML elements.

Linking images

You now know how links work and how to form an image tag, so how do you link an image to another page or site? You can do this by nesting it:

```
<a href="shirts-page.html">

<img src="summer-shirts.jpg"
alt="photo of a button-up shirt" />

</a>
```

The link tag is wrapped around the image, and the entire thing becomes a hyperlink. In fact, you can nest many other elements (headings, for instance) with a link to make them do the same.

Reading code

Something that's useful to know about HTML is that the space between lines and tags isn't interpreted in the browser. Your code will render the following two examples exactly the same in the browser:

```
<p>This is an example paragraph. Now here's a link:

<a href="index.html"><img
src="example.png" alt="description of
the image" /></a>

</p>
```

versus:

```
<p>This is an example paragraph. Now here's a link:

<a href="index.html">

<img src="example.png"
alt="description of the image" />

</a>

</p>
```

The line breaks and indents on the second version help make it easier to visually scan, especially when you're new to HTML. You can use the specific <pre> tag, which does interpret space (useful for poetry) if you need it:

```
<pre>
Learning markup
    can be
difficult      without      space.
</pre>
```

Semantic markup and separation

All the tags discussed so far have inherent meaning behind them. Everything in a <p> tag is a paragraph. An <img> tag contains an image. The term "semantic markup" refers to the fact that a tag's content can be easily understood. That's useful, because if the visual layer was stripped away, those tags still clearly describe the intent of the content. Screen readers for users with visual disabilities depend on this. In the early days of web design, content and style were completely intertwined. That made it difficult to update either one, because you'd have to sift through code that's not relevant. With the separation of HTML and CSS, it's possible to completely change the appearance of a website without touching the content or vice versa. This allows you to clearly focus on the task at hand, whether designing or copywriting. There's another important factor: a style sheet controls the layout of an entire site, not just a page. The amount of time saved increases with the scale of the website.

Spans and divs

Regarding semantic markup, there are a few HTML tags that are meaningless on their own: "span" and "div." They're the empty containers of the Web. A <span> tag displays inline by default, and a <div> tag shows as block. Both tags are useful for the purposes of grouping and styling your layout via CSS, but placing content inside them doesn't add any connotation beyond the visual. It's a good idea to remember to try and use meaningful tags whenever possible. So how are they used? By adding "classes" as attributes to them, which we can style via CSS:

<div class="group-one">

<p>This is a <span class="blue">sentence</span>.</p>

<a href="about.html">

<img src="example.jpg" alt="description of the image" />

</a>

</div>

You can see how several of the tags are nested. That additional slash in the trailing tag helps, but as a designer looking at code it's not always obvious when starting out. That closing </div> tag above is pretty far away from the opening one. Something that's helped me tremendously is by using comments. Here's what one looks like:

<!---you can type anything you want here-->

This might seem to add more complication, but it's useful because it lets you know where groups of tags end. Here's one added to the example from above:

<div class="group-one">

<p>This is a <span class="blue">sentence</span>.</p>

<a href="about.html">

<img src="example.jpg" alt="description of the image" />

</a>

</div>

<!---end of group one-->

See how using the comment makes it visually easier to create a sense of closure? You can feel secure knowing everything is properly nested and move on.

Adding CSS

All the examples so far look pretty dull when previewed in a browser. The browser has default ways of displaying markup if not instructed otherwise. The default Georgia serif font is an example of that. We can override all of this with some simple styling in a Cascading Style Sheet (CSS). This is what the anatomy of a CSS rule looks like:

```
selector {

    property-name: value;

}
```

The selector can be just a generic tag like <p> or it can be a class name like we used in the span or div earlier. Let's change the default font on all paragraphs, make the span text blue, and give the entire group a light gray background color:

```
p {

    font-family: Helvetica, sans-serif;

}
```

```
.blue {

    color: #2874A6;

}
```

```
.group-one {

    background: #ccc;

}
```

Notice the dots at the beginning of the last two examples. They're important, because they denote a class, which refers to the class attributes used in the HTML markup. We're latching onto that content by using the class and then styling it with CSS. Otherwise, generic tags like <p> can just be expressed without the dot. Styling generic tags is useful to set up the general page defaults. Once the basic rules have been laid out, you can be more specific about certain bits of content by using CSS. This is what the "cascade" in Cascading Style Sheets refers to.

Connecting your CSS

The best way to style your HTML is via an external style sheet. This allows you to separate layout from content, keeping everything. To do this, you'll have to save your style sheet. Paste the CSS into a new document in your text editor and save it as "style.css." It's important to add the file extension for everything to work. Now, go back to your HTML doc and add a <link> tag within the <head>:

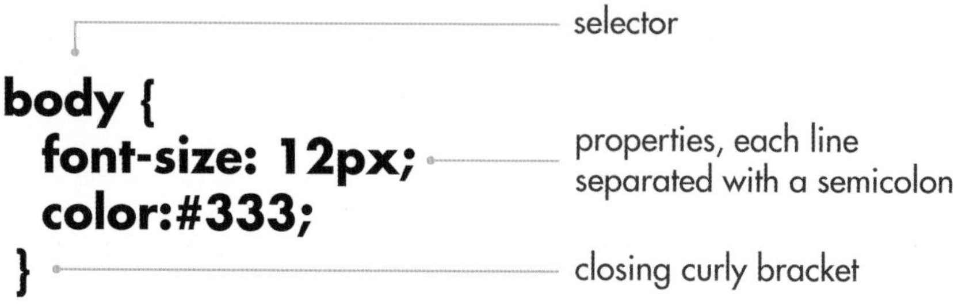

Figure 5.12
CSS tags have their own syntax, and properties are more easily read as individual lines.

body {
font-size: 12px;
color:#333;
}

— selector

properties, each line separated with a semicolon

closing curly bracket

```
<head>

<title>Title of the webpage</title>

<link rel="stylesheet" href="style.css">

</head>
```

You can see two attributes in the link tag, which is self-terminating. The first is the relationship attribute (rel); this tells the browser that this linked file is a style sheet. The second (href) is familiar because you've already used it with links: it simply says where the file is located. After this is complete, save both documents, and they should be synced. Test it out by changing anything in either file, saving, and refreshing the browser.

HACK

If you're using the mouse to save and refresh, you're wasting time and adding undue stress on your wrist in the process. Use keyboard shortcuts to do both in about a second. On a Mac, it's command-S in the file and command-R in the browser.

CSS comments

Just like HTML comments allow you to write notes about the markup, CSS comments can do the same for styling. They start with a slash-asterisk, and look like this:

```
body {

    font-size: 18px;

    color: #333; /*this is just a comment*/

    margin: 2em;

}
```

Color

Hexadecimal codes are a common way of expressing thousands of colors in CSS. They're expressed as a six-digit string of letters and/or numbers. The first pair denote red, the second pair green, and the third blue, within the RGB spectrum.

```
color: #2B5F82
```

All popular design programs have a way of displaying the hex color of anything from type to graphics, so look next time you have the color palette open.

Just do a search for "hex color codes" to find tools on this. Now, save both documents and refresh your browser to see the change live. There are several other ways to express colors in CSS if you need to use transparency. RGBa is the easiest to use, and it is used like this:

```
color: rgba (43,95,130, 0.5)
```

The first three numbers contain the RGB values, and the fourth denotes the alpha (or transparency). The "0.5" value above would be 50 percent transparent.

Styling text

One of the easiest things to style starting out is typography. Using the example from earlier, add a heading and subheads. Then style them with CSS:

HTML:

```
<h1>Jane Doe, Digital Designer</h1>

<h2>Hand-crafted points and pixels
</h2>

<h3>Serving Nonprofits and
Community-Based Institutions</h3>
```

```
<p>Based in Washington, DC, I've been
working professionally for fifteen years.
Please view my portfolio for recent
examples of work.</p>
```

CSS:

```
body {

    font-family: "Times New Roman", serif;

}


h1, h2 {

    font-family: Helvetica, sans-serif;

}


h3 {

    font-weight: bold;

}
```

You're probably asking, where did the body specification come from? Since all visible content is with the body tag, this is an easy method to set everything with a baseline style. The styles for the headings override anything that's already set for the body. This is called "specificity." Also, do you notice how the <h1> and <h2> are grouped? This saves time and space. And the <h3> is using the baseline serif font by inheriting it from the body but adding a bold text weight to differentiate it.

Web safe fonts

Here's the way to think about fonts on the Web. You either assume the font you're using is on most people's devices, or you serve them a custom file that renders the font for them. It's easiest to use what's known as a "web-safe" font. These are the ones that come pre-installed on all devices. The issue is that every operating system (iOS vs. Android, Mac vs. PC) slightly differs in which fonts are standard. Specifying type is near and dear to a designer's heart, so where does that leave us? There's a short list that seems to overlap between most systems. And luckily, a few of them are decent.

- Helvetica
- Arial Black
- Times New Roman
- Verdana
- Courier
- Palatino
- Garamond
- Bookman
- Trebuchet

When specifying fonts, you always use a fallback (i.e., "serif") to default to the basic classification if something goes wrong.

```
font-family: "Times New Roman", serif;
```

Jane Doe, Digital Designer

Hand-crafted points and pixels

Serving Nonprofits and Community-based Institutions

Based in Washington, DC, I've been working professionally for 15 years. Please view my portfolio for recent examples of work.

Figure 5.13 Basic classification and markup of text is the first step in designing web typography.

HACK

Some fonts will only have one or two weights. To get the most mileage, select a font with a family of at least four weights. Don't go overboard here. Adding tons of weights will start to choke up the load time. After all, your website is loading a resource from Google to display these. I recommend 100, 400, and 900 weights for maximum contrast on most fonts. Next, look back to the "embed" tab. This contains two bits of code that you need to copy. The first is an HTML link. Although longer, this looks like the link tag you saw earlier. Paste this directly after the style sheet link but still within the <head> tag. Paste the second bit in your style sheet, for whatever selector you want to target:

HTML:

```
<head>

<title>Title of the webpage</title>

<link rel="stylesheet" href="style.css">

<link href="https://fonts.googleapis.com/
css2?family=Lato:wght@400&display=swap" rel="stylesheet">

</head>
```

CSS:

```
body, h1, h2 {

    font-family: "Lato", sans-serif;

}
```

Save both documents and refresh your browser. You should be looking at a custom font on your web page. You can select multiple fonts and repeat the process if you like. If you're new to font combinations, search for "Google font pairing" to find examples of what other designers have found to be aesthetically pleasing.

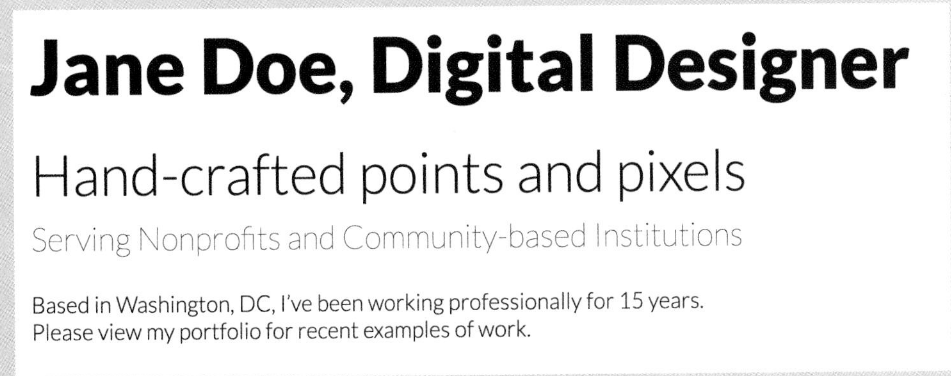

Jane Doe, Digital Designer

Hand-crafted points and pixels

Serving Nonprofits and Community-based Institutions

Based in Washington, DC, I've been working professionally for 15 years.
Please view my portfolio for recent examples of work.

Figure 5.14
Moving beyond the classic web-safe fonts can make even a simple layout look more contemporary.

Using custom fonts

The easiest way to use a custom font is to use one hosted by Google. I've intentionally shied away from mentioning them up to this point, because there are other options for web searches. But for delivering custom fonts, there really is no easier way. If you're someone who has a positive or neutral stance in using Google's digital services, read on. Search for the Google Fonts website. The homepage allows you to filter between categories: serif, sans-serif, display, handwriting, and monospace. I should note that there are a lot of terrible fonts hosted here as well. The last three categories contain most of the common offenders; be critical in your selection. Once you find one that you'd like to use, select it, and choose the weights you'd like, which is a fantastic option for something that's free.

HTML and CSS

Now that we're able to control the style of several HTML elements, it's helpful to go back to some other useful HTML tags. This isn't going to be an exhaustive list of everything available—there are entire books for that. The following are ones that you'll use straight away.

The container

One of the best ways to control the layout of elements on the page is with an outer container. The "container" is simply a div with a class added to it. This is simply nested just inside the <body> element, with all other page content directly within it:

```
<body>

<div class="container">

<!---all content goes here-->

</div>

</body>
```

Adding this container gives you more precision between different screen sizes. For instance, you can set a generic width at 100 percent. This will allow the layout to expand to fill a smartphone-sized screen edge to edge. As you move up in screen sizes, you may want the content to have a bit more breathing room by dictating a maximum width in which the layout stops

Figure 5.15
The container div should be placed just inside the body tag, and it provides control over a flexible layout.

expanding (i.e., 1400px). Adding auto-margin to the horizontal axis ensures that if the screen is sized beyond a laptop width, the container will be centered within its parent element (the body).

CSS:

```
.container {

    width: 100%;

    max-width: 1400px;

    margin: 0 auto;  /*the zero is vertical,
    the auto is horizontal*/

}
```

So a container div ultimately allows you the flexibility to display the overall content width at different screen sizes. This can give your layout some breathing room, prevent overly long lines of text, and generally ensure that everything is centered.

Header content

The <header> tag shouldn't be confused with the <head> tag, which we've already discussed. It's typically just inside the <body> tag and houses the site branding and your navigation menu. The <nav> tag specifically holds the <ul> (unordered list) and <li> (list item) tags that make up your navigation.

```
<body>

<header>

<h1>WidgetCo: Digital Design</h1>

<nav>

<ul>

<li><a href="about.html">About</a>
</li>

<li><a href="portfolio.html">Portfolio </
a></li>
```

```
<li><a href="contact.html">Contact</a>
</li>

</ul>

</nav>

</header>

</body>
```

Note how everything's nested within the <header> tag, and the further nesting of the links inside the navigation menu. If you were to test this without any styling, you'd see a logo stacked on top of a bulleted list. To make things a bit cleaner, let's style the <h1> and make the nav more button-like:

CSS:

```
header {

    text-align: center;

    border-bottom: 1px solid #ccc;

}

header h1 {

    font-family: sans-serif;

    font-size: 2.5em;

    color: #999;

}

nav ul {

    list-style-type: none;

    margin: 0 auto;

    padding: 0;

    width: 70%;

}
```

Figure 5.16
Starting with header content is an easy way to begin a web page.

WidgetCo: Digital Design

About

Portfolio

Contact

```
nav ul li{

    background: #ccc;

    margin-bottom: .75em;

}

nav ul li a {

    display: block;

    color: #000;

    padding: .5em 1em;

    text-decoration: none;

}
```

Footer content

We're skipping to the bottom of the page. Why? Because like the header, footer content won't likely change from page to page. The footer is usually the last HTML element before the end </body> tag. It typically contains copyright and tertiary information and any navigational links that aren't already in the header.

Do you really need a footer? That's a question up for debate, but it does visually signal the end of the page for users. It's also an opportunity to send them to other pages on your website without making them scroll back up. Furthermore, a lot of users intuitively scroll to the bottom of a page to quickly find contact links. Use the following method to show a copyright symbol with HTML character encoding. While we're there, let's add a dynamic time-stamped

Figure 5.17
Placing the footer before any main content makes sense, because it remains consistent between pages.

year with a tiny bit of JavaScript. We can use some CSS to wrangle its position, so it stays at the bottom of the site. This helps if you have short content, so the footer doesn't seem to float in the middle of the page.

HTML:
```
<footer>

<p>&copy;

<script type="text/javascript">

document.write(new Date().getFullYear());

</script>

- WidgetCo.</p>

</footer>
```

CSS:
```
footer {

    position: fixed;

    text-align: center;

    bottom: 0;

    width: 100%;

    border-top: 1px solid #ccc;

}
```

WidgetCo: Digital Design

About

Portfolio

Contact

© 2021 - WidgetCo.

Main content

This will be what changes from page to page, so it makes sense to design it after the header and footer. We can use a new tag to sandwich it directly between the two. The <section> tag is specific and flexible enough to use as a wrapper for the main content of a page and is a block-level element.

```
</header>
<section>
<h1>Jane Doe, Digital Designer</h1>
<h2>Hand-crafted points and pixels</h2>
<h3>Serving Nonprofits and Community-Based Institutions</h3>
<p>Based in Washington, DC, I've been working professionally for fifteen years. Please view my portfolio for recent examples of work.</p>
</section>
<footer>
```

Centering the content

By default, all HTML is aligned left. Certain tags—like paragraphs and some headings—benefit from that alignment. You'll likely want to center much of the content, though. The mobile age has further cemented that desire from users. Rather than trying to center every element, it's easier to center all the content at the body level. This method lets you apply left or right alignment to things that you don't want centered instead. The first thing we need to center is the <body> tag itself, within the outer <html> tag.

```
body {
    margin: 0 auto;
    width: 100%;
    max-width: 1400px;
    text-align: center;
}
```

Remember, the max-width property gives it a hard-stop at a size reasonable to fit on a small laptop. The margin property sets it at the top of the screen (the zero property) and centers it (the second value of auto). So, it's flexible at 100 percent up to a certain point, and then it's centered within the browser window. The text-align property is slightly deceiving. It actually centers all visible content, not just the text. That includes any images, navigation, and divs.

Backgrounds via CSS

In addition to adding background colors, you can also add backgrounds to HTML elements in the form of images. Using the <img> tag is straightforward, but adding them via CSS background property is much more flexible:

```
div {
    background: url(images/sky.jpg)
    center no-repeat;
    background-size: cover;
}
```

There's a lot of information in those short lines: first we're specifying the path to the image, then we're aligning it as vertically and horizontally centered. Finally, we're specifying that it doesn't repeat. If you've ever seen a tiled background image, you can now appreciate that the default

Figure 5.18
This portfolio website features parallax animation as you scroll through introductory content.

GRAND CANYON

June 2014

My freshman year of college I received a call from a longtime friend asking if I wanted to backpack the Grand Canyon with him come summertime. There were only two acceptable answers, "Yes" or "You're coming whether you like it or not." As I had only having car camped with my family before, I decided, "What the hell." Six months and lots of planning later we set out across country taking plane, train, and automobile to arrive at the North Rim of the Canyon. With all of us eager to get our feet wet and start the hike, we set off. The next six days were tiring and tough, but the most fun any of us had ever had on a trip. The process was so simple and pure. The only objective was to make it from point A to point B in however much time it took. The distance and difficult elevation grade went out the window when faced with the incredible views we saw. Needless to say, I was hooked.

method is set to repeat. The second line simply tells the browser to "cover" the entire element with the background image, so that it completely fills the background edge to edge.

Parallax effects

As we defined in Chapter 3, a parallax effect is when the foreground and background layers move at different speeds, creating a sense of depth. By using the background-attachment CSS property, we can "fix" an element in place while scrolling another element "over top" of it. It's a simple method that yields a lot of visual impact because of the implied interaction between the elements. We'll use a <section> tag as an example element:

```
section.parallax {

    background: url("images/fixed.jpg")
    no-repeat;

    height: 50vh;

    background-attachment: fixed;

    background-size: cover;

}
```

HTML:

```
<section class="parallax"></section>

<section>

<p>Some content that scrolls.</p>

</section>
```

In the example above, the first section would be 50 percent of the height of the screen (the "vh" specifies that). The second section (the one without the class) would cover the first one as it's scrolled.

Measurements

Pixels

The most easily understood unit of measurement on the Web is a pixel. It's a dot on your screen. In CSS, it's expressed as "px" and can be applied to most anything, from font-size to the width of an element (tag). Example:

```
img {

    width: 300px;

}
```

Em and rem

These are relative units of measurement—which can be confusing—but they are useful for responsive design because they scale well. One em is equal to the point-size of the font-size of the element it's applied to. If that element doesn't have a declared font-size, it's inherited from the next element up, which is called the "parent element." This could potentially go all the way up the chain to the <body> element if you set the baseline there. Here's an example where the font-size is specified:

```
.group-two {

    font-size: 20px;

    padding: .5em;

    border: .25em;

}
```

Since 20px is 1em here, .5em becomes 10px and .25px becomes 5px. The nice part about using ems is that if you want to scale everything, you only have to change one property (the font-size). Rems are similar to ems but are always based on the font-size of the overall page. This might be helpful so that

any nested elements don't multiply in size (2em based on 1em based on 16px, get it?).

```
.group-two {

    font-size: 1rem; /* =16px */

}
```

Since 16px is the default size, you can end up with weird values in ems to get to relative pixel sizes. For example, to get a relative 30px size, the value would be 1.875rem. Also, when you declare the <body> element in pixels, you're setting it for all viewports (mobile and laptop).

HACK

We can eliminate some of the decimal points by declaring the <html> element as 62.5 percent. This also solves the screen-size problem because it's based on the percentage of the viewport, not a fixed pixel.

```
html { font-size: 62.5%; } /* =10px */

body { font-size: 1.6rem; } /* =16px */

h1 { font-size: 3rem; } /* =30px */
```

See how much easier that is to calculate? Now everything is based on an even ten-pixel value and more logical to scale up. This method is employed by a lot of professional web designers because of those advantages.

Percentage

We just saw that it's possible to use a percentage-based value as a unit of measurement in CSS. I don't recommend it for everything (again, calculations), but it's a great unit for certain elements such as images and large layout blocks. For

example, if you want your images to take up 100 percent of the screen width on a mobile screen, it's pretty effortless. But what about a larger screen? A huge image on a laptop-sized viewport could quickly get annoying, so we can combine percentage with max-width.

```
img {

    width: 100%;

    max-width: 800px;

}
```

That gives us the best of both worlds; the image scales nicely, but there's a hard stop at 800px. Note that percentage works in relation to any parent elements. For instance, if an element is specified as 1000px wide, any element inside set to 100 percent would render as 1000px. Eighty percent would become 800px, and so on. You can take advantage of this parent–child relationship to make sure that an image inside a div fills it completely. The parent div, could then be set to 50 percent.

```
.image-block {

    width: 50%;

}

.image-block img {

    width: 100%;

}
```

Vw and vh

These units are based on the viewport (the screen). Either unit is equal to 1/100 of the overall vertical (vh) or horizontal (vw) size of the screen. These might be useful in certain situations because they are not dependent on any parent element. For instance, if you want a full-screen image for an introductory section, you could wrap it in a link that leads to a section further down the page and use vh.

HTML:

```
<body>

<div class="intro-content">

<a href="#section-two">

<img src="splash.jpg" alt="interior of office" />

</a>

</div>

</body>
```

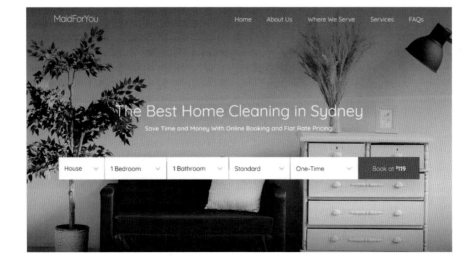

Figure 5.19
Using 100vh for a background image size is an easy way to fill the entire screen.

CSS:

```
.intro-content img {

    height: 100vh;

}
```

Zero as a value

Any time a unit of measurement is expressed as a zero, you don't have to include the measurement, because zero equals the same thing in all forms:

```
img {

    margin: 0;

}
```

The Box Model

The way that HTML elements (tags) are displayed in the browser relies on what's called the Box Model. It starts with the element itself, which is the innermost box. Directly around that—no matter if it's an image, heading, paragraph, etc.— lies the padding. It's the first amount of "space" that surrounds an element. The border is next. The size can be as large or small as needed, and the border can even be rounded by using the border-radius CSS property. The last thing is the margin. This is the space between everything associated with that element (including the border) and the others around it. A lot of my students are initially confused about the difference between the padding and margin. Sometimes, just throwing a "test" border around an HTML tag is a good way to see the difference. You can then experiment by adding padding, which makes the rectangle bigger. Then add the margin, which will move the rectangle within the layout.

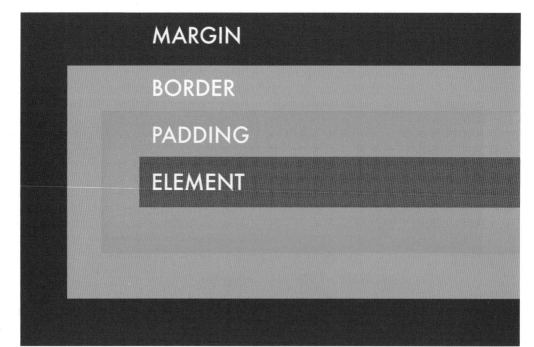

Figure 5.20
Understanding the Box Model will demystify differences between padding and margin.

```
h1 {

    border: solid 1px red;

    /* add padding and margin to test */

}
```

Inheritance

HTML tags that are nested in other tags are called "child elements." If CSS properties aren't specifically expressed for the child, it usually inherits the property of the parent tag. If the parent doesn't specify, it goes further up the chain or defaults to the browser default (16px font-size, for instance).

HTML:
```
<article>

<p>This is a test sentence</p>

</article>
```

CSS:
```
article {

    font-size: 1.5em;

}
p {

    /* paragraph inherits article font-size */

}
```

Responsive and retina images

To further optimize for both mobile screens and the increased pixel density of devices, you can take advantage of exporting images specifically suited to smaller screens, and images outputted at 2x and 3x pixel density. Saving images with these specifications can be easy enough. Just crop mobile images to a specific width and save with a unique file name (the "s" denoting small):

header-image-s.jpg

Most design software also allows you to output 2x and 3x images automatically through export options:

header-image-2x.jpg

How do you target these images for specific contexts, though? The answer is using the "srcset" attribute in your <img> tags:

```
<img alt="description of image"
srcset="header-image-s.jpg 600w,
header-image-l.jpg  1200w">
```

The two images linked in the srcset attribute above (delineated by commas) are followed by widths. The browser will automatically select the best source for the current width of the viewport window. It requires a bit more production but avoids the problem of serving large images for all screens. Similarly, the srcset attribute can be used to target device pixel density:

```
<img alt="description of image"
srcset="header-image-s.jpg,
header-image-m.jpg  2x,
header-image-l.jpg  3x">
```

The markup above offers the "regular" 1x image first and offers two additional options at 2x and 3x densities. The browser will serve whichever is appropriate for the device pixel density. There are more attributes and parameters that can be explored, including the <picture> element for more precise art direction on the Web.

Positioning

At a certain point, you'll grow tired of looking at content in the default flow, which is known as "static positioning." There are four additional methods that can be used to position HTML elements, giving you a bit more variety in how to present it visually:

Any element with this "offset" class would be positioned 50px away from the top and left of its normal (static) position. This is a no-nonsense solution for moving content "away from" other things on the page. Use it to increase negative space and open the layout.

Relative

The next method that's easiest to understand is "relative positioning." Adding a bit of space to any of the four sides causes the element to be positioned relative to its normal position. The amount is determined by how much space you add. For instance:

```
.offset {

   position: relative;

   top: 50px

   left: 50px

}
```

Absolute

The name says it all here. Absolute positioning is quite effective when you want to lock an element in place on the page. Using the same four directions we used with relative positioning, you can place something exactly where you want it:

```
.exact {

   position: absolute;

   top: 100px

   right: 50px

}
```

Figure 5.21
Offset positioning
can help you
achieve layouts
that have
organic qualities.

This would cause an element with the "exact" class to be positioned 100px from the top of the page, and 50px from the right, unless it's positioned in a parent element that's set to relative positioning. In that case, the measurements start from the edges of the parent element. Absolutely positioned elements also have no bearing on the positioning of other elements in the layout. They're removed from the normal page flow, which is something to note.

Fixed

We briefly explored this method earlier when testing out a <footer> tag. Fixed positioning is perfect for header and footer content, fixing them to the top or bottom of the page even when scrolled. It's relative to the four corners of the screen, making it easy to "fix" in any position.

```
header {

    position: fixed;

    top: 0;

}
```

The previous header tag would stay put at the top of the screen and stay there as content is scrolled behind it. If you've ever seen a floating button labeled "go to top," that's another instance of the fixed position property in action.

Sticky

The newest and most flexible positioning method is a hybrid of sorts. It assumes the relative position, until the viewer scrolls past it when it then becomes fixed into place. This is useful when you have a bit of content that you want to highlight further down the page.

```
.sticky-content {

    position: sticky;

    top: 50px;

}
```

The fact that sticky positioned content is dynamically positioned by the scroll means that you can effectively manipulate the hierarchy of content through a long amount of information. The above example would scroll and then become "fixed" 50px from the top of the screen.

Complex layout

Float

At a certain point, you'll want options beyond the block and inline content models. Float properties have been around for a long time in CSS, and they allow you to "float" images within text content. This kind of text wrapping is reminiscent of traditional print-based layout and allows for a more organic flow of content. The two options for a CSS float are left or right. Adding a bit of margin around the element you're floating is advisable, too, so it's not directly touching other content.

```
Img {

    float: left;

    margin-right: 10px;

}
```

In the past, the float property was used to create complex page layouts—well beyond what it was designed for—because of limitations in CSS layout. Since the arrival of Flexbox and CSS Grid, it's been more or less relegated to its original purpose.

Flexbox

Flexbox was introduced as a "flexible box model" in an effort to alleviate many of the problems associated with distributing layout items evenly or flexibly. It allows you to nest several items in an outer container and align them horizontally *or* vertically inside that space (in the form of rows or columns). Layouts that were difficult to achieve using floats and positioning—such as vertically centering content nested in a parent element or making different columns the same height—are easily achieved. The true value in using Flexbox is the way the container element adapts to different screen sizes. Several properties are customizable, including the flow of content (column, row), and the ability to "wrap" to more than one line of items.

```
div {

    display: flex;

    flex-flow: row wrap;

    align-items: center;

}
```

There are two basic elements to work with in Flexbox: the outer container element (div, section) and the inner items or elements. Each has many available properties that are customizable depending on how you'd like to feature the content. Search for "a complete guide to Flexbox" to get an in-depth tutorial from CSS Tricks, which is a reputable source.

CSS Grid

When CSS Grid was introduced, it was a game-changer for complex layouts. Previously, the only way to effectively lay out content in both rows *and* columns was through using parent elements to form each row, with floated elements inside each row to form columns. This required a lot of nesting and floating, with a lot of custom CSS rules making things work behind the scenes. Those kinds of layouts are much easier to achieve with CSS Grid. One of the most valuable aspects of a grid layout is the ability to use the fractional (fr) unit of measurement, which represents the "available space" left in a grid. Here's an example:

HTML:

```
<section class="outer">

<div class="col"></div>

<div class="col"></div>

<div class="col"></div>

</section>
```

CSS:

```
.outer {

    display: grid;

    grid-template-columns: 300px 1fr 1fr;

    grid-column-gap: 20px;

}
```

Let's explain the above. First, we set up a generic section named with an "outer" class. Nested inside that are three div elements named with "col" classes. The class names can be changed to anything you'd like. The CSS is where it gets interesting. We specify the outer container as using grid layout. We then specify the width of our inner divs with the "grid-template-columns" property, saying that the first "col" is 300px wide and the following two are one fractional unit each. That means whatever space remains after the initial 300px is neatly divided by the last two divs. The final "grid-column-gap" property is essentially the "gutter" in classic graphic design parlance, or the space between the columns. Mixing fixed units (pixels) and completely fluid units (fractional units) gives you a lot of control with respect to prioritizing content and screen sizes. This is just one of the many aspects of fine-grain layout available with CSS Grid. Similar to what I've mentioned above regarding Flexbox, search for "a complete guide to CSS Grid" to get the authoritative—and very long—guide from CSS Tricks.

UNSTUDIO

Category ⌄   Status ⌄   Location ⌄   ✕ Remove filter

Arnhem Central Masterplan
1996

Mercedes-Benz Museum
2001

Xingdong New Area
2019

New Budapest Bridge
2018

Figure 5.22
CSS Grid allows for precise control over different-sized content in rows and columns.

Designing in the browser

This concept has been fairly common for well over a decade now, and much of what I've introduced in this chapter—write a bit of code, preview it, and tweak—follows the line of thought. Many of the design programs we use to design for an interactive web experience are themselves built using static compositions. High-fidelity prototyping often involves mocking up dozens of potential pages on a website before a single line of code is written. For high-stakes situations where business or reputation is on the line, that makes sense. But for simple websites, working directly from one or two representative page designs can be good enough to start building from. This is usually enough to work out basic things such as colors, font pairings, negative space, and hierarchy. From there, you can build out the components in code. Marking up and testing things piece by piece is a solid approach: start with the outer page container, then the header, and footer. When you get to the main content, tackle that in chunks as well. Using this method, you can directly learn from the implications of writing and editing code by troubleshooting as you move along. Designing in the browser can have its drawbacks, though: if you can't execute your vision using HTML and CSS, you may settle for something lesser. A series of those kinds of compromises can result in what many call a "Frankensteined" site, where things just aren't working out aesthetically.

Designing buildable layouts

Remember, the medium itself is flexible, and it's important to design layouts that can be reworked if needed. Designing pages that work well as a single column is one way to start. Complex layouts can be accurately achieved using Grid Layout or Flexbox, two tools that open the true power of CSS styling. But if you try to learn them before the basics, you'll spend more time getting frustrated than making actual progress. Your first page layouts should embrace classic design sensibilities and build upon simple typography, well-chosen imagery, and a carefully considered color palette. Here are some concepts to consider:

- Use one or two typefaces that pair well.
- Center everything at the <body> element. It's much easier to align individual elements left or right.
- Create contrast by utilizing scale. Sub-headlines should be noticeably larger than body copy, and headlines should scale up from there.
- Control hierarchy through the use of negative space. What do you want users to see first, second, and third?
- Have consistency of treatment. The pages on your site should look like they belong together.
- Have clarity of function. Important call-to-action buttons should communicate their intent.

Cutting through the noise

World-renowned designer Michael Bierut (2014) has said that "The internet is both illuminating and blinding." What's been discussed here is the tip of the iceberg. Most designers won't ever reach the mid-range coding abilities of a true developer. Still, even knowing the basics of how to translate your visual layouts can be game-changing. It's a huge competitive advantage not to have to outsource basic web pages. Whether a proof of concept, a rough draft, or just an experiment, the ability to understand markup will separate you from many other designers. When you're first starting, the small victories of just "getting something to work" can inspire you to dig deeper. Use them to build your skills as far as your curiosity takes you. You'll empower yourself to build your own basic projects.

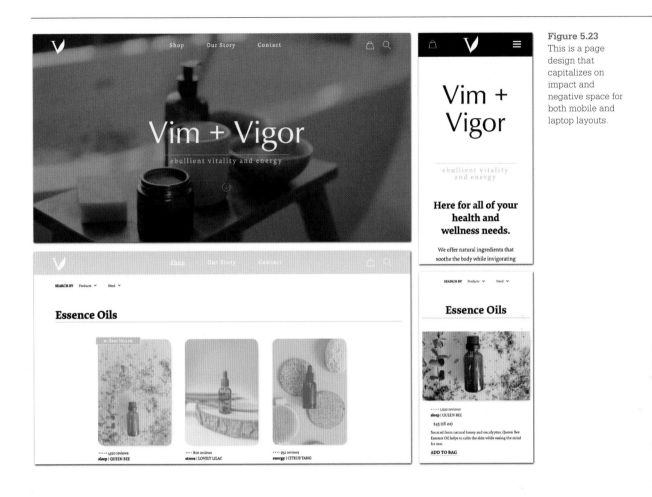

Figure 5.23
This is a page
design that
capitalizes on
impact and
negative space for
both mobile and
laptop layouts.

Figure 5.24
This category
menu for the
UNSTUDIO
website features
playful interactive
and dimensional
typography.

Design an HTML and CSS typographic poem that builds on basic markup and styling skills presented through a design lens.

DESCRIPTION

Design a web page featuring a poem, which pairs word and image in a dynamic way. This project will allow you to showcase a visually impactful web design project in your portfolio without diving into the coding deep end. Styling a resume in HTML and CSS is a typical beginner web design project. This alternative gives you a bit more creative freedom in terms of layout and presentation, and is a bit more forgiving on the technical side.

SPECIFICATIONS

The short poem should be styled using at least two fonts. You may use multiple weights within each font. Use some kind of imagery to contrast the text. This can be done using photos, illustration, or background images. Remember, you can easily show organic edges and transparency by using PNG images. Since poetry doesn't always read well on mobile devices because of irregular lines and spacing, we're only going to design for 1400px "laptop" width. This also keeps the project approachable from a code perspective.

Figure 5.25
This basic mood board captures moods and visual themes for a typographic poem.

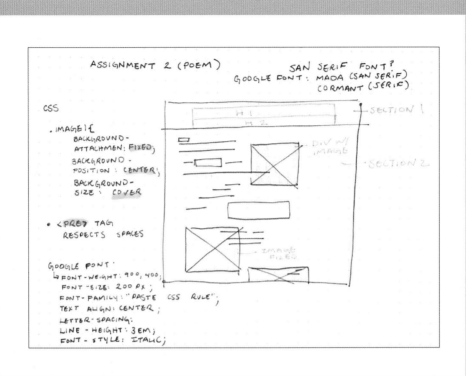

Figure 5.26
Sketches help
ensure that you
aren't just
arbitrarily
designing while
coding in the web
browser.

RESEARCH AND INTENT

Search on the Poetry Foundation's website for any poems that seem interesting. Look for particular moods and words that you might be able to bring attention to, both visually and typographically. Be subjective and personal in your choice—this is one of the rare opportunities to do so in a design project. You'll have a lot more fun if you choose something that resonates with you.

METHODOLOGY AND CONTENT

A poem that's between 100 and 300 words is the perfect length for this exercise. This will allow for some scrolling, while keeping it reasonable. Copy the text, poet, and any attribution, and save it as a text file. Begin searching for images that might serve as complementary or counterpoint to the text.

Avoid cliché and obvious image associations at all costs. Knowing that metaphor is often used as a poetic device means that you should steer clear of literal interpretation of imagery. Contrast and juxtaposition are often a much better choice.

SKETCHES

Begin some rough compositions of how blocks of text might be arranged on the page. You can simply use different lengths of horizontal lines to denote text, while writing out some of the individual words you'd like to highlight. Make notes about type styles and imagery as well.

Figure 5.27
Utilizing some
lesser-known tags
like <pre> allows
for unconven-
tional text
presentation.

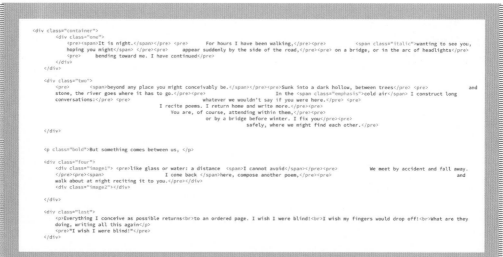

Figure 5.27
Utilizing some lesser-known tags like <pre> allows for unconventional text presentation.

MOCK-UP

A quick digital mock-up will ensure that you're designing with intention when it's time to build it in code. Design in a 1400px-wide composition; the height can vary. Here's where you'll have a chance to test out the colors and typefaces you have in mind. Speaking of type, be sure to select Google Fonts to keep things simple. There are plenty of decent pairings to choose from there.

MARKUP AND STYLING

With your mock-up for reference, begin marking up your content with code. Start with a container-classed div just inside your body tag. Add sections within the container and paragraphs within the sections. The <br> tags can be used to break lines, and <span> tags can isolate individual bits of text.

EXPERIMENTING AND TESTING

Make sure that all your HTML tags and CSS rules are properly closed, and test in a browser. Make adjustments as needed. Experiment with different positioning methods, margins, and padding. For a "layered" look, try placing images via both HTML <img> tags and CSS backgrounds. Use different weights of the fonts you've chosen for contrast. You can deviate from your mock-up a bit if you feel inspired.

GETTING IT ONLINE

One of the most convenient aspects of sharing and presenting web design projects is that you just need a link to do so. However, getting the files online requires a few things—namely, hosting. If you're a student, your school may provide hosting free of charge. Otherwise, commercial hosting can be purchased for a nominal fee (a few dollars a month). You'll also need an FTP (file transfer protocol) application. Cyberduck is free and works with both Mac and PC. I'm not going to get into detail about how to transfer files via FTP (there are a lot of tutorials available), but it involves connecting to your host, copying from your local computer to your remote (online) folder, and testing it by typing the link in your browser. Keep all files (HTML, CSS, images) in a single folder; use an intuitive name to keep the link short, for example: mywebsite.com/web-poem.

GOALS AND OUTCOMES

A notable project will be visually adventurous with all text styled as CSS. It may be tempting to design some text with other software and export it as an image, but resist this. Being able to control the typography natively is one of the challenges of this assignment. The images that you chose to complement the poem should add visual impact. The finished product should stand up to any other design work in your portfolio. In the end, this exercise should allow you to experiment with basic markup and create something worth showing. Since it's just a single page with one layout width, it should be achievable in a few days instead of weeks.

Figure 5.28
This entry-level web design project is visually adventurous enough to show within a portfolio.

REFLECTION AND REVISION

Now that your files are online, test them in a few browsers to make sure there aren't drastic differences. Compare the final product to the mock-up you designed. Is it close to what you had imagined? Did you make any changes along the way that embraced the spirit or mood of the poem? That's great. Did you settle for something because you struggled with the code? If so, that's something to resolve while the project is fresh in your mind. If you need to troubleshoot, start with the most basic elements (body, container) and work your way down to more specific ones. Once any challenges are dealt with, compare this to your other design work. Does it visually complement the poem you chose? Is it dynamic enough? If not, dive back in and push the contrast a bit.

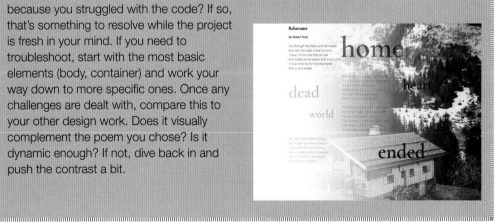

Figure 5.29
Words and images styled with CSS can set the visual backdrop for a poem's web page.

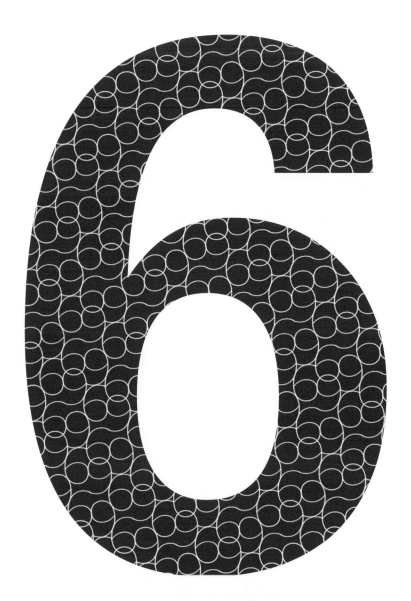

Emerging Technologies

Figure 6.1
A head-mounted display offers a completely immersive virtual reality experience.

The term extended reality has emerged during the last few years to represent the next frontier of digital design, as we move beyond screens. It represents virtual, augmented, and mixed reality environments, which range from extrasensory to completely immersive. It's first helpful to explain some commonalities and differences between the three environments.

Virtual reality (VR)

Think of the classic image of someone wearing a headset that shuts out the world around them—that's virtual reality. The concept has existed in the public eye since the early 1990s, when the nascent technology was rolled out on the heels of NASA research. Popular magazines of the era predicted that we'd all be decked out in VR gear by the end of that decade. The hype never materialized, but why? For one, it was quite expensive. Most headsets were at least US$2,000 at the time, and few home computers had the processing power to run the software. And for those who shelled out the cash and a fast machine, the quality of the experience was a big letdown. Blocky graphics and unreliable performance didn't match up to the slick marketing images. The equipment was relegated to the dusty closets of the few who bought it.

Fast forward to 2012. A start-up called Oculus successfully crowdfunded a campaign to build a new head-mounted-display (HMD). This would become the Oculus Rift, one of the first commercially released VR headsets in twenty years. It delivered better graphics, and the overall user experience was better—less glitchy. And the price? US$599. Still not an inexpensive piece of hardware but attainable for those who were interested. Larger companies, such as HTC and Samsung, followed suit and we've found

ourselves in the midst of a VR renaissance. Though VR has come a long way, it hasn't quite yet hit the tipping point. One of the missing factors is the human element. Despite the best efforts of science fiction, we're not ultimately looking to replace our reality but assist it. Recreating experiences in digital form is novel, and it's the reason that VR has done well in the gaming sector. Augmented and mixed reality are primed to help us weave emotion into the digital experiences and fill them with surprise and delight.

Augmented reality (AR)

If we're to be honest, another reason why VR has taken so long to catch on is because of the user isolation. Being locked in a virtual world is a dream come true for some but a bit scary for others. Augmented reality provides us with an option that shares the same spirit of VR but with the ability to stay in our own environment. In the last few years, sophisticated AR has allowed 3D images to be viewed in a way that makes for a very rich experience. Specifically, it means that the images are spatially oriented so that they seem to move with the real environment. Older technologies were more like a heads-up display. That's where a two-dimensional graphical overlay is slapped onto a background, but it moves with the viewing

frame instead of being anchored in the environment. The original Google Glass wearable optics were an example of this.

The first AR experiences were created in the early 2000s and started to be commercially viable by 2008. The timing was crucial because that's when smartphones finally started to become ubiquitous. Instead of a purpose-built headset, the screen can be leveraged from an existing device. Having a built-in camera is critical because it allows virtual images to be inserted on top of a live video feed. This is how the "augmented" part of AR works. The medium has taken off in recent years, with a variety of apps and tools being released. As phones and tablets have increased processor speeds, the quality has increasingly improved.

Eyewear capable of displaying augmented content does exist, and most display graphic overlays in the form of a heads-up display. These emerging glasses will first be used to offload screen content from devices into our field of vision, but they may become more interactive as the technology progresses.

Mixed reality (MR)

As the most recently developed area of the XR space, mixed reality has the most potential to deliver the picture that sci-fi has painted for us. If you've ever seen any Marvel films, you've seen the concept of immersive augmented reality or mixed reality. It was finally made real by Microsoft's HoloLens in 2016. There have been a few other devices that have been contenders, but this seems to be the last frontier for developing emerging tech in the field. Why is that? Because MR bridges the physical world with the virtual environment, combining the experience of virtual *and* augmented realities. Some VR headsets allow this through a live camera feed, meaning you're actually looking at the physical world through a camera. This is an attempt at extending what's already been developed for VR in an MR experience, and it works fairly well as a proof of concept. However, viewing the experience through a camera for extended periods of time doesn't do much to alleviate the motion sickness and fatigue often associated with VR. There's also the issue of bulkiness and discomfort; it's a lot of gear worn on and around the head. The mixed-reality consumer models are more like masks or goggles that allow you to see the world around you through your own eyes instead of a camera. These devices project a sort of dimensional hologram onto the lens or

Figure 6.2
Augmented reality takes advantage of the devices we already use to present digital content on screens.

Figure 6.3
Mixed-reality headsets present the best of augmented content in real-world space.

viewing surface. In doing so, they're capable of creating immersive 3D experiences seen through your own eyes. They also allow you to interact with digital objects in real space using hand gestures.

You probably know someone who uses several monitors for productivity. You might even be one of them. Some of the biggest predicted growth in MR is as a monitor replacement. Imagine a screen with your files, emails, apps, and images. Except it isn't a screen, it's your field of vision. This exists for VR technology right now, but the form factor has prevented wide adoption. Mixed-reality devices have been slow to come to the market, but the promise of increased productivity might be the thing to ultimately push them into the mainstream. These mediums are still being developed for case uses, with continued growth expected in the future. So how do you start designing for them?

Workflows

In other disciplines of digital design, the methods and tools for creating are fairly straightforward. The workflow includes sketches, paper prototypes, visual design, interaction prototypes, and end-use development. We've become really good at designing two-dimensional experiences for flat screens and devices. Most of the digital tools we currently use are made specifically for doing so. Designing for XR seems like the Wild West in comparison. Even something as simple as sketching becomes more difficult when we must consider perspective. What's the right approach when fledgling digital tools seem to appear every six months, and yet none of them seem like good solutions? It's important to realize that not that long ago, the mobile design landscape was much the same. There weren't two familiar iOS and Android ecosystems but dozens of platforms that looked and felt very different. Mobile design patterns hadn't been developed, and designers were throwing a lot of things at the wall to see what would stick.

Design vs. development

I should note that when talking about development for XR, this differs a bit from the simple markup that we discussed in the last chapter on web design. Development in this emerging space has so far relied on differing platforms like Unity, Unreal Engine, ARKit, and ARCore. Some of these have a graphical interface that allows designers to do some preliminary composition in the actual rendering engine. This can be valuable when you want to test the ability for basic interactions. For the most part, though, professional output in these mediums is developed by those with specific skills: scripting, textures and shading, and game physics. These particular skills rarely fall within a designer's purview. It's important to understand the fundamental possibilities of the various development platforms, but prototyping is best done with a workflow that a designer can more quickly iterate with. Some smoke and mirrors are necessary to present what's essentially 2D output into a 3D experience. Most of the prototyping that a digital designer can easily engage with *considers* space and dimension, while presenting the content in a way that's visually convincing but not totally interactive. Higher-fidelity methods designed in 3D engines allow for real interactivity but require more time and development skills.

UX considerations

Depth or lack of familiar controls is an important consideration when designing UX for extended reality. You must ask yourself: How does a user begin to engage with your experience? What kind of instruction (if any) will greet them upon donning a head-mounted display? Will they be guided to an initial on-boarding experience for first-time use? What about subsequent sessions? Or do you want a stripped-down environment that sparks inquiry and exploration?

The implications are much different than designing for the devices we're used to. In VR particularly, the user can't just "look away" and reconnect with the real world. Of course, they can for AR and MR experiences, but these are still much richer than the multitasking realities of the present. The designer has the power to create something that commands attention hard to come by in the twenty-first century. On the other side of the coin, it also means

that you can make a user dizzy with confusion if you aren't hyperaware of the decisions you make.

Some issues to address from the outset:

- Will the user be instructed on how to begin?
- What are the perceived and actual properties (affordances) of the environment? How complex or simplified is it?
- What controls are initially revealed?
- How quickly can the user jump in and interact with the experience? Can they pick up from a previous session if they have a spare fifteen minutes?
- What physical constraints need to be considered (i.e., range of motion, seated or standing position of user)?

Designing and prototyping for VR

Aspect ratio of composition

In thinking about the field of view for VR, a 360-degree photo is the best way to establish it. When viewed normally, these photos look like a funhouse mirror, but when viewed spherically, it's a fully immersive experience. There are specific

cameras that are made to capture 360-degree photos and video at high resolution, but there are also smartphone apps that do a good enough job for a prototype. Equirectangular images (say that three times) have a 2:1 aspect ratio, meaning the width is twice the height.

Figure 6.4
An equirectangular photo forms a virtual background when wrapped in a spherical 3D environment.

Rather than looking at them straight on, it makes more sense if you print out the photo and join the two ends in a circle. Now, you can get a sense of the environment around you.

UI and environment

There's a range of possible environments for VR applications, from complex ones where new objects can be created and manipulated, to simulators where you're viewing a predetermined experience. The layout and design of the environment is important because it's the first thing a viewer sees when they put on a headset. Many experiences feature a 360-degree photo or computer-generated landscape. This background is known as a "skybox" in VR parlance. The complexity of the skybox needs to be reconciled with the user interface. For instance, a complex interface will clash with an environment that's too detailed. At the opposite end of the spectrum, the user might get bored with a sparse environment if the controls are minimal. This isn't as important in augmented or mixed reality because the user can also view the real world around them. In VR, though, it's important for users to feel grounded on a solid plane, with a scale that feels similar to real life. Imagine an interface floating hundreds of feet in the air above a skyline. That situation could not only be distracting, but might cause real anxiety in many users.

Viewing hierarchy

A user is likely to first look towards the center and slightly down with respect to the field of view. That's where our natural gaze sits. The horizontal periphery is next, followed by the ground and sky. Whether or not you'll want to put an interface directly in front of the user depends on the context. For a home screen or hub, a menu might make sense there. For experiences that are deeper—where something is being manipulated—the controls are better situated at waist level. Also, left-to-right motion seems easiest while standing, and looking up and down is more comfortable while seated.

Input UI for VR

We've gotten efficient at using a mouse, trackpad, or fingers to manipulate various devices. Many people can text with two thumbs almost as fast as they can type. This extends easily to the AR realm, because we're still using fingers as a way to interact on a smartphone or tablet. But our collective dexterity is still basic when it comes to inputs for VR. Sci-fi films make it seem natural, but hand-tracking gestures are still not widely understood by most and must be learned to be effective. Best practices of spatial UI are being written as we experiment with them, but the most reliable inputs a designer can currently rely on are these:

Gaze

This involves looking intently at an interface or button. Since there's no cursor, there needs to be a signal that the thing you're looking at has been activated. A hover effect (color or depth change, etc.) seems to be the best way to indicate that. Gaze can be used in combination with a controller button as well (i.e., look at button in VR, see hover effect, press button on external controller).

Pointer

This method uses the controller in much the same way as we currently use a mouse or trackpad. A beam is often used to help visualize what's being pointed at. This allows for a bit more precision where needed. Note that for VR applications, a rendered controller appears in space for this to work.

Figure 6.5
A controller offers direct manipulation of VR objects, but it requires some user confidence to master.

Direct interaction

Moving, rotating, and scaling objects in 3D space is best done through some sort of gesture with a controller. This means pressing a button in combination with moving the controller directionally. Handheld controllers are taxing to use for extended periods (especially when two are involved), so this should be a consideration. Learnability is also a factor in using controller buttons.

Hand tracking

All signs point to the eventual adoption of hand tracking as the holy grail of inputs in the long-term. The technology has become reliable, but *occlusions* caused by the user's own hands throw a wrench in the mix. This happens when one finger is obscuring another from a certain angle. And like I mentioned, complex gestures must be collectively learned in order for mass adoption.

Backgrounds, color palettes, and fatigue

Classic design principles have taught us to use contrast and complimentary color schemes to create hierarchy. This works well in flat design, where the negative space is just that. In VR, the skybox might be expressed as a photo or picturesque rendering. This is much more vivid and saturated than most of the backgrounds we're used to seeing in digital experiences. This is no doubt one of the factors

contributing to the fatigue that people often associate with VR experiences. You may find that to avoid these kinds of symptoms (especially for lengthy periods of time), you'll need to slightly mute UI components, calls-to-action, etc. Of course, dimming or slightly blurring the background is an option as well. The context of the experience you're designing for will dictate whether you can do this: it's less effective if a user is standing and expected to physically move around in a space.

Text in VR

The resolution of text in current head-mounted displays affects the legibility of text in XR. They're not quite on par with the pixel density of the devices we've become accustomed to. Aliasing (the jagged appearance of curved or diagonal lines) becomes more pronounced in HMDs, making certain typefaces tricky to use. These are the same issues we once faced with type in early web design. Here are some basic considerations when designing type for VR:

- Avoid text with delicate serifs. Bodoni and Didot look great in print, and they've looked good on most devices over the last few years. But until the fidelity for headsets increases across the board, they're not ready for prime time in VR. Using a typeface that was designed for digital use (such as Open Sans) is a good start.
- Scaling large blocks of text may temporarily solve legibility problems, until you realize it's obscuring the field of view. Line length (the width of a column of text) decreased with the shift from print to computers, and from computers to devices. This compounds even more for VR: limit line lengths in the field of view to around thirty characters to avoid additional fatigue.

Figure 6.6
Text in VR can be an issue when distance from the user and angles are taken into account.

- Measurements that we're used to (points, pixels, ems) don't immediately translate to VR, because they don't account for angles and distance. Google created an angular unit of measurement to represent one millimeter viewed from one meter away. They call it a "distance independent millimeter," or DMM. It's a bit of a stretch to immediately understand, so here's a general rule of thumb when designing with measurements we're already familiar with: 20px is a comfortable minimum text size at 1 meter (just over 3 feet) away. This, of course, needs to increase if text content is placed further away from the viewer.

Using sound

Sound is a tricky topic when we're talking about digital design. People expect to hear sounds in a captive experience, such as watching a video, but get annoyed if an app or website makes sounds. You're mentally prepared for the former and surprised by the latter. Immersive experiences break those preconceived expectations for now—you're not going to annoy anyone at a coffee shop. Planning for audio to help with some content delivery can free some of our dependence on text in VR. The additional benefit is that you can lessen any scaling or legibility issues, or cluttering the field of view. Spatial sound can also be used to cue a user or give them a sense of presence, since it's in stereo. For instance, you can use an alert sound that's spatially tuned if you want to call attention to a secondary menu or dialog that's behind the user in VR space. This will cause them to instinctively turn their head to follow the sound.

Putting it into practice

Sketching in 360 degrees

I've waxed on about the benefits of sketching and paper prototyping for the other disciplines mentioned thus far, but it takes a bit of imagination to extend that into the 3D space. A spherical perspective grid is very useful in viewing the sketched prototype with a head-mounted display.

There are a few downloadable grids that designers experimenting in XR have developed. Designer Vova Kurbatov has produced some of the easiest to understand, in my opinion. It's a bit odd to see it at first: you'll see familiar vertical grid lines, each one measuring 10 degrees of the left-to-right view. You'll also see horizontal lines

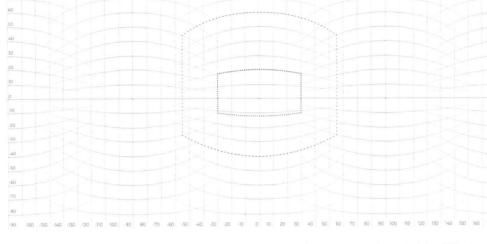

Figure 6.7
An equirectangular
grid takes some
getting used to,
but it allows
you to sketch in
VR space.

that curve both up and down as they move away from the center. They each represent 10 degrees of the up-and-down view. The places where these curved lines converge create a set of cylindrical shapes. Those shapes represent what we then see directly in front of us at the center of the grid, to the left and right sides, and—to the extreme left and right—behind us.

Drawing curved sketches on this grid takes a few minutes to get used to, but the benefit of doing so is the fact that you can snap a photo and view them in VR. Using a

smartphone app and a primitive VR viewer like Google Cardboard is a perfect companion to the lo-fi spirit of the sketch. At about 80 degrees of view, it will feel like you're looking through goggles. The experience isn't quite up to par with higher-end headsets, but it's easy to quickly share because it's portable and inexpensive.

It's best to start simple: create a few basic menus floating in the center of the grid and view it quickly to get a feel for it. Then try drawing interfaces or objects on the left and right panels, or behind you.

HACK

A trick that will help you understand this warped grid more quickly is to do an internet search for an equirectangular photo. Print out the photo at the same 2:1 cropped size as your curved grid, and then simply trace over the contour shapes of the photo. Viewing the result in a 360-degree app will give you some immediate satisfaction and inspire you to continue sketching on your own.

Content areas

Remember those sketches where you drew a menu behind you? They're fun to experiment with, and it is important to work through the initial excitement of knowing they're possible. Ultimately, though, it's good to apply some UI principles to practice. Starting at the center line again, objects in our extreme periphery sit at –90 degrees on the left and 90 degrees on the right side. It's possible to feature content here, but it shouldn't be something a user would need to constantly interact with. Reserve the far sides for lesser used or tertiary content that can support the main interface. The area past 105 degrees in either direction is actually the area behind you (again, think of wrapping the grid in a circle, end to end). It's what VR pioneer Mike Alger calls the "curiosity zone," and it's an interesting opportunity with which to surprise or delight the user. Again, nothing that depends on functionality should live here. The content height is also important; about 60 degrees up and 40 degrees down from the center is the most we can expect a user to comfortably look.

Figure 6.8
The viewer's immediate periphery is a consideration for VR user interfaces, but the 360-degree sphere is also a possibility.

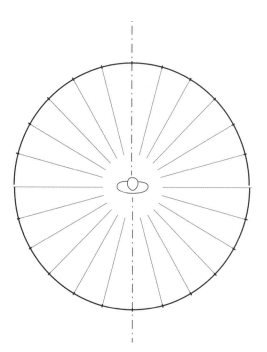

Body ergonomics

Whenever we learn something new, we tend to overdo it. Diets, exercise, a new hobby ... we've all done it. So, after sketching your first drafts of a fully wrapped 3D experience, it's time to rein it in a bit. Physically, you could look all around in a full circle. Practically, this isn't possible for very long. Body ergonomics—what's comfortable for a period—dictate some constraints on where objects should be in space. Determining the position of the user is important in designing the VR space around them. For instance, are they sitting or standing? If you've had a chance to try out a headset, chances are you were standing. However, it's obvious that a seated position is more comfortable for longer stretches. UX constraints will likely dictate how long the typical experience lasts (what kind of tasks, level of complexity, etc.) and whether a seated or standing position is preferred. For immersive experiences that capture the dynamic ability of VR, standing in a virtual room with content surrounding you is quite engaging. It's physically easier to look in your periphery while standing—you can twist your body a bit to accommodate.

For applications that focus on productivity or creativity, a seated position might more realistically dictate UI placement. Our first sketches might show interfaces at eye level, but it becomes clear that they aren't sustainable for long periods of time. Imagine trying to work a typical eight-hour day by manipulating content with your hands straight out in front of you. We know that people inherently look slightly down while at rest, and our current tools are already in that zone. While seated, our mouse, trackpad, and keyboard are there. But even while standing and using a device, we tend to keep them at chest level. Do some people-watching and notice very few people are holding smartphones up at eye level. So, logic would dictate that users would be most comfortable with primary tools at about 30 to 40 degrees below center.

Vertical head movement is slightly easier while seated and looking up is sometimes associated with curiosity. Think about when you're brainstorming or trying to recall something: many people look to the sky. Knowing that, content above 20 degrees up from eye level has an opportunity to engage with people in a more whimsical way. A user could literally "look up for inspiration" to view their upcoming weekend plans or recent photos. Anything past 60 degrees becomes awkward, though; we almost never look straight up for more than a few seconds.

Field of view and periphery

Expert opinions in the field vary on this, but it's mostly agreed that an area of continual focus is about 30 degrees in either direction. Simply find the center line of the grid and count three lines left and right of that. Make a mark in either direction. Count two lines vertically up from the center, and two lines down from it. That's your prime-time viewing area, where it's easy to naturally focus. Now, count two-and-a-half lines beyond either horizontal mark and make two more. That's 55 degrees in either direction. Recalling that 40 degrees down and 60 degrees up start to push our vertical limits, we can draw a rectangle based on these measurements to establish the maximum field of view. It's the furthest that it's comfortable to view and interact with in a sustained way. I say rectangle loosely here, because of the curved grid.

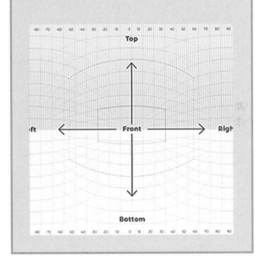

Figure 6.9
Establishing the field of view is helpful in making sense of the 360-degree grid.

Distance and depth

Thinking about measurements on the Z-axis isn't something most digital designers are used to. Even for typical motion graphics, the Z-depth is implied. Unless you've had some exposure to the physical (industrial, architectural, or interior) design disciplines, it's not likely you've had a need for true 3D modeling. So, it's somewhat comforting to know that our first prototypes for VR also use implied 3D. Essentially, we're wrapping a long image in a circle and putting the user in the center of it. Interfaces can have real dimension in VR, and we can leverage that concept with a bit of imagination. When designing flat content to be viewed stereoscopically, we can add perceived depth using familiar graphic design principles. Scale is an obvious way to demonstrate distance. Objects nearer to us appear larger and crisper. Those in the distance are smaller, lighter, and perhaps a bit softer. A short drop-shadow can make a button "float" in front of a larger group of elements. Transparency also creates a sense of depth, so being able to see overlapping components helps sell the trick. Initial concepts can be quickly put together with these methods. There are four distance zones to consider for VR content:

- The "immediate space" around the user is within 1 meter. The personal bubble should be carefully considered so as to not cause claustrophobia or VR-induced fatigue. In his text *Designing for Mixed Reality*, Kharis O'Connell (2016) describes the distance of 50–70cm as the "interaction plane." This is where common UI controls are most easily manipulated because it doesn't require us to physically move. Again, this will likely be near waist level, because of ergonomics. Stay away from anything closer than a half-meter because the eye strain is immediately uncomfortable.
- The "principal space" beyond that is between 1 and 10 meters. Three-dimensional opportunities are great in this area, because our "binocular disparity" is stronger. This has to do with the distance between our eyes creating different angles, thus creating a sense of depth. That depth is very pronounced here; experimenting with layered menus or content that could be toggled could be interesting since the visual payoff is impressive. This is the primary area for content: not crowding our personal space, but close enough to easily see and read. The ability to toggle primary content in and out of

this zone is also an interesting thought—like a virtual counterpart of minimizing and maximizing windows on our laptops. A user could pull content into this zone, closely interact with it, and then push it back out for easy access later. Gaze or pointer interaction is appropriate here.

- The "secondary space" is between 10 and 20 meters. The 3D option is possible in this space, though it rolls off steadily at the outer limits. The parallax effect is still convincing enough to create a sense of depth at this distance. Since gaze or pointer-based input becomes less reliable, this is an ideal distance for content that doesn't require direct interaction.
- The "distant space" represents anything past twenty meters, and content is essentially rendered flat in perspective. It does add to the overall atmospheric depth of the scene, though, so consider lightening and blurring any elements at that distance. Text is illegible here, as is anything that a user would need to focus on.

UI density

Organizing content around the fixed size of a display is one of the first steps in considering a user interface. We've become really good at progressive enhancement: optimizing for mobile screens and being more liberal with larger ones. But what happens when the screen disappears, and content is all around us? For one, the UI density needs to be reconsidered. Designers need to decide how interfaces will be treated in space. What kind of UI controls will be revealed, and where will users have to look to use them? Will they be fixed in the environment, or locked in the user's field of view like a heads-up display? Since there's so much more space available, the temptation is to show more available controls. I encourage you to try this once and test it in a cardboard viewer. The claustrophobia will likely be palpable and accompanied by the desire for negative space. The field of view is important to respect, but you also don't want to crowd the areas around it like the cockpit of a plane. The gestures available to you from controllers, hands, or eye gaze create opportunities to show and hide additional menus. And remember, the interface needs to be learnable, so consider current UX expectations and affordance when designing it. As technology improves and VR becomes more ubiquitous, new ways of interacting will become more accepted.

Panel shapes

Our first experiments with sketching on the grid can yield some interesting insight. If you follow the curved lines of the 360-degree grid, you'll end up with flat-faced elements. Some of the first UI panels we might envision will likely be flat since that's what we're used to. A flat panel is best used for content that's nearer to the user. An example would be a to-do list or virtual notepad that can be quickly toggled in order to add to it—something within reach. Several existing applications feature a palette that allows a user to choose paint colors to apply to dimensional drawings. The shortcomings are apparent for wider applications, though: it's tough to read text while in perspective. Flat panels in an accordion layout are the logical progression to this, and they solve some of the legibility

issues. They're also similar to the way we currently arrange multiple displays. So, those interested in VR from a work-productivity perspective might skew toward this layout. If you draw straight lines on the 360-degree grid, they become curved stereoscopic panels. Curved panels present the content around the user, which takes advantage of the environment. It's important to carefully consider the skybox (background) when using curved panels. What's behind them? Is the contrast too strong? A flat panel can easily be placed against a wall in a 360-degree photo environment, but a curved panel becomes more obvious. Again, this isn't a suggestion to "fill up the space" in the circle around the user.

Navigating spaces

Depending on the type of experience, the user might be seated or standing, stationary or moving around. In a classic workspace scenario, a designer must think about the immediate environment. The near and middle distance become interactive zones, and the background becomes just that. But for situations where the user is expected to navigate a virtual space, it gets a bit more complicated. Unless a user is standing in a very large room, they might not be able to walk very far. Many VR devices require a user to define the physical boundaries of a space. Placing the user in a virtual theater is now a classic way of allowing for limited

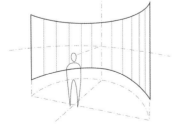 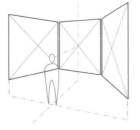 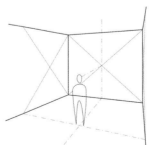

Figure 6.10
Different panel sizes can be displayed in various configurations around the user in virtual space.

Figure 6.11
Popular digital design software can be hacked to design for VR space with some basic calculations.

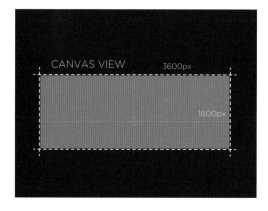

physical navigation with respect to constraints. Allowing people to "teleport" throughout an experience using virtual markers has been a way to solve the distance issue. Thinking about how different spaces will look and feel as part of a larger one is essential in ensuring a fluid user experience. Essentially, designing several compositions that are connected through interaction is the method used to create a much larger one.

Digital prototypes

After you've spent some time sketching your ideas and viewing them spatially, you'll want to test a digital version. Use whatever application you feel most comfortable with. Full resolution equirectangular images for current VR applications range in size, to roughly 7200 × 3600px at full resolution. We can halve that for the sake of speed and file size, giving us a composition of 3600 × 1800px to work with. It's still a large canvas size given most digital design dimensions, but it's certainly more manageable. Our skybox background will live in this space, and it may be photographic in quality or more abstract, depending on the context. We need to consider the field of view and periphery next. A 1200 × 600px layer or artboard represents about a third of the overall 360-degree view and allows you to

create some content in the field of view and periphery. This should be centered within the larger composition, and you can use a bit of transparency (10–20 percent) for some added dimensional effect.

Previewing these digital designs in a cardboard viewer or head-mounted display is the next step. With a wider overall view (about 110 degrees), it will feel more comfortable. Export the overall composition as a PNG file (to allow for the transparency), and open the image in a 360-degree app such as GoPro VR Player. If you have a headset connected, you should be able to view it directly from the application. Put on the headset and look around your scene, testing where you've placed content.

Figure 6.12
The UI view can be established from the overall canvas size.

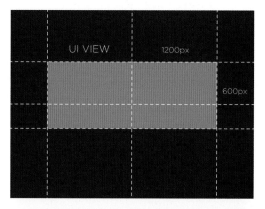

Figure 6.13
Using transparency and offset positioning can have a spatial layering effect when viewed in VR space.

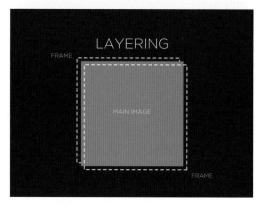

Prototyping with interactions

At this stage, you're viewing the content from a fixed position in the center of the equirectangular photo. Dynamic interaction isn't possible through this kind of prototype, but several tools have the ability to connect different compositions together through visual hotspots. Essentially, by staring at a UI element that has been designated as a link, you use a gaze control to "click through" to the next composition. It's intuitive and serves to link several scenes together as part of a larger experience. Some back-and-forth with revisions at this stage can save a lot of time during development, so the ability to create with basic 2D-design tools is a game-changer. Adobe XD utilizes a plug-in called DraftXR that lets you preview in WebVR on a smartphone or even a headset. Many other software developers are actively trying to reconcile the lack of resources available to designers who are trying to break into VR but lack development skills. As the medium approaches a tipping point, there will no doubt be additional tools that bridge the gap between development and proof of concept.

Prototyping with animation

Sometimes it's necessary to show a version that features the fidelity of the digital prototypes but also shows the dynamic interaction that they're lacking. After Effects is a useful tool for this because some basic 3D work is possible with it. If you require vertex-based "true-3D" rendering, that's best achieved with Cinema 4D. Luckily, the two programs integrate quite well in creating hi-fi mock-ups that can show interaction animation. It's possible to view these in both 2D and 3D, which After Effects has afforded in the past few years. When would you need this animated prototype as an option? When the stakes are high enough, and the investment of time and money become clear. A 2D rendering showing interaction is great to show clients or stakeholders who are remote, or don't have direct access to a headset. Of course, showing them something closer to the real thing with an HMD can be much more convincing. I should add that this process itself can become time-consuming. At the end of the day, you might ask yourself, "How many steps and mock-ups must I create before I can build the real thing?" Remember, the goal is to reduce time in development where you'll likely have to outsource labor. Consider that your barometer when deciding how far to prototype.

3D design and development

For a designer, prototyping in 3D space can be a valuable skill to add to your digital repertoire. It's a major step in the workflow, which includes all UX implications beforehand, and the development process afterwards. The visuals in the digital prototyping stage are impressive to view stereoscopically, but this is the first time a client or stakeholder can really experience what the finished product might look and feel like. Being able to move and interact with the content in real space just isn't matched by anything else. There are a few options to consider when choosing how to prototype in 3D:

A-Frame
A-Frame VR for the Web might be a good starting point for those already comfortable with HTML. It's progressed steadily and is nearly as fast as stand-alone VR applications. The other major benefit is that there's nothing to install because it runs on a browser. You can literally start by creating an HTML file. It's cross platform and supports most headsets, both basic and high-end.

Unity

This is now the most widely adopted platform for VR development. It's free, uses C# scripting, and features an intuitive interface. The best part: there's no initial cost. There are fees associated with its advanced tiers (you won't need them) and an online asset store where you can purchase pre-made components. There, 3D designers sell everything from rendered skyboxes to detailed interior furniture. There are also free components to use if you search thoroughly. I've found that most of the components are useful for those in the gaming industry, and less so for digital designers. They're still quite helpful in learning the basics of the program.

Unreal Engine

This is the other major VR platform worth mentioning. I'll say straight away that it's more complicated as a development tool. This is mostly because it relies on C++, a more difficult object-oriented language to grasp. The community knowledge around the platform is also much smaller than that of Unity, so there are less publicly available resources. Unreal is also free; they make money on a similar asset store and royalties on professional applications created with it. Where it shines is in its high-end graphics rendering. The scripting curve with Unreal is not really a viable option for those who are hoping to jump in and experiment, though.

HACK

Unity looks very different to any design software you're used to. Search for the phrase "learn Unity in one hour" for options that cut through the noise to get started right away. Though complex actions—like teleporting from one scene to another—require scripting knowledge, designers can jump in through a method called "grayboxing." It's become a common practice, first made popular by VR designer Alex Chu. Think about it as "wireframing in VR." You start by dropping in generic elements (which are gray) in blank composition to see how big it looks, and how easy it might be to interact with. It's a low-stakes way of feeling how things like distance and proximity work in native VR, and it doesn't require that you learn scripting or befriend a developer. Search for "ProBuilder" in the Unity Asset Store to get a free plug-in that allows you to easily start building.

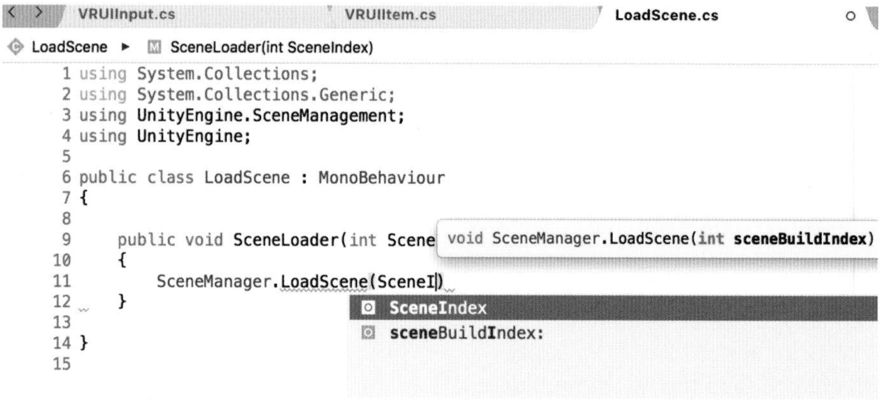

Figure 6.14 Some programming is necessary to do more than the most basic of testing in Unity.

```
       VRUIInput.cs              VRUIItem.cs              LoadScene.cs

   LoadScene  ▸    SceneLoader(int SceneIndex)

   1  using System.Collections;
   2  using System.Collections.Generic;
   3  using UnityEngine.SceneManagement;
   4  using UnityEngine;
   5
   6  public class LoadScene : MonoBehaviour
   7  {
   8
   9      public void SceneLoader(int Scene    void SceneManager.LoadScene(int sceneBuildIndex)
  10      {
  11          SceneManager.LoadScene(SceneI)
  12      }                                    SceneIndex
  13                                           sceneBuildIndex:
  14  }
  15
```

Takeaways

The design process for VR becomes much more straightforward after we've unpacked some of the technical requirements. The dimensionality adds another layer of consideration, but it's quite doable for most designers. What you need to remember is that UX is just as (if not more) important, and UI can be presented in a variety of ways. Design should start with pencil on paper, progress to digital methods, and only move to development software when and where appropriate. For a portfolio piece, I would recommend stopping short of development, because the entry-level aesthetics will likely fall short when compared to your other work.

Designing and prototyping for AR

Defining differences

Augmented reality is distinct from VR by the fact that it merges the real world with a digital one. The immersion is less extreme, and the bar to entry is a bit lower in many ways. AR doesn't utilize headsets but is able to leverage the devices we already use daily: smartphones and tablets. Tourism and retail are consumer-facing industries that have already taken advantage of this medium. In my opinion, "non-gaming" AR apps are crucial to furthered growth, and we're seeing those offerings increase steadily.

A complicated canvas

We were able to demystify and define a canvas size to start working with VR. So, what about the same for AR? Well, it's a bit open-ended, because it depends on the context. For instance, some AR apps are based on geolocation. Users can even influence where AR objects are based in that example, so the "canvas" is infinite. On the flip side, a popular way to use AR is through a "marker," an image that activates the augmented content when scanned via a device camera. Here, the canvas could be as small as a few feet. Because you're not limited to an external environment, the possibilities are more flexible in AR. Moving beyond a rectangle and thinking about the experience as a scene rather than a screen is essential to utilizing the medium. Using the method of designing connected spaces in VR can be extended here as well. You might consider mapping several rooms in a building and folding AR content into those spaces. Mocking up how content responds in each room as separate compositions becomes a way to think about starting.

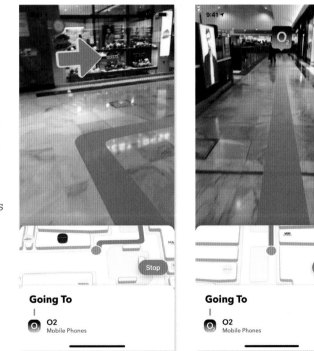

Figure 6.15
Non-gaming applications are essential for furthering the pace of augmented-reality experiences.

UI interaction in AR

Because augmented reality is restricted to rectangular views, the added complications associated with VR (like field of view and periphery) are somewhat negated by the fact that content is framed by a device. There are four basic ways to feature content and interactions in AR:

Static, fixed to screen

This represents the traditional heads-up display that was popular in first-generation AR wearables such as Google Glass. This is the go-to solution for content that needs to be easily available to users. This is known as "persistent UI" because it stays in view. Information and data are most likely to live here, with menus accessed in more intentional ways.

Static, fixed in space

Content viewed in AR is most commonly presented in this way. It allows the user to shift the frame (their device) to view it from different positions and angles. Most content that's triggered with an AR marker is shown this way, as it allows you to easily explore the dimension of the content. The Actu Paris project by French designer Laura Normand plays on this idea. The posters themselves are minimalist, featuring abstract geometric shapes and color. Once activated in AR, volumetric shapes spring from the flat layout and informational text appears. This is well suited for content that needs to be tightly controlled and presented in a specific manner.

Figure 6.16
Augmented elements fixed in 3D space offer users the ability to explore the environment with a device.

Figure 6.17
Using 2D printed matter as a base layer can provide interesting results when paired with augmented content.

HACK

Any 2D objects fixed in 3D space might be difficult to see or read (text, for example) at different angles, so a crafty method is to "swivel" them towards the user. This is known as "billboarding" in AR jargon.

Dynamic and movable

Many AR apps feature content that can be interacted with in a dynamic way: creation, deletion, and manipulation. For example, the IKEA Place app evokes its namesake by allowing users to envision what furniture would look like in their homes. The products are shown as 3D assets in augmented space and can be moved around in X, Y, and Z space, rotated, and dropped in place. Experiences that leverage this level of interactivity fully embrace what's possible in AR, because the outcomes are open ended. Rather than viewing an experience as a designer has predetermined, the user is directing the flow. Of course, it also gives the user the ability to present content in a way that might not be intended or desired. It requires giving up a certain level of control that might be at odds with a piece of prescriptive design. Apps that are intended as tools fall naturally into this category.

Occlusion

One of the most difficult issues to solve with AR is occlusion, which deals with rendering virtual objects behind real ones in the viewer's eyes. This helps define depth in an augmented space—without it, the 3D object would just appear pasted in the foreground. As technology has evolved, so have the effects of realistic immersion within AR. In situations where virtual 3D objects are fixed in space for the user to simply view, this is less important. However, for more complex scenes where integration with real-world objects is key, occlusion is necessary for a believable experience. Some AR experiences aren't as convincing because virtual objects are always placed in the foreground, regardless of their intended depth in Z-space. Advances in this technology have been game-changing for the medium. Apple's ARKit, for example, introduced "people occlusion" as the software matured. This allows for pushing content recognized as a person by the camera into the midground, with augmented elements in front of it. This was a significant step, and most high-level AR experiences followed suit.

Transparency and content

Content with transparency is important for some AR applications, especially if it's to be layered in an environment. Navigation apps also utilize some transparency to not block the viewer's path. This becomes even more important as augmented reality makes the leap from devices to things such as car windows. A heads-up display needs to be useful without hindering sight.

HACK

Regarding transparency, somewhere around 80 percent opacity is the magic number. Content is easily seen while still giving an idea of what's behind it. The ability to see overlaid content in a transparent way opens up opportunities for storytelling. Showing "what could be" over an existing background or scene is a clever way to do so.

Prototyping on paper

Much like the 360-degree grid for VR, several sketch sheets exist for AR. Designer Sarah Tan's is one of the easiest to understand. It's an augmented reality ideation template that captures ideas and sketches for two states: how the experience is launched through the device camera, and how content and interaction happen afterwards. Many AR apps need an image trigger or room scan to launch, so it allows you to envision that first important step. How the content can be interacted with is also important. Can it be moved or rotated? Does any screen-based UI activate or change the content? Clarifying ideas (i.e., whether there's animation or sound) at the start can save a lot of time. This template also nicely addresses those questions. Vova Kurbatov also has a minimalist two-point perspective grid that's worth looking at for drawing out more detailed sketches. You can decide where to place the horizontal plane, and quickly get started from there.

Figure 6.18
Sarah Tan's augmented-reality ideation template is perfect for conceptualizing and visualizing an experience.

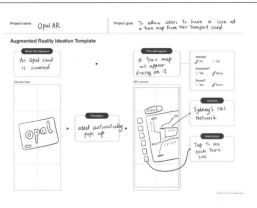

Figure 6.19
Imagining creative uses of AR technology is what makes the medium so exciting for designers.

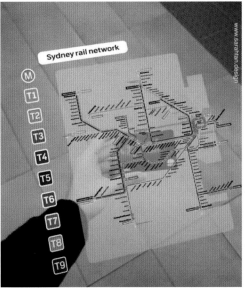

scene with an iPhone, and the ruler could be rotated horizontally so the content was always facing the user. Issues such as distance, scale, and legibility are easily tested in minutes via this method. Even more, these designers were able to prototype higher-fidelity versions by filming the scene and animating the button in Keynote, of all applications. How did it work? Quite well. It's an important lesson for us to learn as designers because we tend to use complicated tools early and often. These are often a time suck, and we end up changing everything anyway. It takes some imagination to use crude tools in an unorthodox way, but it's all in the service of time.

> **HACK**
>
> There are a few "mid-fi" animation tools—such as Principle—that have pre-built movements and transitions. They're less clunky than the methods described above but require far less time than something like After Effects.

Hybrid methods

The built-in device camera is an overlooked asset for prototyping. After all, it's the same angle and focal length that a user will see the experience through. At an AR conference, designers at Apple described using paper cutouts, clear rulers, and tape to mock up an AR proof of concept. It's funny but also brilliant. They simply designed AR content inside 2D buttons, printed them out in color, and cut them out with scissors. These "buttons" were placed in a scene by mounting them to a clear ruler and having someone hold it from above. A second person could film the

Digital prototyping

There are several AR prototyping tools designed to mock up realistic experiences without having to code. I'm reticent to even name them, because several companies have tried—and failed—to find traction in this space in the last few years. Adobe Aero seems to be one that's robust enough to stick around. It features the ability to design and build in a computer-based application and test the AR in a mobile one. It's an ideal setup because you're using each environment in the way it serves best.

Using Augmented Reality (AR) in Legal Contracts

Hi-fi mock-ups with animation

After Effects is well suited to design lush, animated previews of augmented experiences. Its tracking and 3D capabilities are complex enough to handle the task but easy enough to understand if you're familiar with the program. The built-in camera tracker analyzes motion in the source video and lets you add 3D components that are associated with a point in motion. This lets you mock up content that's fixed in space, and it looks quite convincing. You can also create content that's fixed to the composition, like a heads-up display. Simply create new layers above the video and animate from there.

Figure 6.20
One novel use of augmented content is to shed light on complex tasks such as legal contracts.

HACK

After setting a 3D Camera Tracker in After Effects, make a selection of motion-tracked points and control-click to define the ground plane and origin (the 0,0,0 point in X,Y,Z space). All subsequent 3D objects will then be oriented relative to this plane. My students use this method to prototype AR graphics, and the results are often portfolio worthy. Plus, it's a lot easier to share work that's created this way because the output is in the form of a traditional video. People don't need to use devices to see the AR output, which might be the difference in getting your work seen. This is *the* way to go if you want a polished look that's easy to view and share but don't want to deal with actual development (and coding).

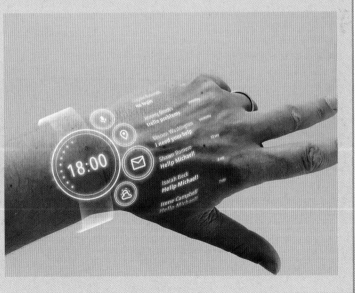

Figure 6.21
This is the future we were all promised by sci-fi films, and hacking After Effects can help us imagine it.

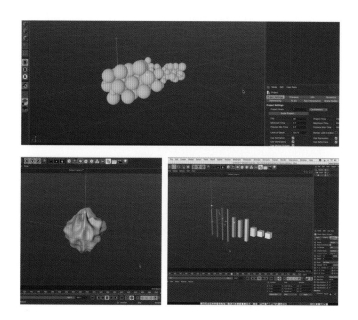

Figure 6.22
Cinema 4D allows the creation of "real" 3D content, which can then be imported into AR projects.

AR for art

There are several platforms that allow for AR experiences to be triggered using the marker image discussed earlier. Artivive is the most widely used, and uses a computer-based content creation tool in conjunction with a mobile viewer app. It's quite easy to use and there are free options available to students. It can also show both static and animated output. For those looking to experience some low-stakes AR design that's paired to a two-dimensional companion piece, this is a fun option.

Development

As with VR, final development needs to happen in an environment suitable for platform-ready export. It's worth knowing a bit about the various development workflows capable of creating final assets. While development in other disciplines has been streamlined and democratized—designers can easily create and publish a website—the AR development sphere is still highly specialized. The professional-level tools are outside the skill set of most digital designers. My advice is to learn enough to know the differences between these workflows, but lean on a developer when the time comes to build it for public use.

True 3D animation

The most difficult kind of content to create in After Effects is dynamic 3D content. Because of the lack of a true node-based engine, objects are 2D in 3D-rendered space. You can extrude basic shapes and type to be more convincing, but anything beyond that requires the help of a true modeling application like Cinema 4D. The other issue is showing the interaction: a finger or hand would need to be green-screened or rotoscoped and placed over virtual content to look realistic. My suggestion: you'll know when, and if, you have to extend mock-ups to this level. The time needed is worth considering, but if the stakes are high enough, go for it.

Figure 6.23
Professionally developed AR apps are the icing on the cake, but they require deep resources to launch.

AUGMENTED REALITY DEVELOPMENT TOOLS

ARKit
A suite of tools first launched by Apple comprises the ARKit package. Built with Swift and xCode programming languages, it leverages the iOS device's camera, processors, and sensors to allow for augmented reality interaction. As mentioned, the latest version allows for some substantial breakthroughs such as the occlusion of 3D objects. This is a code-based workflow that requires significant development skills. However, it does interface directly with Reality Composer, an Apple offering with a graphic interface. It's like a visual sandbox for ARKit, and allows those with no experience in 3D to experiment with a pre-built library of components.

ARCore
Google's Competitor to ARKit has many of the same capabilities. Motion tracking, environmental intelligence, and lighting are all part of the software's features. It's better at mapping large areas than ARKit but not at occlusion. Otherwise, we might consider it a tie in terms of features and rendering.

Unity
Most of the caveats (and possibilities) of designing for VR in Unity also apply to AR, so I won't repeat everything I've already outlined. However, it's worth mentioning that their AR framework bundles features from both ARKit and ARCore in a single workflow. That could save time versus developing separately for each platform. Another time-saving advantage of Unity is a drag-and-drop component library for object interactions and gestures. For designers not put off by development, this could be a defining factor in which method to choose.

Unreal Engine
As with Unity, Unreal features a framework that unifies iOS and Android platforms into a single pathway. An AR project template features an example project that highlights the possibilities of the platform.

Web AR
Since many AR experiences require a mobile app, there are sticking points in getting users to install a purpose-specific app. WebXR is a big step toward native web-based AR for everyone, and a huge leap for the medium. Initiating an experience from a web page is a huge win for the medium going forward.

Mixed reality: prototyping for the final frontier

Towards an evolution

Though they've been the slowest to mature to a commercial market, mixed-reality headsets showcase the true possibilities of the XR disciplines. Right now, they're still cumbersome, expensive, and haven't quite lived up to their potential. But as various companies race to build more powerful and affordable versions, they're no doubt going to command a lot of attention. Up to the current point, games and industrial applications have largely driven the growth of XR. Productivity and utility will be the factors that eventually push it over the edge. Being able to negotiate immersive experiences while still being "in the real world" is a strong pull and will be a milestone once it reaches the masses.

Interaction in MR

Most of what's possible with mixed reality is a combination of the best that VR and AR offer. But there are some notable additions, mostly because hand gestures are a big part of MR. The ability to see and use your hands (instead of rendered hands like in VR) is valuable, and decoupling interactions from a controller is the first step in making things more natural and accessible. Some common MR gestures within the field of view include:

Air tapping: such as pressing a mouse button or touching a device screen.

Tap and hold: such as a long press on a mobile device.

Open manipulation: a freeform method of moving spatial content within an experience.

Open/closed hand: selecting an object or content and manipulating it.

OK sign/thumbs up: confirming an action or sequence.

Open/closed pinch: selection and fine manipulation of a specific object or an object within a group.

Open/relaxed pointer: used to target and activate, like a hover. Also used to scroll through content in the field of view.

Transparency in MR

On VR headsets, the real world is obscured, and colors are much more pronounced and saturated. Since holographic content is being projected through additive light, there's transparency involved in an MR display such as the HoloLens. The content is being added to the existing light of the real world, and this is consequential with respect to brightness and opacity. Lighter colors, including white, are a bit translucent. One-hundred percent black is rendered totally transparent (think about it—how would you "project" black light?). Keep this in mind when designing interface colors in MR. If you need a dark color, a 15 percent gray for all three RGB values may work. For content in the field of view, transparency helps with practical matters. After all, you don't want the user walking into something accidentally. Translucency (where only some light passes through) is better for text legibility, especially on larger content panels. A slightly blurred image is best for a background because it softens the details. Knocked-out white text can be read easier against it.

Paper prototyping

If you're sensing a pattern, you'll know that a sketch sheet is the first step in prototyping an MR experience. The familiar 360-degree grid becomes useful

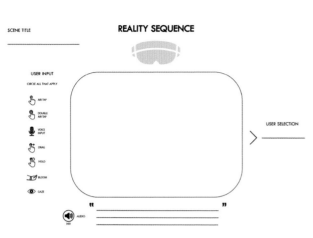

SCENE TITLE

REALITY SEQUENCE

USER INPUT

CIRCLE ALL THAT APPLY

AIR TAP

DOUBLE AIR TAP

VOICE INPUT

DRAG

HOLD

BLOOM

GAZE

AUDIO

USER SELECTION

resource that I've found quite useful is by Lillian Warner, a UX researcher and educator. Her XR design template includes a field of view layout for each scene, and gestures that can be quickly selected and associated with interactions.

Figure 6.24
Mixed reality can be fuzzy to digitally present, so some pre-conceptualization helps to frame the experience.

Digital prototyping in MR

Since the user is viewing the experience via headset, most of the prototyping methods used for VR can apply to mixed reality as well. The equirectangular images, digital tools, and 360-degree photo viewer can help stitch together a realistic scene.

for prototyping the UI, background, and overall field of view. You also might explore sketches a bit further since gestures are more widely available. One

HACK

For digital prototyping in MR, the background image is key: using a photo that looks like a believable environment would sell the concept of MR better than a futuristic scene that feels out of context.
Remember, this is VR in the real world. So, a typical scene might be in an office or living room. Anything too manicured might seem like a game or virtual world, which it's not.

Figure 6.25
Creative imagination of an MR experience can be designed and presented with the tools we use now.

Prototyping interactions

We know that the digital prototyping methods we hacked for VR aren't meant to show complex interactions, and they won't

when reimagined for MR either. So how do you show the variety available in mixed reality, since they're core to the medium? Cue After Effects.

HACK

When prototyping interactions, take photos making various gestures with your hands against a white background. You can easily clip them out in Photoshop. You can then use the same animated process we discussed in prototyping augmented reality to show the interactions. Position the clipped-out hand gestures to appear in the timeline right before an interaction happens. It won't matter much that they're static; this is a prototype, remember?

Hybrid methods

There have only been a handful of consumer-grade headsets that have delivered on the promise of MR. In fact, several companies have formed, released headsets, and dissolved within the span of a few years. It's a complex medium, the prototyping methods available are as well. Anything realistic and truly interactive would probably verge too close to actual development, and it isn't likely we'll see anything that solves this dilemma soon. The VR hybrid methods we covered are probably your best bet, combined with a good dose of imagination required to leverage them for MR concepts.

Mixed reality development

Unity: The Mixed Reality Toolkit (MRTK), developed by Microsoft, interfaces directly with Unity. It seems to be the best medium-specific development tool for MR and will likely be a valuable tool moving forward. It was created as a development asset for the HoloLens, but it is an open-source project that can also support other devices. Note that since this is a Microsoft product, it's PC only.

Spectator View: An interesting bridge between a prototype and development, Spectator View (another Microsoft product) acts as a showcase for mixed reality. It lets people see what a HoloLens user is seeing and interacting with, but on a 2D screen. Pretty convenient for showing a larger audience the potential of MR without headsets. This also directly interfaces with Unity.

Figure 6.26
Leveraging UI and UX considerations for digital and physical applications is exciting territory.

Unreal Engine: The XR Framework in Unreal Engine extends to mixed reality. Their camera component allows mapping of real space, and developers are actively producing content with it. Unreal also has a Mixed Reality Capture framework that can composite people into a virtual environment. I'd describe it as "mixed reality-ish," and the setup and calibration seem quite complicated for now.

Future considerations

The unknown factors are the big "if" in the XR space, and the eventual flattening out of the rapid tech adoption cycle will be a big one. Now, it's difficult to keep up with current tools and capabilities, much less understand the intricacies of each. There's also a huge chasm between early adoption and mass consumption, which is why we've seen so many companies shutter their doors a few years after starting. The "if you build it, they will come" approach didn't stick when applied to XR. The organizations with enough money to invest in large-scale storytelling— and the ability to ride it out—have become major players. It's akin to the browser wars of the Web in the late 1990s. When the dust eventually settles, it will be interesting to see what standards have remained, and what has completely changed. The workspace implications and a push toward increasing efficiency will need to be a driving factor if the discipline is to move beyond gaming. That's already happening at enterprise levels but is slowly filtering down to consumers. Practical application and cost will surely ease that process. For designers, adopting current UI and UX practices for a physical environment is the key takeaway. The opportunities for digital designers will no doubt be huge, and those with the abilities to jump into this space can expect to be rewarded both creatively and financially.

XR DESIGN EXERCISE

Create an augmented reality proof of concept that leverages the digital design skills, tools, and hacks that you've learned. Present a video experience that looks and feels real.

DESCRIPTION

Design a ten-to-twenty-second proof of concept that showcases augmented reality for a brand, business, or imagined future technology. This project will utilize motion graphics to show what an AR experience will look like from the user's perspective. It will also allow you to push the experimental boundaries of a concept and give you a portfolio piece that showcases the imagination possible with AR, while sharing it in a way that's easy for anyone to view.

SPECIFICATIONS

Create an AR conceptual experience that's exported as video. It should be long enough to get the idea across but short enough to technically execute. An actual AR experience is great as a final product, but it usually needs to run as a stand-alone app. For this exercise, we'll build something that looks and feels like a real experience but can be viewed as a video and shared online. You'll use camera tracking in After Effects to convincingly "place" digital content in a video clip.

RESEARCH AND INTENT

Brainstorm concepts that would fit in the concise time limit, prioritizing experimental concepts. This is your chance to run wild since there's no development at stake. Futuristic technologies that don't yet exist or ideas that aren't commercial are great if they're visually compelling.

Merging different kinds of media, such as physical and digital, is one technique. One of the very early AR experiences was a magazine ad for MINI, which used a marker image. Viewing that image on a computer webcam triggered the AR experience, allowing you to see a 3D vehicle in space by turning the magazine. Doing so featured the product—a car—in a unique and interactive way. The physical/digital interaction is a sticky one, and it allows us to extend brands across mediums.

If you're thinking about an experience for a brand or business, find a way to connect an interaction to what that entity does. IKEA Place is an app that scans a room and allows you to place and move—you guessed it—IKEA furniture. Popular AR apps let users see their face with different make-up effects. Sure enough, those have been created by companies selling cosmetics.

On the flipside, if you're pursuing something completely experimental and fun, creativity is something you should highlight. An app that lets you draw or trace over a spatial environment or pull color palettes from your field of view are some ideas my students have explored.

METHODOLOGY

How will the experience start? Is a marker image used or environment scanned? You'll probably only have enough time to show one or two interactions: think about what those might entail. Will they be self-generated or require direct interaction? The former would be more indicative of dynamic animation in the display as you move through the experience. The latter might require you to use hand gestures to make something happen.

CONTENT

You'll need a video to serve as the background. It needs to be smooth, crisp, and show an environment that works well with your concept. You have a couple of options to source this: free stock websites or filming it yourself. A stabilized smartphone video provides good enough quality. If you want to use the spatial audio from the video clip, make sure there are no audible distractions when filming.

SKETCHES

Start with Sara Tan's augmented-reality ideation template to get a sense of what the project goals are and how to start shaping the UI. If you want to explore a bit more fidelity, you can add additional sketches that are more in depth. Write out a rough timeline for what's going to happen. A basic storyboard template might help you commit to this task.

Figure 6.27
A quick storyboard can help establish a scene and pacing for an augmented-reality concept.

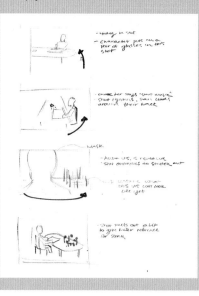

DIGITAL DESIGN

After importing your video footage, start designing the UI assets. While you can work in whatever software you're comfortable with, designing directly in After Effects can save time. You won't have to create shapes from imported layers or re-key text. Hide all the UI layers and return back to your footage, trimming anything extraneous. Select the layer and select track 3D camera from the tracker menu. Depending on the length and complexity of the clip, this will take a bit of time to process. The shorter duration of the project should keep it reasonable, though.

TECHNICAL STEPS

You should end up with a bunch of tracked points throughout the footage. Select several points that originate from the "floor" of the composition. The bull's-eye target that appears should look like a tabletop, parallel to the ground. Command-click and choose "set ground plane and origin." This will effectively set the position coordinates to zero for X, Y, and Z, and it eliminates the need to work with odd numbers when manipulating the position of other objects. Then, choose one or more points that stay persistent throughout the clip and control-click and choose "create null and camera." This adds a null object, which we know from Chapter 3 is a flexible blank layer. It also creates a 3D camera that places the null object in a fixed position within the moving footage. This is the part that will make everything look convincing because, once you parent any layer or comp to the null object, it locks it into place within the footage.

MOCK-UP

With those specific steps completed, animate the interactions and pre-comp them in their own layer (Layer > Precompose). Parent the comp to the null object, and you should have an animation that's fixed in space. You can use the null object to make transformations that affect the animations as a whole, like rotating the entire thing 90 degrees or scaling it up in size. Make sure that the "continuously rasterize" switch is checked so that everything is crisp.

ADDING THE FOREGROUND

If your concept calls for it, you may want to film your hands "touching" the digital content you've just designed, to make it seem real. To put things in perspective: the video of the environment serves as the background, the digital content the midground, and tactile interaction the foreground. You can practice "acting out" the gestures you'll want to use (tapping, swiping, etc.). Record hand gestures to video when you're ready. If you do it against a neutral background, you can rotoscope them in After Effects. This will effectively "clip out" moving hands in video, giving you a foreground to add. Spend the time needed on this method because choppy rotoscoping can take down the overall quality a few notches.

Figure 6.28
These are screenshots of an AR project, which feature rotoscoping to realistically place augmented content in the midground.

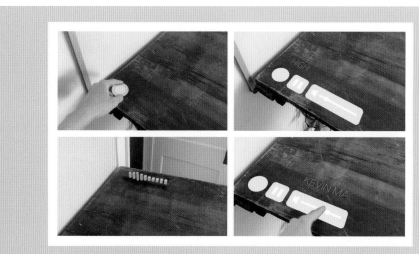

TESTING

Render and view everything in real time to make sure your content is well positioned with respect to the environment (i.e., it looks natural) and that the pacing is good. A nice final touch is to add an introductory branded scene that sets up the content. Add any audio cues now that the animations are finished, remembering the levels we discussed in Chapter 3.

REFLECTION AND REVISION

Ask yourself the simple question: "Does this look like I'm viewing an AR experience through the lens of a participant?" If not, things to consider in making it feel more realistic are: the scale of the digital content in relation to the background; angles of content relating to perspective; and the responsiveness of the interactions and animations. Maybe it's the background video that just didn't work? The best options will show a defined sense of ground and space bounded by walls or architecture. Filming in an open meadow won't give you that definition. Re-shoot any video if needed, and make sure any rotoscoped layers look believable and smooth.

GOALS AND OUTCOMES

The method used for this project is what many tech companies have used to sell the concept of AR to the masses. It's much easier to view a "slice" of a fringe technology in a medium that's already commonplace than to deal with additional tech requirements. Building a prototype that actually works in AR is possible with the tools we've discussed, but simply calling attention to a portfolio piece is much more difficult that way. Both methods are important to show the breadth of your skills, but this technique should get the most bang for your buck. If it doesn't look realistic enough, that advantage is lost. Sweat the details when it comes to finessing this piece. A successful project will spark the imagination for most viewers and show that you're well versed in emerging technologies. We've used skills from UX, UI, and motion graphics to build this, so evaluate those against their respective disciplines. The final deliverable should be a video that can be shared easily and widely via websites and social media.

Epilogue

AIGA's Design Futures Research project yielded this from its research in bridging digital and physical experiences:

> People transition across devices, environments, and activities in continuous communication and service activities. Users expect technology to provide seamless, unified experiences, even when moving among messages and services from different sources.
>
> AIGA (nd)

This statement is evidence of how design has changed over the last twenty years. Traditional roles of the past have changed in terms of their scope and duties. Art directors are now expected to be digitally proficient across an array of media. Most designers cannot simply get away with creating logos and branding for a living unless they have carved out some sort of niche for themselves.

The days of learning your craft and then gracefully applying it for another thirty years are gone. The software revolution of the 1990s was a drastic departure from the calculated, tactile approach to design production. And yet, contemporary design output makes the 1990s seem like the dark ages. Graphic design disciplines are slowly escaping the overarching identity forged over the last century, yet many of my incoming students still talk about "magazine design" as an early interest.

And, while I'm sure there are still many magazines being produced, I haven't bought one in a decade. What this illustrates is the push and pull that seems to dictate the meandering narrative that's being rewritten.

Always learning

Learning multidisciplinary skills early in your career is crucial. Ways of working haven't been fully cemented yet and new workflows aren't a total system shock. In my own teaching experience, third-year design students were often frustrated by learning HTML/CSS and motion graphics. They were able to manipulate their traditional graphic design work at a fairly high level and were now back at the drawing board. Since then, I've started teaching those disciplines to second-year students with much more success. Don't rush to find a niche—specialization will inevitably find its way into your work, and your personal style will likely have a hand in that as well. Most creatives will job-hop throughout their career, and reinvention may be necessary to navigate the waters of a constantly changing landscape. Having to brushup in a discipline that you've previously learned is like riding a bike: you'll be slow at first, but you won't need the training wheels again.

The next shift

As design and technological skills converge, some of the low-hanging work will inevitably need to shift. Many specializing in logo and identity work have pivoted to now include motion and animation as part of that identity. And indeed, artificial intelligence can now algorithmically design decent-looking

Figure 7.1
The marriage of physical and digital mediums holds the biggest promise for future technologies.

Figure 7.2
Designers might find themselves producing for several mediums for a combined sensory experience.

Figure 7.3
Laura Normand's packaging design combines physical and digital output.

posters in seconds. Designing around complexity and large amounts of data are skills already in demand, and we can expect that to continue. "Experience design" is an umbrella term that's been used in recent years to describe the decoupling of distinctly siloed disciplines and include any design output that's experienced by a user. This could be a book, a website, extended reality experience, or physical event. As the connectivity between physical objects and digital devices increases, we'll see output "handed off" back and forth between mediums.

That convergence of output will require young creatives to have skills across a breadth of disciplines and think holistically. Many businesses once thought of graphic design as the window dressing of their content and products. Now, many designers find themselves in leadership roles where design is considered as part of early strategy. Methods of production that once required heavily specialized knowledge are now becoming automated and we can expect software to make another big leap. There are several visual website builders that have finally come into their own as professional tools, yet knowing how to code still makes those tools more useful.

There's no doubt that access to technological processes that were once esoteric will open room for a lot of clutter. We've already seen that in the glut of video content that floods social media. Work that's able to cut through that clutter will

become premium, and refined messaging through various media will be prized.

Bringing it around

The "intuitive spark" is one of the things that hooks in young designers. It's the witty expression or emotional connection that makes work memorable. Print has long been an outlet for championing that spark, and we're seeing it played out in digital media. Emerging technologies are always a bit rough aesthetically, but we eventually find a way to bring aesthetic harmony and human connection to them. Teaching how to harness that powerful mix of unexpected connections that make something memorable is honestly more difficult than anything discussed in this book. But it's comforting to know that it's the thing that will always be in demand. The challenges of problem-solving, visual storytelling, and distillation of content mean something new to tackle every day, through whatever medium we find ourselves in.

Image credits

5.12 Courtesy of David Hardy
5.13 Courtesy of David Hardy
5.14 Courtesy of David Hardy
5.15 Courtesy of David Hardy
5.16 Courtesy of David Hardy
5.17 Courtesy of David Hardy
5.18 Courtesy of Thomas Koehler
5.19 Courtesy of Tyler Honeycutt
5.20 Courtesy of David Hardy
5.21 Courtesy of Jillian Hobbs
5.22 Courtesy of LAVA
5.23 Courtesy of Hayley Gillespie
5.24 Courtesy of LAVA
5.25 Courtesy of Jerelle Ocampo
5.26 Courtesy of Jerelle Ocampo
5.27 Courtesy of Jerelle Ocampo
5.28 Courtesy of Jerelle Ocampo
5.29 Courtesy of Joshua Pizza

Chapter 6:
6.1 Courtesy of David Hardy
6.2 Courtesy of UNIBOA
6.3 Courtesy of Bram Van Oost
6.4 Courtesy of David Hardy
6.5 Courtesy of Jesper Aggergaard
6.6 Courtesy of David Hardy
6.7 Courtesy of Vova Kurbatov
6.8 Courtesy of Vova Kurbatov
6.9 Courtesy of Vova Kurbatov
6.10 Courtesy of Vova Kurbatov
6.11 Courtesy of David Hardy
6.12 Courtesy of David Hardy
6.13 Courtesy of David Hardy
6.14 Courtesy of David Hardy
6.15 Courtesy of Dent Reality
6.16 Courtesy of Laura Normand
6.17 Courtesy of Laura Normand

6.18 Courtesy of Sarah Tan
6.19 Courtesy of Sarah Tan
6.20 Courtesy of Sarah Tan and Anne Wong
6.21 Courtesy of Vova Kurbatov
6.22 Courtesy of Haroon Matties
6.23 Courtesy of David Hardy
6.24 Courtesy of Lillian Warner
6.25 Courtesy of Vova Kurbatov and Inna Sparrow
6.26 Courtesy of Gleb Kuznetsov
6.27 Courtesy of Haroon Matties
6.28 Courtesy of Haroon Matties

Epilogue:
7.1 Image courtesy of IDEO
7.2 Courtesy of Laura Normand
7.3 Courtesy of Laura Normand

References

AIGA (nd), 'Design Futures Research', AIGA website, no date. Available online: https://www.aiga.org/resources/design-futures-research (accessed 18 March 2022).

Bierut, Michael (2014), 'Michael Bierut Graphic Designer - The Creative Inflience Ep.13', Vimeo website, 24 June. Available online: https://vimeo.com/99025203 (accessed 18 March 2022)

Cox, Norm (2015), 'The 3 Line Menu Icon: What is a Hamburger Menu?', Small Business Trends website, 21 January. Available online: https://smallbiztrends.com/2015/01/3-line-menu-icon-hamburger-menu.html (accessed 18 March 2022).

O'Connell, Kharis (2016), *Designing for Mixed Reality*, Sebastopol, CA: O'Reilly Media.

Index

Note: Page locators in *italic* refer to figure captions.